BIRDS IN KANSAS

University of Kansas
Museum of Natural History

Public Education Series No. 12
Joseph T. Collins, Editor

BIRDS IN KANSAS

VOLUME TWO

Max C. Thompson

Department of Biology
Southwestern College
Winfield, Kansas

&

Charles Ely

Department of Biology and Allied Health
Fort Hays State University
Hays, Kansas

Foreword by John E. Hayes, Jr.
Western Resources

UNIVERSITY OF KANSAS
MUSEUM OF NATURAL HISTORY

The Public Education Series is intended to provide publications on natural history for the people of Kansas. This volume is the result of studies sponsored, in part, by the Museum of Natural History at the University of Kansas, Southwestern College, Fort Hays State University, the Kansas Biological Survey, the Kansas Department of Wildlife and Parks, and the Kansas Ornithological Society.

Distributed by the University Press of Kansas
Lawrence, Kansas 66049

Library of Congress Cataloging-in-Publication Data

Thompson, Max C.
   Birds in Kansas.

      (Public education series / University of Kansas, Museum of Natural History; no. 11–12.)
   Includes index.
   Bibliography: p.
      1. Birds—Kansas—Identification. 2. Birds—Kansas—Geographical distribution. I. Ely, Charles A. (Charles Adelbert), 1933–   . II. Title. III. Series: Public education series ; no. 11–12.
QL684.K2T47   1989   598.29781   89-5017
ISBN 0-89338-026-1 (v. 1)
ISBN 0-89338-027-X (pbk. : v. 1)
ISBN 0-89338-039-3 (v. 2)
ISBN 0-89338-040-7 (pbk. : v. 2)

This publication is funded in part by the Chickadee Checkoff of the Nongame Wildlife Improvement Program of the Kansas Department of Wildlife and Parks. All persons filing a Kansas income tax form have an opportunity to make a special contribution that is earmarked for conservation of nongame wildlife. Do something wild! Make your mark on the tax form for nongame wildlife.

Dedicated to our colleagues
who waited so patiently
and continued to provide us with new data

FOREWORD

In *Kansas Wildlife,* Joe Collins had this to say about birds: "Their overwhelming numbers contribute the most to the variety of Kansas, while the mammals, reptiles, and amphibians play an important but nonetheless supporting role in enriching the number of creatures that inhabit our state." *Birds in Kansas, Volume Two* clearly demonstrates this variety; our state boasts a surprising mixture of avian life. That diversity, that richness of wildlife, depends upon our environmental vigilance.

As pressures continue to build on an ever-dwindling natural environment in Kansas, it is important that field guides such as *Birds in Kansas* be available to interest and inform those who would save the habitats of these delightful creatures. With the publication of this volume, the Museum of Natural History, University of Kansas, has produced a complete set of field guides about the vertebrate animals of Kansas, a remarkable achievement and a commitment to informing the people of our state about their precious natural heritage.

Western Resources is committed to improving life for all living things, including birds. We think that *Birds in Kansas, Volume Two* is eloquent testimony to the beauty and wonder of our state, and we agree with Joe Collins when he said, "Wildlife is biodiversity. And biodiversity is the essence of a wilderness environment. It is what we seek for our souls after a hard week of work. It is what we must have to restore our sense of balance in a people-dominated world that seems more and more out of balance and at odds with Mother Nature. I consider it the responsibility of all people to act as stewards of our natural environment." Without the diversity that birds and indeed all wildlife bring to our state, we would all lead duller lives. In an effort to display that diversity and encourage its preservation, Western Resources is pleased and proud to support the publication of this book.

John E. Hayes, Jr.
Chairman of the Board, President,
and Chief Executive Officer
Western Resources

PREFACE

This work represents the final volume of a two-part work on Kansas birds. The position of Kansas in the continental United States has provided ornithologists and birdwatchers with an excellent opportunity to become acquainted with a large number of species, not to mention the many surprise birds that continue to fly into the state. Since Volume One was published in 1989, two more species, the Pyrrhuloxia and Fish Crow, have been added to the state list. This brings the total number of species, verified and hypothetical, recorded within the borders of Kansas to 426. Undoubtedly, as more birdwatchers and ornithologists comb the state, more new species will be added to the state list.

As mentioned in the preface to Volume One, these volumes are not intended to be a scientific work but to provide the layperson with a means to determine the distribution of birds within the state. Some records may seem to have scant data to support them. This is only because it was not possible to go into an extensive discourse on each species. These data will appear in a more scientific work.

Without the amateur birdwatcher, this series would not be nearly complete. The Kansas Ornithological Society and its members have been of tremendous help in compiling data and providing us with dates of occurrence. Data are still needed on many species, as the following accounts will show.

For data, photographs, and assistance in the field, we would like to thank Sylvia Albright, Jerry Arnold, Ron Barkley, Terry Barnett, Byron Berger, the late Amelia Betts, Walter Boles, Bessie Boso, Jan Boyd, Roger Boyd, the late Ivan Boyd, Margaret Boyd, William Brecheisen, John Brockway, Martin Brockway, Tim Broschat, Fred Burgess, Steve Burr, Ted Cable, Thomas Cannon, Stephen Capel, Joan Challans, Wallace Champeny, Calvin Cink, Randy Clark, Lorena Combs, Jeffrey Cox, John Davis, the late Charles Edwards, Effie Edwards, Guy Ernsting, Elmer Finck, Thomas Flowers, Stephen Fretwell, Jo Garrett, Robert Glazier, Bob Gress, Charles Hall, Steve Hansen, Erma Henley, Larry Herbert, Jane Herschberger, Ken Hollinga, the late Lloyd Hulbert, Allen Jahn, Marion Jenkinson, J. C. Johnson, Jr., Nanette Johnson, Kenn Kaufman, Katharine Kelley, Steve Kingswood, Robert Kruger, Bill Langley, Dan Larson, Robert LaShelle, John LaShelle, Dan LaShelle, Patricia Latas, Bill Layher, Eugene Lewis, Eulalia Lewis, Renne Lohoefener, Paul Long, Edmund Martinez, Jim Mayhew, Lloyd Moore, Mary Louise Myers, Jay Newton, Art Nonhof, John Palmquist, James Parker, James Piland, Jean Piland, William Piper, Galen Pittman, Dwight Platt, Barb Pratt, the late Martin Pressgrove, James Ptacek, Margaret Ptacek, Mrs. W. H. Qualls, Mike Rader, the late Orville Rice, David Rintoul, James

Rising, Marvin Rolfs, Stan Roth, Jr., Richard Schmidt, Steve Schmidt, the late Ed Schulenberg, Jean Schulenberg, Tom Shane, Frank Shipley, Theodore Sperry, Dennis Stadel, Donald Stout, Robert Sutherland, Marie Swisher, Allen Tubbs, Don Vannoy, Byron Walker, Barbara Watkins, Michael Watkins, Robert Wells, Celia White, Gerald Wiens, Kevin Wills, Robert Wood, Eugene Young, Dennis Zehr, and John Zimmerman.

We would like to especially thank Sebastian Patti and Earl McHugh, who criticized the first draft of this manuscript. Marvin Schwilling and Scott Seltman provided input into the final draft.

We dedicate this book to the amateur birdwatchers and ornithologists whose past works and observations have made it possible.

Max C. Thompson
Charles Ely
1 November 1991

CONTENTS

Towhees, Sparrows, and Longspurs

Blackbirds and Orioles

INTRODUCTION

The history of Kansas ornithology and bird distribution and vegetation can be found in the introduction in Volume One and is not repeated here. Because readers may have only one volume with them, we are repeating the explanation of species accounts.

Amateur birdwatchers should be reminded that it is not possible to identify every bird observed. Even the best observers make mistakes, but only the best will admit it!

EXPLANATION OF SPECIES ACCOUNTS

Since this is a general work, we use a minimum of citations, many of which are available in most public libraries. We include citations where the reader is likely to question a comment or may want additional detail. Other citations refer to published photographs or items of special interest to Kansas birdwatchers. Unless otherwise stated, our comments refer to birds and their activities *in Kansas*.

Names: Common and scientific names and the sequence of species follow the American Ornithologists' Union Checklist (6th edition) and subsequent supplements.

Maps: For each species, a small outline map indicates by black dots the counties in which a species has been reported. These reports may be specimens, literature records, or sight records. Obvious sighting errors are not included. Those species that breed in the state may have open circles on the map indicating that a definite breeding record is in hand for that county. Only records indicating a nest, nest building, eggs, parents carrying food, or young birds too immature to have flown in from elsewhere were considered. Sightings during the breeding season but without the above qualifications were rejected.

Data were provided by many observers, chiefly members of the Kansas Ornithological Society, and are from a database maintained by Ely.

Photographs: A photograph, often taken in Kansas, is provided for 177 of the 207 species treated in this second volume. The photographs are the work of 32 Kansas wildlife photographers unless otherwise noted. We are grateful to these individuals for allowing us to use their photographs.

Status: This section is a general statement defining the occurrence of a species. If a species has been taken only a few times in the state, or if its status is still in question, additional detail is provided. Since this is a general work, our terms are defined broadly rather than quantitatively:

Regular: Occurs in about the same numbers, in about the same
                areas each year
Irregular: May vary each year in numbers or distribution
Local: Present and/or breeds at only a few localities or is widely
                scattered over a larger area
Casual: Occurs in very small numbers most years
Vagrant: Occurs rarely but can be expected every few years
Accidental: Far out of its normal range or movement pattern and
                not likely to appear in the near future

Indications of abundance refer to presence in proper habitat and
are also qualitative:

Rare: Only a few individuals seen in a season
Uncommon: Small numbers present, but found on most birdwatch-
                ing trips
Common: Easily found, usually in numbers
Abundant: Present in large numbers, usually widespread and con-
                spicuous

The status of a species is complicated by the fact that it may be resident, but the individuals present may be either permanent residents
(e.g., Northern Cardinal), from both resident and migratory populations (e.g., American Crow), or from summering, wintering, and transient populations (e.g., Mourning Dove).

Period of Occurrence: We provide extreme dates of reported occurrence
and main migration periods. Comments on variation from normal patterns and/or variation within the state are sometimes provided. Data
are from a database compiled and maintained by Ely.

Breeding: A brief life history is given for each regularly breeding species.
Included are the basic data concerning nesting habitat, nest location
and construction, egg colors, clutch size, incubation period, nestling
period, and often courtship and care of the young. This information
is from basic sources such as Bent (various years) and Terres (1980).
Breeding is reported only when an active nest, eggs, or dependent young
have been reported and documented. Both recent and historical accounts are included when available, as are changes in status or distribution.

Habits and Habitat: Here we provide information on where the
species is most likely to be found at various times of the year ecologi-
cally and (usually) geographically. We include interesting or unusual
behavior and observations both from personal experience and from
the literature.

Field Marks: For most species we provide no more than brief comments on identification, but where confusion with other species in Kansas is a definite problem we provide more specific comments. For difficult groups such as flycatchers and fall warblers, it is imperative that readers refer to one or more good field guides. Unless otherwise stated, most field marks refer to the male.

Food: The food preferences of each species are included. Data are from personal observation and the literature mentioned previously.

An Olive-sided Flycatcher (*Contopus borealis*). Photograph by Dale and Marian Zimmerman.

New World Flycatchers (Family Tyrannidae)
Olive-sided Flycatcher
Contopus borealis (Swainson)

Status: The Olive-sided Flycatcher is an uncommon transient statewide.

Period of Occurrence: This flycatcher is most numerous during May and again during late August and early September. Extreme dates are 20 April to 7 June and 6 August to 4 October. The nesting reported by Goss (1891) is either an error or a *lapsus*.

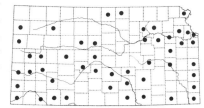

Habits and Habitat: The Olive-sided Flycatcher nests in coniferous and mixed forests west and north of

Kansas, but individuals may linger within the state into June. As with other wood-pewees, it is usually first noted by its call — a loud, emphatic three-note affair accented on the middle syllable and slurred downward on the third. This distinctive call is often interpreted as "hic-three-beers." This species is nearly always seen perched on the exposed tip of a dead branch, often a treetop. From here it calls and sallies forth to capture flying insects, usually returning to the same or a nearby perch.

Field Marks: The large bill and head and short neck give this species a "bull-headed" appearance. In color, its wide dark flanks contrast with the white breast and mid-belly. The patches of white feathers that can sometimes be seen on the sides of the lower back above the tail may help to identify this species. However, these patches are often not visible on a bird perched high overhead.

Food: The Olive-sided Flycatcher feeds on a variety of flying insects, including flies, ants, bees, and beetles. It is said to be especially fond of honeybees.

A Western Wood-Pewee (*Contopus sordidulus*). Photograph by Roger Boyd.

Western Wood-Pewee
Contopus sordidulus Sclater

Status: The Western Wood-Pewee is an uncommon transient and a rare local resident in the extreme west and occurs eastward to central Kansas during migration. It probably nests in riparian situations in the extreme west.

Period of Occurrence: Confirmed specimens have been taken between 29 April and 17 September. Sight records, chiefly free-flying, nonsinging

individuals, have been reported
primarily between 4 May and
16 June and 1 August and 19
September. Most reports are during May and September.

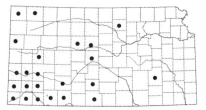

Breeding: Nesting has not yet been
documented from Kansas, but
singing males have been seen repeatedly on territories in suitable
habitat. The most likely records to date are from Cheyenne, Morton,
and Rawlins counties. The nest is a flat cup placed on the top of a dead
horizontal branch at a moderate height. It is constructed of plant
fibers and shredded bark tied together with spiderwebs but typically
without a covering of lichens. It is lined with fine grasses, plant down,
and occasionally feathers. The clutch is two to four, usually three,
creamy white eggs with brown blotches and speckles on the larger end.

Habits and Habitat: Summer birds in Kansas have been in cottonwood
groves with sparse understory along the Republican and Cimarron rivers,
in riparian habitat near open fields, and on an abandoned farmstead
near Beaver Creek. During migration individuals also occur in urban
parks. The species is most easily found by its distinctive call "che-
beeer," the second note slurred downward. Birds call and feed from
open perches, often within two meters of the ground if vision is un-
obstructed by vegetation. Additional fieldwork is necessary to determine the status of the two wood-pewees in Kansas. Wood-pewees with
the eastern song type have been reported from extreme western Kansas,
and the two forms may possible hybridize. It is interesting that all
wood-pewee songs heard at Hays have been of the "eastern" type but
that all specimens (none taken while singing!) are "western" by plumage
characteristics.

Field Marks: The two wood-pewees cannot be identified in the field except when singing, and even hand-held birds are extremely difficult
to distinguish. Many hand-held individuals can be distinguished only
by measurements and close comparisons of known specimens. Even
songs may be confusing—see Kaufman (1990) for descriptions and cautions.

Food: The diet of the Western Wood-Pewee is primarily ants, bees,
wasps, and flies supplemented with other flying insects and occasionally berries.

An Eastern Wood-Pewee (*Contopus virens*). Photograph by Gerald J. Wiens.

Eastern Wood-Pewee
Contopus virens (Linnaeus)

Status: The Eastern Wood-Pewee is a common transient and summer resident in eastern Kansas and a progressively rarer transient westward. It presently breeds westward in riparian habitat to Kingman, Russell, and probably Jewell counties. Breeding farther westward requires confirmation.

Period of Occurrence: Confirmed specimens have been taken from 9 May to 23 September. In the east it is most numerous from early May to early October with extreme dates of 18 April and 18 October. March and early April dates are suspect, as many have been of Eastern Phoebes! Farther west, where it is a transient only, extreme dates are 4 May to 18 June and 10 August to 18 October.

Breeding: It nests in deciduous forests and in riparian habitat westward along the major rivers to north-central Kansas. It is common and widespread west to Clay, Ottawa, and Republic counties and local (often in oak groves) westward. The nest is a shallow cup saddled on a horizontal branch far from the trunk at moderate to high elevation. With its lichen-covered exterior it resembles a knot and is often invisible from the ground. It is built of plant fibers, stems, and spider egg sacs tied together with spiderweb and lined with plant down and fine hair. A nest is most easily found by following the female as she returns to it. The clutch is two to four, usually three, creamy white eggs blotched and speckled with brown at the larger end. Most laying in Kansas is in mid-June. The incubation period is 12 to 13 days, and it is single brooded.

Habits and Habitat: This flycatcher usually feeds from an exposed but shady perch from which it darts out for flying insects. It also snatches an occasional insect from foliage or a spiderweb. It is especially active in early evening. The typical song is a three-note, drawn-out whistle, "pee-ah-weeee," which rises, then falls. It has other songs, including a two-note "pee-ah"; that song, however, is very different from the song of the Western Wood-Pewee. It sings most actively at dawn and dusk.

Field Marks: This species differs from the Eastern Phoebe in having wing bars, a more slender build, a yellow lower mandible, and very different behavior. Remember that the immature Eastern Phoebe also has wing bars but differs from the wood-pewee in posture and heavier-appearing body. Wood-Pewees lack the distinct eye ring of various Empidonaces.

Food: The Eastern Wood-Pewee feeds on flying insects, especially flies, ants, beetles, and small moths, and occasionally eats berries. Although a high proportion of its prey is very small insects, Bent (1942) reports an adult feeding an intact Red Admiral butterfly to one of its young.

A Yellow-bellied Flycatcher (*Empidonax flaviventris*). Photograph by B. D. Cottrille for the Cornell Laboratory of Ornithology.

Yellow-bellied Flycatcher
Empidonax[*] *flaviventris* (Baird & Baird)

Status: The Yellow-bellied Flycatcher is a rare transient in eastern and central Kansas and is casual in the west.

[*]The genus *Empidonax* is a confusing group of nine *very* similar species that can be reliably identified in the field *only* when singing. Even hand-held individuals require careful examination; most require use of measurements and characters not included in standard field guides; two can be reliably identified only by direct comparison with known specimens. It is not possible to identify all *Empidonax* in the field. Birders attempting to identify *Empidonax* in the field should study both the descriptions *and the cautions* given by Kaufman (1990). The following comments on periods of occurrence and, to a lesser extent, status are based largely on specimens, hand-held birds, and singing males and may require future modification.

Period of Occurrence: Most confirmed records are during May
and September. Extreme dates
for specimens and hand-held birds
are 24 May and 5 June and 1 August through 7 October. Sight
records extend these dates to
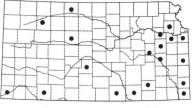
2 May and 24 October. April dates are suspect.

Habits and Habitat: During migration the Yellow-bellied Flycatcher occurs in deciduous forest and riparian growth, usually frequenting undergrowth or the lower branches of trees from which it feeds in
characteristic flycatcher fashion.

Field Marks: The Yellow-bellied Flycatcher is the only *Empidonax* in
Kansas with both a yellow throat and a yellow eye ring, but it closely
resembles the Cordilleran Flycatcher. The song is an explosive "pse-
ek" and an ascending whistle "pur-wee," but individuals in Kansas are
usually silent.

Food: This species feeds on flying insects, chiefly beetles, bees, ants, wasps,
and small moths. It snatches small caterpillars and spiders from vegetation and occasionally eats small berries.

An Acadian Flycatcher (*Empidonax virescens*). Photograph by B. D. Cottrille for the Cornell Laboratory of Ornithology.

Acadian Flycatcher
Empidonax virescens (Vieillot)

Status: The Acadian Flycatcher is an uncommon transient and summer resident in the east and a casual transient elsewhere. It is presently known to breed west to Cowley and Atchison counties.

Period of Occurrence: Specimen records span the period 5 May and 15

September. Sight records extend
this period to 30 April and 30
September. Sight records from
central and western Kansas are
suspect. An immature taken in
Ellis County on 27 July is undoubtedly a stray.

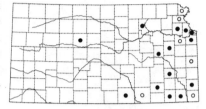

Breeding: The Acadian Flycatcher breeds in shady bottomland deciduous forest. Most nests have been in either the northeast or southeast,
but it nested once (1964) in Cowley County. The nest is a woven shallow basket of stems and plant fibers tied together with spiderwebs and
suspended hammocklike from the fork of a horizontal branch of a small
tree or shrub, often near water. Long streamers of grass or other fi-
brous material trail from the base of the nest, giving it a "trashy" appearance but perhaps also providing camouflage. Egg laying is in late
May through early June. The clutch is two to four, usually three, white
to buffy white eggs marked with scattered brown dots at the larger end.
The incubation period is 13 days, the nestling period is 13 to 15 days,
and it is single brooded. The female alone builds and incubates, as with
other members of the genus, but both parents feed the young.

Habits and Habitat: During migration the Acadian Flycatcher also occurs in upland deciduous forests, where its behavior is like that of other
Empidonaces. It typically perches in deep shade, usually within 16
feet of the ground, and is relatively inactive.

Field Marks: The song is a sharp "tee-chip" accented on the second syllable and repeated several times per minute, accompanied by a tail flick.

Food: This flycatcher feeds chiefly on flying insects, especially beetles,
wasps, bees, ants, and small moths; caterpillars; and occasionally berries.

Alder* Flycatcher
Empidonax alnorum Brewster

Status: The Alder Flycatcher is probably a common transient statewide.

Period of Occurrence: Specimens identified by Allen R. Phillips fall within the time periods 13 to 29 May and 29 July to 12 September.

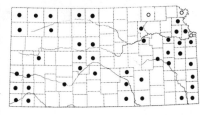

Habits and Habitat: Stein (1963) confirmed that this and the nearly identical Willow Flycatcher are sibling species that occupy overlapping ranges without interbreeding. They differ in song type, nesting habits, and to some extent ecology — this species nests farther north and prefers less open, wetter nesting areas. In Kansas both species occur in riparian habitats, deciduous woods, edge areas, and parks and during migration have identical habits. Both occur primarily in thickets of shrubs or in low to moderately tall trees. They capture flying insects from exposed perches.

Field Marks: Although more olive (less gray and white) and larger than the Least Flycatcher, the Alder Flycatcher cannot be safely identified in the field except when singing. The typical song is of three notes, accented on the second and slurred downward on the third, and usually represented as "wee-bee-o." The call has been described as a buzzy "zshreer."

Food: The Alder Flycatcher feeds primarily on beetles, aphids, wasps, flies, moths, caterpillars, and occasionally small berries.

* "Traill's Flycatcher" is an entity involving two sibling species (Alder and Willow Flycatchers) that can be identified reliably only by song type ("wee-bee-o" and "fitz-bew," respectively) or by direct comparison of hand-held individuals. The combined species occurs statewide with confirmed migration records from 28 April through 12 June and 3 July through 28 September.

A three-year (1967–69) migration study in Ellis County (Ely 1970) showed an extended fall migration, with adults passing through from 23 July to 16 August and immatures from 16 August to 12 September. The spring migration extended from 12 May through 12 June but with a pronounced peak (87 percent) during the period 20–25 May. Numbers present were greatly affected by inclement weather and subsequent "fall-outs" — the grounding of migrants during a night of low visibility, fog, and drizzle.

A Willow Flycatcher (*Empidonax traillii*). Photograph by Mike Hopiak for the Cornell Laboratory of Ornithology.

Willow Flycatcher
Empidonax traillii (Audubon)

Status: The Willow Flycatcher is a common transient statewide and a rare local summer resident in the northeast. It has bred recently in Doniphan and Wyandotte counties. A nest report from Marshall County (1886) is possible, but one from Ellis County (1933) is almost certainly an error.

Period of Occurrence: Specimens identified by Allan R. Phillips are for the period 12 May through 12 June and 16 August through 15 September. Extreme dates for sight records outside the breeding range (mostly unconfirmed) are 27 April through 6 July and 25 July through 26 September. There are also mid-summer records from central and western Kansas.

Breeding: The nest is a compact cup of weed bark, plant fibers, and grass lined with plant down and fine grasses, sometimes with feathers in the rim. It is usually placed in a crotch and may have streamers of plant material hanging from its base. Anderson found seven nests near the Missouri River in Wyandotte and Doniphan counties (Johnston 1964a). All were in willows from four to 14 feet above ground. Most held three or four eggs laid in mid-June. Eggs are creamy white, spotted and blotched with brown at the larger end. The incubation period is 12 to 15 days, the nestling period is 13 or 14 days, and the species is single brooded.

Habits and Habitat: During migration the Willow Flycatcher occurs in all wooded and edge habitats, and its behavior is essentially like that of the Alder Flycatcher. It prefers low perches in undergrowth.

Field Marks: The song is a wheezy, two-note "fitz-bew" accented on the first syllable.

Food: It feeds on flying insects, especially bees, wasps, flies, and beetles, and occasionally on berries.

A Least Flycatcher (*Empidonax minimus*). Photograph by Uve Hublitz for the Cornell Laboratory of Ornithology.

Least Flycatcher
Empidonax minimus (Baird & Baird)

Status: The Least Flycatcher is a common transient statewide.

Period of Occurrence: This species is most common during May and from early August through late September. Specimen records are 26 April through 28 May and 3 July through 24 September; sight records are from 20 April to 6 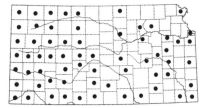 June and as late as 20 October. We have no evidence of breeding in Kansas; mid-summer reports are apparently southbound migrants.

Singing males have been reported on the unusual dates of 5 April (Rooks County), 19 June (Osage County), 27 June (Linn County), 19 July (Shawnee County), and 15 September (Shawnee County).

Habits and Habitat: This is the *Empidonax* most familiar to Kansas birders. The Least Flycatcher was formerly widely known as the "chebéck" because of its song. It sings persistently in spring and occurs in all open wooded and brushy habitats, including dooryards, parks, and roadsides. It is equally widespread in fall, and its characteristic low "whit" is a common sound. It feeds from exposed perches at almost any elevation and is easier to find and observe than other Empidonaces. It also snatches insects from tree trunks and leaf surfaces.

A three-year migration study (1967–69) in Ellis County (Ely 1970) showed a slow gradual fall migration without any major peak. Adults (easily recognized by their worn plumage) passed through from 16 July through 23 August, overlapped briefly by immatures, which were present from 15 August to 24 September and with a straggler on 16 October. In spring most males arrived during the first half of May; most females during the latter half.

Field Marks: Although smaller and paler (more gray and white) than other Empidonaces, the Least Flycatcher can be reliably identified in the field only by song — a sharp "che-beck" accented on the second note and uttered with a flick of the head and a twitch of the tail.

Food: The diet of this species is flying insects, including beetles, bees, ants, and moths; small caterpillars; and occasionally small berries.

A Hammond's Flycatcher (*Empidonax hammondii*). Photograph by Dale and Marian Zimmerman.

Hammond's Flycatcher
Empidonax hammondii (Xantus de Vesey)

Status: The Hammond's Flycatcher is apparently a vagrant in fall in western Kansas.

Period of Occurrence: There are five specimen records, all from Ellis County during the period 8 September to 4 October of the years 1961, 1966, 1970, and 1971. One handled by Martinez near Great Bend, Barton County, 22 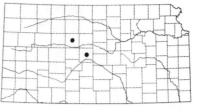 and 23 September 1974 was not verified nor were several recent sight records from Morton County.

The first specimen was brought in by a cat in Hays; the others were mist-netted in low riparian growth bordering Big Creek near Hays. The species summers in conifers in the Rockies and westward and moves to lower elevations during migration. In summer it usually feeds at moderate to high elevations in trees but during migration descends to much lower levels. It is a typical *Empidonax* in behavior. The song, not expected in Kansas, is described by Bent (1942) as "sep-ut, tsur-r-rp, tseep," and the call is "pip" or "chip" (male) or "tweep" (female). It characteristically flicks its wings (and tail) more often than do other Empidonaces while foraging.

A Dusky Flycatcher (*Empidonax oberholseri*). Photograph by Dale and Marian Zimmerman.

Dusky Flycatcher
Empidonax oberholseri Phillips

Status: The Dusky Flycatcher is a low-density transient in western Kansas and is casual eastward to Trego County (once).

Period of Occurrence: Specimens have been taken between 29 April and 17 May in Finney, Seward, and Morton counties, and an apparent "early fall" transient was taken in Trego County on 22 June. There are also unconfirmed fall 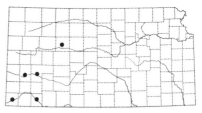 sightings from southwestern Kansas. This is probably the most regular of the "western" Empidonaces in Kansas (10 specimens from 1950 and 1962–1967), occurring usually along the Cimarron and Arkansas rivers.

Habits and Habitat: All Kansas specimens have been taken in riparian situations, usually in cottonwood groves or in saltcedar thickets. In its

breeding range the Dusky Flycatcher occurs in relatively dry areas —
deciduous shrub, aspen groves, open deciduous woods, and logged-
over slopes.

Field Marks: The territorial song (not yet reported in Kansas) has been
described as "sebit! djuree, pswee" or "chip-zee whee," with the second
note low and blurred. It flicks its wings and tail less often than does
the Hammond's Flycatcher and appears larger and slimmer in general
appearance; however, all sight records are suspect.

Gray Flycatcher
Empidonax wrightii Baird

Status: The Gray Flycatcher is a vagrant in extreme southwestern Kansas. The only valid record is a specimen taken in cottonwoods along the Cimarron River, northeast of Elkhart, Morton County, on 29 April 1967. There are several unconfirmed sight records from September.

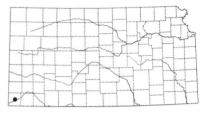

It regularly occurs in sagebrush and pinyon-juniper woodlands of the Great Basin east to central Colorado. The song, not expected in Kansas, is a two note "tu-wheet" or "pee-ist" or a "chualup! seeal," the first note emphasized. A possible field character is its habit of typically dipping its tail downward gently rather than forcefully and then allowing it to return. It is the palest and grayest of the Empidonaces.

A Cordilleran Flycatcher (*Empidonax occidentalis*). Photograph by Dale and Marian Zimmerman.

Cordilleran Flycatcher
Empidonax occidentalis Nelson

Status: The Cordilleran Flycatcher is a vagrant in western Kansas.

The Western Flycatcher has recently been split into two species that are indistinguishable in the field except for different songs. The few Kansas specimens are of the Rocky Mountain species, the Cordilleran Flycatcher. Two of the three Kansas specimens are from the Cimarron River south of Rich-  field, Morton County, on 3 and 5 September 1952. The third is from Big Creek near Ellis, Ellis County, on 5 September 1971. A report of a singing bird on the Cimarron River near Elkhart on 26 May 1984 (Scott Seltman) is probably valid. The few fall reports are unconfirmed.

The "Western Flycatcher" is a widespread western form that prefers moist woodland. All Kansas specimens were taken in riparian growth. The typical song is a rising "whee-sit" accented on the second note. It typically has a yellow throat and a white, tear-shaped eye ring. It also flicks its wings and tail simultaneously as does the Hammond's Flycatcher.

Black Phoebe
Sayornis nigricans (Swainson)

Status: The Black Phoebe is a possible vagrant but is considered hypothetical until a specimen or photograph is obtained.

Period of Occurrence: There are two unconfirmed March reports. One was from north of Elkhart in Morton County and the other from Topeka, Shawnee County; the latter was probably a Slate-colored Junco. The Black Phoebe is a 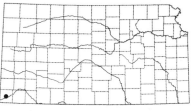 species of the southwestern United States where it is largely resident and usually occurs near water. It is a typical phoebe in behavior but with the color pattern of a well-marked and very dark Slate-colored Junco. The song is a "ti-wee, ti-wee," with the first note ascending and the second descending, and the call is a loud "chip."

An Eastern Phoebe (*Sayornis phoebe*). Photograph by Bob Gress.

Eastern Phoebe
Sayornis phoebe (Latham)

Status: The Eastern Phoebe is a common transient and summer resident in the east, becoming progressively less common westward where it is rare and local in summer. There is presently no breeding record southwest of Finney County.

Period of Occurrence: The Eastern Phoebe is most numerous from mid-March to mid-October but with extreme dates of 28 February and 19 November.

Breeding: The nest is usually placed on a ledge or girder under a bridge over or near water. Natural sites such as cliffs and rocky outcrops and outbuildings are used less frequently. The nest is a cup or half cone of plant stems, moss, algae, rootlets, and mud lined with hair and fine grass. The clutch is three to six, usually four or five, white eggs. The incubation period is 14 to 16 days; the nestling period about 14 or 15 days. It is double brooded, with the second clutch frequently laid in the same nest without refurbishing. Most first clutches are complete by mid-April; most second clutches by early June. Klaas (1962) reported a high incidence of cowbird parasitism in second clutches in Douglas County.

Habits and Habitat: The Eastern Phoebe is our first flycatcher to return in spring. It is one of our best-known birds, often nesting near humans, especially in rural areas near water where it nests on window ledges, in wells, and so on. Successful nesters tend to return to the same spot in successive years, as demonstrated by Audubon a century and a half ago. Nesting birds may become disorientated and build several nests side by side simultaneously. Harrison (1975) reported six complete nests (two with eggs) and 22 partial ones on a single bridge beam.

In Ellis County (Schuckman 1971), Eastern Phoebes nested in low density, apparently because of reduced habitat rather than competition with the Say's Phoebe. The Eastern Phoebes occupied small or low bridges over streams that had flowing water during at least part of the nesting cycle and always had trees or shrubs in the near vicinity. When such bridges were replaced by larger structures of concrete, and vegetation was cleared within 100 yards of the structure, the phoebes moved elsewhere. In one year seven of 13 nests (and their incubating females) were destroyed by a single flood at night. Other mortality was due to mites, snakes, and raccoons.

Field Marks: The song is an emphatic "fe-be" or "fe-bit," "fee-o-bee." It is very different from the clear, whistled "fee-bee" of the Black-capped Chickadee with which it is often confused.

Food: The major food items of the Eastern Phoebe are flying insects, including beetles, wasps, ants, flies, grasshoppers, and moths; caterpillars; spiders; and berries. It has also been reported eating tiny fishes.

A Say's Phoebe (*Sayornis saya*). Photograph by Dale and Marian Zimmerman.

Say's Phoebe
Sayornis saya (Bonaparte)

Status: The Say's Phoebe is a common transient and summer resident in the west, becoming progressively less common eastward. It has been reported east to Washington, Lyon, and Harvey counties.

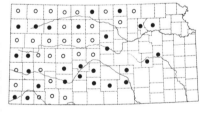

Period of Occurrence: The Say's Phoebe is most numerous from mid-March to mid-October but with extreme early dates of 19 February and 2 March and with some individuals lingering into November. Individuals have survived until at least 30 December in Morton County.

Breeding: In Ellis County the Say's Phoebe returns only three to six days later than the Eastern Phoebe but begins nesting a full two weeks later (Schukman 1971). Nests are placed under bridges, on rocky outcrops, and in caves along stream beds and in man-made structures such as sheds. Nest sites are not restricted to riparian growth or even to the vicinity of water. The nest is an open cup of plant stems and plant fibers lined with grass or hair. Mud is rarely used and never as extensively as in the nests of the Eastern Phoebe. The clutch is three to seven, usually four or five, white eggs. The incubation period is about 14 days; the nestling period about 16 days. It is double brooded; in Ellis County most first clutches are completed in late April or early May, second clutches in late June. Nests are not anchored with mud, and in the Ellis County study a number were blown down by high winds; those built atop Barn Swallow or Eastern Phoebe nests fared better.

Habits and Habitat: The Say's Phoebe is definitely a bird of open country, rarely noted near trees except perhaps in an isolated farmstead or dry stream bed. The song, though not loud, carries well, and in prairies the bird is frequently heard before it is seen. Adults usually feed from a low perch, often a yucca stalk, fence line, or rocky outcrop. They either dart out after flying insects or drop to the ground, bluebird fashion. Wolfe (1961) noted that in Decatur County, before the turn of the century, it nested so frequently in hand-dug wells that it received the local name of "well bird."

Field Marks: The usual song is a plaintive two-note "phe-ur," with the second note drawn out. The Say's Phoebe appears noticeably larger than the Eastern Phoebe and presents a noticeably pinkish appearance below and a contrasting black tail. Like the Eastern Phoebe it frequently "wags" (dips and spreads) its tail while perched.

Food: The food of this species is chiefly flying insects, including bees, wasps, flies, beetles, and moths; it also feeds on millipedes, sow bugs, spiders, and some berries.

Vermilion Flycatcher
Pyrocephalus rubinus (Boddaert)

Status: The Vermilion Flycatcher is a casual early spring visitor to south-central and southwestern Kansas.

Period of Occurrence: The two spec-imens and all dated sight records are within the time period 4 to 28 April. The first specimen, an im-mature female, was collected in Morton County in 1967. In April 1973 five were found dead in a

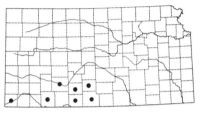

yard near Protection, Comanche County, following a blizzard, and Marie Swisher sent one to the University of Kansas, where it was preserved. The sight records are from Barber, Ford, Kiowa, Meade, and Pratt counties.

Habits and Habitat: In its breeding range the Vermilion Flycatcher oc-curs in savannahs, often in open riparian situations. It is rare and local in the states bordering southwestern Kansas but has bred in Okla-homa, and an eventual nesting in south-central or southwestern Kansas would not be unexpected. Postbreeding movements northward and eastward are common. The nest is an inconspicuous flat cup decorated with lichens and placed on a forked, horizontal branch of a low tree. The female builds the nest and incubates alone, but the male assists with the feeding of the young. The male has a spectacular courtship flight in which he rises vertically from a perch with crest raised and feathers erected and with quivering wings flutters down to the female, all the while repeating a series of "pit-a-see" notes. It is a typical flycatcher in behavior, sitting upright on an open perch and flying out to snatch insects from the air or ground. Males are very pugnacious toward their own and other species but are usually fairly tame and easy to approach. The usual call is a sharp "peet."

Field Marks: Adult males are unmistakable; females and immatures have white throats and streaked breasts with patches of yellow or salmon on the belly.

Food: Food of the Vermilion Flycatcher is primarily insects, especially grasshoppers, beetles, and bees.

An Ash-throated Flycatcher (*Myiarchus cinerascens*). Photograph by Dale and Marian Zimmerman.

Ash-throated Flycatcher
Myiarchus cinerascens (Lawrence)

Status: The Ash-throated Flycatcher is apparently a casual transient and an occasional summer resident along the Cimarron River in extreme southwestern Kansas. Sight records need verification. It was considered "fairly common" in Morton County during May 1950 (Graber & Graber 1950).

Period of Occurrence: Specimens as well as sight records from Morton County fall within the period 29 April to 16 September. There is an

additional specimen from Meade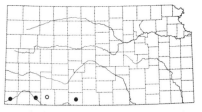
County (8 June) and sightings
there between 28 June and 22 August. There are unconfirmed reports from Sedgwick (7 August),
Seward (4 June to 3 July), and Comanche (13 and 14 May) counties.
The Ash-throated Flycatcher nested in Meade County in 1983, 1984
(probably), and 1985 and probably in adjacent Seward County in 1984
(Boyd 1985).

Breeding: This southwestern species breeds in Kansas very rarely and
locally. The nest is typically in an old woodpecker hole, a natural cavity, or a bird box. The nest is built of stems and other plant material;
it is lined with grasses, roots, and hair and often includes shed snake
skins, bits of cellophane, plastic bags, and so on. The clutch is four or
five creamy white eggs, lightly marked with brown and lavender spots
and streaks.

Habits and Habitat: The Ash-throated Flycatcher replaces the Great
Crested Flycatcher in much of the arid southwestern United States, but
in southwestern Kansas both have been seen in the same cottonwood
groves. In adjacent Oklahoma and Colorado it occurs in riparian situations, chiefly cottonwood groves along streams; in pinyon-juniper
woodlands; and in dry canyons. It feeds both from exposed perches
and by gleaning prey from branches and leaf surfaces while foraging
in low vegetation.

Field Marks: This flycatcher resembles a small, very pale Great Crested
Flycatcher but has a distinctive song — a clear, whistled "chew boo."

Food: The Ash-throated Flycatcher feeds primarily on flying insects, including ants, large flies, bees, wasps, cicadas, grasshoppers, and moths;
caterpillars; spiders; and some berries.

A Great Crested Flycatcher (*Myiarchus crinitus*). Photograph by Bob Gress.

Great Crested Flycatcher
Myiarchus crinitus (Linnaeus)

Status: The Great Crested Flycatcher is a common transient and summer resident in eastern and central Kansas, becoming rare westward where it is restricted to riparian habitats and occurs very locally.

Period of Occurrence: The Great Crested Flycatcher is most numerous from late April through early September but is much less noticeable after nesting and during the fall. Extreme arrival and departure dates are 10 April and 16 October, respectively.

Breeding: The nest is typically at a moderate elevation in a natural tree cavity or an old woodpecker hole; bird boxes and man-made structures may also be used. In 1887 a pair nested in a cannon on the statehouse grounds, Topeka, but the nest was destroyed when the cannon was fired (Goss 1891). The nest is composed of whatever vegetable material is available plus paper, cloth, and so on. The Great Crested Flycatcher is famous for including a shed snakeskin or its modern equivalent — cellophane, plastic, and such items. The clutch is four to eight, usually five or six, creamy white eggs heavily marked with brown spots and scrawled lines. It is single brooded, with most egg laying in early June. The incubation period is 13 to 15 days; the nestling period is 14 or 15 days. Both sexes build, but all incubation is by the female. Pairs frequently return to the same nest site in successive years.

Habits and Habitat: This species occurs in all wooded habitats from deciduous forests to towns and riparian growth. It is a very noisy bird during spring and is most easily found by its call. It uses a variety of scolding calls as it harasses large birds and squirrels in its territory. It is also highly territorial toward other males. Although the Great Crested Flycatcher prefers edge or clearings in forests, it normally perches within or beneath the canopy and is not easily seen; it rarely perches on exposed wires as do kingbirds. It feeds both by sallying out from these perches and by gleaning insects from branches and leaf surfaces. It is generally a quiet bird after nesting is completed.

Field Marks: The only other Kansas flycatcher with reddish brown in the wings and tail is the smaller and much paler Ash-throated Flycatcher. The present species has a very distinct call, a loud, emphatic "wheep." It also has several more complex calls, including a rapidly repeated "whip-whip-whip."

Food: The Great Crested Flycatcher eats a large variety of insects, including dragonflies, beetles, bees, ants, butterflies and moths, flies, and caterpillars; it also eats spiders, a variety of berries, and an occasional small lizard.

A Cassin's Kingbird (*Tyrannus vociferans*). Photograph by Dale and Marian Zimmerman.

Cassin's Kingbird
Tyrannus vociferans Swainson

Status: The Cassin's Kingbird is apparently an irregular transient and possible summer resident in extreme southwestern Kansas. It is often confused with the Western Kingbird, and sight records need confirmation.

Period of Occurrence: The only specimen is from Morton County (26 May 1950); additional sight records from there are between 24 April and 26 May and 5 to 22 September. There are additional unconfirmed sight records north to Cheyenne and east to Russell counties.

Habits and Habitat: The Grabers (1950) saw from one to four individuals on several occasions during the years 1950 to 1953. All of these were in the weedy pastures and slopes bordering the Cimarron River rather than in the riparian growth, which largely consisted of cottonwoods. Schwilling (pers. comm.) considered it fairly common there during 1951 and estimated a total of 12 to 15 birds. None was found during numerous visits during the 1960s, but there have been several reports since the early 1970s. It is a typical kingbird in feeding behavior, nesting habits, and pugnacity but is said to be calmer and quieter than the Western Kingbird, with which it sometimes occurs.

Field Marks: The most distinctive note is "che-bew," "che-queer," or a low nasal "queer." The Cassin's Kingbird also utters a series of loud, harsh, rapid, repetitive "ke-ke-ki-deer" notes. Its white throat contrasts with a gray breast and upperparts. It also has a narrow buffy white tip to the tail rather than white outer tail feathers.

Food: The Cassin's Kingbird eats largely insects, including bees, wasps, flies, grasshoppers, and caterpillars; it is also said to eat more berries than other kingbirds. Ohlendorf (1974) reported one capturing a juvenile harvest mouse (*Reithrodontomys*) weighing 5.5 grams.

A Western Kingbird (*Tyrannus verticalis*). Photograph by Robert C. Bearse.

Western Kingbird
Tyrannus verticalis Say

Status: The Western Kingbird is a common transient and summer resident except in extreme eastern Kansas, where it is rare and local and probably still expanding its range. It is most common in western Kansas.

Period of Occurrence: The Western Kingbird is most common from late April through early September; extreme dates are 2 April and 25 September with stragglers to 16 and 19 October. Spring arrival is usually near 22 to 26 April.

Breeding: The nest is a bulky cup of plant materials, paper, string, and rags lined with roots, matted plant down, and hair and placed on a horizontal branch of a tree or occasionally a utility pole, windmill, or other man-made structure. Bent (1942) reports nesting in a variety of unlikely sites, including an old woodpecker cavity. The clutch is three to six, usually four or five, creamy white eggs with brown blotches and spots and gray or lavender spots. The incubation period is 12 to 14 days, probably by the female alone. It is normally single brooded. Most egg laying is during mid-June, with young fledging in early to mid-July.

Habits and Habitat: This kingbird is also widely known as the Arkansas Kingbird. It occurs in all edge habitats, most frequently in riparian habitat, shelterbelts, and farmsteads, and in residential areas. In west-central Kansas it outnumbers the Eastern Kingbird in those habitats but is outnumbered by the Eastern Kingbird in tree groves in rangeland. The early literature suggests a notable range extension eastward since the turn of the century. It is a very pugnacious species, harassing any large bird or mammal near its nest. However, it is tolerant of many small birds that often nest in the same isolated trees. It is extremely noisy during the early part of the breeding season, giving special calls at dawn and even during the night near street lights. It usually feeds from an exposed perch but may on occasion feed on or very near the ground in recently plowed fields. After nesting, some individuals wander, a few reaching the East Coast. It apparently does not usually gather in large flocks in fall, though Roger Boyd observed 45 over Baldwin on 27 August and Ely counted 43 along a one-mile stretch of utility lines in Edwards County on 13 August.

Field Marks: The Western Kingbird is yellow-breasted with a black tail, having a white outer edge on the outer tail feathers; the pale gray breast shows little contrast with the white throat. The most common call is a sharp "kip" or "whit"; it also uses a variety of twittering and sputtering calls; one has been described as "pkit-pkit-pkettle-dit," accented on the last note.

Food: The Western Kingbird feeds primarily on bees and grasshoppers, with smaller numbers of caterpillars, butterflies, bugs, and moths; it also eats some spiders, millipedes, and berries.

An Eastern Kingbird (*Tyrannus tyrannus*). Photograph by Bob Gress.

Eastern Kingbird
Tyrannus tyrannus (Linnaeus)

Status: The Eastern Kingbird is a common transient and summer resident statewide but is more common in the east.

Period of Occurrence: This kingbird is most common from late April

through early September; extreme
dates are 2 April and 8 October.

Breeding: Courtship involves an erratic, zig-zag, tumbling flight accompanied by shrill chattering.
The nest is usually on a horizontal branch within seven feet of the
ground, but it may be in a fork of a shrub, on a dead snag, or even on
a utility pole or other man-made structure. The nest is a bulky cup of
weed stalks and plant stems with an inner cup lined with roots, plant
down, and hair. The clutch is three to five creamy white eggs marked
with conspicuous irregular gray blotches and brown spots and speckles. Both sexes build, but only the female incubates. The incubation
period is 13 or 14 days; the nestling period about 18 days. It is single
brooded, with most egg laying in June and with most young fledging
during early and mid-July.

Habits and Habitat: The Eastern Kingbird usually feeds from an exposed
perch from which it sallies out to capture flying insects. It is aggressive
toward large birds and may briefly alight on its foe's back while peck-
ing at its neck or head. A common flight pattern is to hover with quivering wings just above vegetation. In much of its range it is called "bee
martin" in response to a presumed preference for honeybees — a preference not supported by analyses of stomach contents. It migrates
during the day in loose flocks, and in spring individuals can often be
seen resting briefly on low perches before moving on and being replaced by others. Large flocks have been reported in fall, as at the Konza
Prairie near Manhattan, where John Zimmerman observed large flocks
feeding on dogwood berries. The effect of weather on concentrations
was noted by Byron Walker, who saw 470 birds along Route 54 near
Kingman on 11 September 1975. All were gone on the 12th, following a 50-degree drop in temperature in just two days. Pete Janzen reported a flock of 110 in Sedgwick County on 28 August. On its wintering
grounds in northern South America the species wanders about in
large flocks, feeding largely on fruit in the tops of tall forest trees.

Field Marks: No other kingbird combines a black and white pattern and
a black tail broadly tipped with white. Its calls include a "kip-kip-kip-
per-kipper" and a series of shrill "dzep," "dzeet," or "tzee" notes repeated
in various combinations and speeds.

Food: Food is primarily insects, including bees, wasps, ants, large flies,
cicadas, grasshoppers, moths, and caterpillars; spiders; and a variety
of berries, fruits, and rarely seeds.

A Scissor-tailed Flycatcher (*Tyrannus forficatus*). Photograph by Bob Gress.

Scissor-tailed Flycatcher
Tyrannus forficatus (Gmelin)

Status: The Scissor-tailed Flycatcher is an uncommon to common transient and summer resident in southern and eastern Kansas, becoming rare northward, and is only casual in the northwest. In Kansas, it reaches its greatest breeding density in the southern tier of counties in the central part of the state. Numbers decrease sharply but in a radial manner northeastward to Cloud County (Zimmerman 1978). There was a noticeable range expansion into northeastern Kansas during the early 1950s.

Period of Occurrence: The Scissor-tailed Flycatcher is most numerous from mid-April to early October; extreme dates are 26 March and 6 November. In most of the state peak numbers are during the migration period — late April and October.

Breeding: The courtship of this species includes a spectacular "sky dance" in which the male performs a vertical zig-zag flight (a line of sharp-angled "VVVV's"), chattering loudly while opening and closing its long tail. At such times he may ascend a hundred feet into the air. The nest is a shallow cup of plant stems, string, bits of paper, and plant down lined with rootlets, plant down, and hair and placed on a horizontal tree limb or a man-made structure, such as a windmill, at low to moderate elevations. The clutch is two to six, usually three or four, white eggs with large brown spots and gray under markings. The female alone builds the nest, incubates, and does the bulk of the feeding of the young. The male perches nearby and actively defends its territory. The incubation period is 12 to 14 days; the nestling period about 14 days. It is apparently single brooded in Kansas. The family tends to remain together as a unit until ready to migrate. Postbreeding birds wander, and the species regularly reaches the Atlantic coast and Canada.

Habits and Habitat: This trim, exquisite species is one of our most popular and admired birds. It is a typical kingbird in most of its activities. It prefers open country with scattered trees, where it sits on an exposed perch, especially a fence or utility line. It feeds primarily on flying insects but also snatches insects from the ground and occasionally from exposed vegetation. Its normal flight is swift with rapid wing beats and tail folded. It readily harasses large birds and potential mammalian predators. It is usually intolerant of other species. Although highly territorial during the height of the breeding season, scissor-tails tend to occur in variably sized flocks at other times. Males continue to roost together at night even while nesting, and after nesting they are joined by females and immatures. These flocks may number 250 or more individuals. Thompson found over 1,000 at a roost in the Oklahoma Panhandle. In southern Mexico, a wintering area, Ely once counted 438 individuals leaving a small roosting thicket about one acre in size. The call is a "kip" or "tuk"; among its other vocalizations is a twilight song that consists of a series of "pup-pup-pup" notes. It also gives a number of rather explosive, sputtering calls.

Field Marks: Adults are unmistakable with their long, forked tails; immatures are browner but have similar pattern and show pink on the sides.

Food: Half of the diet of this species is said to be grasshoppers and crickets; it also eats wasps, moths, caterpillars, spiders, and some berries. It eats seeds, but only rarely.

A Horned Lark (*Eremophila alpestris*). Photograph by Bob Gress.

LARKS (FAMILY ALAUDIDAE)
Horned Lark
Eremophila alpestris (Linnaeus)

Status: The Horned Lark is present all year and is most common in central and western Kansas. Presumably, summer populations are resident, augmented by transients and winter birds at other seasons.

Period of Occurrence: The Horned Lark occurs during all months but is most conspicuous October through April.

Breeding: Nesting begins very early, with courtship and establishment of territories by early March. The nest is a shallow cup placed in a depression either near a grass clump or in a completely bare area. It is constructed of grass stems and lined with finer grasses, plant down, hair, and feathers. The clutch is three to six, usually four, grayish white eggs heavily spotted with brown. The incubation period is 11 days, but the nestling period is short (about 10 days), and young often leave the nest before capable of flight. The first clutch is started very early (by 3 March in Ellis County), perhaps as an adaptation to avoid cowbird parasitism. The young begin forming flocks by mid-April while the female begins a second clutch. Peak nesting statewide is late March–early April and late May–early June, for first and second clutches respectively.

Habits and Habitat: The Horned Lark occurs in areas of low or sparse vegetation such as fallow fields, cultivated fields (until the ground surface is covered by vegetation), disturbed areas, and grasslands. The male sings from a low perch and also has an impressive flight song presented most frequently before dawn. In this the male ascends several hundred feet into the air and circles with a hovering flight while repeating a complex series of twittering notes. The call has been described as "tsee-titi," accented on the first syllable. In western Kansas it occurs in small flocks during spring and summer and in flocks of hundreds to many thousands during fall and winter. During periods of heavy snowfall, large flocks congregate along newly cleared roads, and many are killed by passing vehicles. A common local name is "snow-bird." Local populations may move south in fall; at any rate their numbers are augmented by transients from farther north.

Field Marks: At close range the face markings are unmistakable. The "horns," small tufts of black feathers above the forehead, are difficult to see except at close range and when in a good position. At other times note its habit of walking rather than hopping and the contrasting light brown upperparts, white belly, and black tail.

Food: During the nesting season the Horned Lark feeds on a variety of insects, including caterpillars, ants, wasps, grasshoppers, and bugs gleaned from vegetation or captured on bare ground. Seeds of grasses, weeds, and waste grain are the predominate food at other seasons.

Purple Martins (*Progne subis*). Photograph by Bob Gress.

SWALLOWS (FAMILY HIRUNDINIDAE)
Purple Martin
Progne subis (Linnaeus)

Status: The Purple Martin is a common transient and summer resident in eastern Kansas and an uncommon and local summer resident in the west. It breeds west to Decatur, Scott, and Stevens counties but with few nestings yet recorded from the extreme southwest.

Period of Occurrence: This species is most common from early April through August; extreme dates are 2 March and 28 September. Later dates, several to 14 November, are unlikely and need verification.

Breeding: The Purple Martin is colonial; in Kansas it uses artificial bird boxes in towns. Most successful colonies are 12 to 25 feet above ground in open areas with utility lines or similar perches nearby. Each male begins defending a compartment and ledge upon returning, and each female eventually selects one of these sites. Nesting begins three or four weeks after returning, usually mid-April to mid-May. The nest is a cup of plant stems, grass, and mud lined (by the male) with green leaves.

Some nests are very sparse; others completely fill the space available. The clutch is three to eight, usually four or five, white eggs. In eastern Kansas most eggs are laid between 20 May and 7 June (Olmstead 1955). The incubation period is 15 or 16 days, the young fledge in about four weeks, and the species is single brooded. Both sexes share nest-building duties, but only the female incubates. Both sexes share in feeding the young.

Habits and Habitat: This is the first swallow to return in spring, the actual date depending on local temperature and weather conditions. A few adult males arrive first, sometimes two weeks before the first pair, followed by the first females and then the year-old birds. These scouts sometimes succumb to severe weather and at times are literally trapped inside houses by snow and ice. The Purple Martin has a number of chirping and gurgling calls and a pleasant song. The flight, alternately flapping and sailing with broad triangular wings, is distinctive. Martins face competition for nest sites from House Sparrows and especially European Starlings. Olmstead (1955) saw actual egg removal by sparrows and found one female martin trapped in her chamber by a House Sparrow nest. Gaunt (1959) saw starlings eating martin eggs, but Thompson has seen martins pummel starlings and drive them away from houses.

Like other swallows, martins spend much of their time on the wing, even drinking and bathing while in flight. Near colonies some birds may be active at night. Martins assemble into huge flocks prior to the fall departure, usually from mid-July to mid-August. A flock of 20,000 was reported in Wichita on 17 September. These nocturnal roosts are frequently in shade trees in towns and cities and shared with robins, grackles, and other species — to the dismay of local human residents. On occasion, large numbers are killed illegally by misguided individuals to "protect human health," as occurred recently in Wichita. Such ignorance should not be excused!

Field Marks: Males are unmistakable blue black, not purple; females and immatures, brown above and light below, are much larger than any other Kansas swallow. Surprisingly, some observers confuse male martins with starlings!

Food: The food of the Purple Martin is primarily flying insects, especially ants, wasps, beetles, grasshoppers, dragonflies, and flies; at times insect prey is snatched from the ground. In numerous areas martin populations are encouraged as a potential means of insect control.

Tree Swallows (*Tachycineta bicolor*). Photograph by David A. Rintoul.

Tree Swallow
Tachycineta bicolor (Vieillot)

Status: The Tree Swallow is a common transient and rare, local summer resident in eastern Kansas and is an uncommon to rare transient in the west. In recent years it has bred, locally, at large reservoirs west to Barton County.

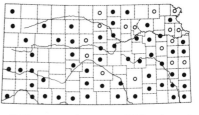

Period of Occurrence: The Tree Swallow is most common as a transient from mid-April to mid-May and from late August through September. Spring arrival is usually early April. Extreme dates are 8 March and 24 October. Occasional individuals have remained near open water to 31 January (Wilson Reservoir, Russell County).

Breeding: The nest is in a cavity, usually an old woodpecker hole, and is typically over water. Most Kansas nests have been in standing, drowned timber at large reservoirs. At Cheyenne Bottoms in 1977 a pair occupied a bird box erected by Edmund Martinez. The nest is a cup of dried grass lined with feathers. The clutch is four to six, usually five, pure white eggs. The incubation period is 13 to 16 days, the young fledge in about three weeks, and the species is single brooded.

Habits and Habitat: The Tree Swallow is widespread in Kansas during migration, usually with other species of swallows and most often near water. The first flocks arrive soon after the first martins appear, usually at lakes or reservoirs where they feed low over the water surface and rest on nearby bare vegetation. Later they appear in flocks of mixed species. Large roosting flocks can be found in cattail growth at Cheyenne Bottoms, especially in fall. A few individuals linger until the last open water freezes; one taken at Cheyenne Bottoms on 15 December was picking dead insects off the surface of the ice. Late sightings of swallows are most likely to be of this species.

Early nesting sites were limited to northeast Kansas along the major rivers, but the recent flooding of standing timber during the building of large reservoirs has allowed a marked increase in both numbers and extent of breeding range. A nesting colony at the Marais des Cygnes Wildlife Management Area, first noted in 1979, grew to over 100 pairs, then gradually declined, and eventually disappeared as the snags rotted and fell (Schwilling 1990). Recent nestings in bluebird boxes in Jewell and Reno counties suggest that the species will take advantage of nest boxes placed in suitable habitat.

Field Marks: In good light the green or blue back of the adult is conspicuous, and in all plumages the pure white underparts are distinctive. The white of the face does not extend upward behind and above the eye as in the Violet-green Swallow.

Food: Most of the year the Tree Swallow feeds on flying insects, chiefly beetles, ants, flies, and wasps. During migration berries (and rarely a few seeds) are taken when inclement weather eliminates flying insects. The use of bayberries on beaches of the Atlantic coast is well documented.

A Violet-green Swallow (*Tachycineta thalassina*). Photograph by Bob Gress.

Violet-green Swallow
Tachycineta thalassina (Swainson)

Status: The Violet-green Swallow is a casual visitor, usually in fall. It has bred once in Kansas.

Period of Occurrence: Most sightings have been at the Cheyenne Bottoms during late September; extreme dates are 8 August and 4 November. From one to three individuals were reported at the Cheyenne Bottoms at various

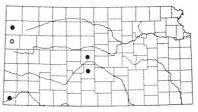

times during six of the 14 years during the period 1972 to 1985. There are unconfirmed sightings in fall from Jefferson, Johnson, Morton, Sherman, and Stafford counties. A published spring record from Shawnee County is rejected. A pair bred in Wallace County in 1987.

Breeding: The discovery of an active nest in Wallace County by Stan Roth and students on 3 June 1987 was a great surprise. Two males and a female were seen at a rock outcrop, and a male was observed carrying nesting material into a cavity in the bluff. On 17 and 18 June Marvin Schwilling visited the site and saw only the female — apparently feeding young in the nest (Schwilling and Roth 1987). The typical nest, constructed of grasses and lined with feathers, is placed in a natural cavity in a tree or in a cliff face, woodpecker hole, or crevice in a man-made structure. The clutch is four to six pure white eggs. The incubation period is 14 or 15 days, and the species is single brooded.

Habits and Habitat: Most sightings in Kansas are in fall, when a few individuals join the huge flocks of swallows congregating at such favored spots as Cheyenne Bottoms. At such times the birds alight on dirt roads and utility lines and can sometimes be approached quite closely.

Field Marks: The Violet-green Swallow can be distinguished from the similar Tree Swallow by the white of the face, which extends above and behind the eye and clearly outlines it. If seen from above, white patches on the sides of the upper tail coverts are also distinctive.

Food: Food of the Violet-green Swallow is exclusively flying insects, including flies, ants, termites, beetles, and moths.

A Northern Rough-winged Swallow (*Stelgidopteryx serripennis*). Photograph by Bob Gress.

Northern Rough-winged Swallow
Stelgidopteryx serripennis (Audubon)

Status: The Northern Rough-winged Swallow is a common transient and uncommon summer resident statewide. It is least common in southwestern Kansas.

Period of Occurrence: This species is most numerous from mid-April to mid-September; in most years spring arrival is 7 to 10 April; extreme dates are 15 March and 22 October. Winter sightings are probably of immature Tree Swallows.

Breeding: The nest is placed within a cavity, often at the end of a bur-row in a steep-faced stream bank or road cut. Other nest sites in-clude rock outcrops as well as drain pipes and other man-made structures. This swallow is usually a solitary nester, but two or three pairs may nest in close proximity. The nest is a shallow cup of grass lined with fine grass but not feath-ers. The clutch is four to eight, usually five or six, pure white eggs. The incubation period is 14 to 16 days; incubation is chiefly by the female. The nestling period is 19 to 21 days; the species is single brooded, with most young fledged by mid-July and most birds leaving the nesting area shortly thereafter.

Habits and Habitat: The Northern Rough-winged Swallow normally oc-curs near water, from tiny streams to large reservoirs, but also in the vicinity of road cuts or similar nest sites. Adults forage low over the ground over farm ponds and grassland or other open country. This species is much more widespread than the similar Bank Swallow with which it is often confused. Many early reports of Bank Swallows in cen-tral and western Kansas, including those of a few pairs nesting in banks, were undoubtedly this species.

Field Marks: The grayish or brownish throat is distinctive in all plumages. The name rough-winged refers to the short, stiff, hooked barbs on the outer vane of the outer primary of adult males, which can be seen (or felt) only when the bird is in the hand.

Food: The food of the Northern Rough-winged Swallow is entirely fly-ing insects, including wasps, ants, bees, flies, and beetles.

Bank Swallows (*Riparia riparia*). Photograph by David A. Rintoul.

Bank Swallow
Riparia riparia (Linnaeus)

Status: The Bank Swallow is a common transient and local summer resident in eastern Kansas and an uncommon transient in the west. It may have bred there formerly. It is often confused with the Northern Rough-winged Swallow.

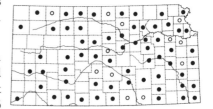

Period of Occurrence: Specimen records are between 29 April and 29 September; extreme dates (sight records, some doubtful) are 26

March and 7 April and 3 October. Most migration is from late April to late May and mid-August to mid-September.

Breeding: The Bank Swallow is highly colonial, with nesting colonies of 10 to several hundred pairs. The nest is in a burrow, usually in a steep-sided sandy bank of a river or stream, but in some areas road cuts, gravel pits, or even sawdust piles at sawmills are used. Burrows are usually near the top of the bank, sometimes only a few inches apart; they extend inward about two feet before inclining upward to the nest chamber. The nest is a platform of grasses and usually lined with feathers. The clutch is four to six, usually five, pure white eggs. The incubation period is about 15 days, and young fledge in about three weeks. The species is single brooded. There are no recent, documented breeding records west of Jewell and Stafford counties.

Habits and Habitat: Adults often select and defend a burrow dug in previous years. When a new burrow is needed or an old one needs repair, both sexes participate. Sexual pursuit is a common part of the courtship. Both members of the pair sit at the burrow entrance and sing together. Breeding is sometimes delayed by high water that undercuts the river banks. In eastern Kansas in 1961 nesting was delayed about one month, with the peak of egg laying around 12 July (Johnston 1964b). Bank Swallows are most obvious during migration, when they flock with other swallows, and at the breeding colonies.

Field Marks: This is a small swallow with a white throat and belly separated by a contrasting brown breast band. It also differs from the Northern Rough-winged Swallow in its flight, which is typically low and more fluttery and erratic.

Food: The Bank Swallow's food is almost entirely flying insects, with ants, wasps, termites, true bugs, beetles, flies, and moths predominating, and some caterpillars.

A Cliff Swallow (*Hirundo pyrrhonota*). Photograph by Roger Boyd.

Cliff Swallow
Hirundo pyrrhonota Vieillot

Status: The Cliff Swallow is a common transient and local summer resident statewide. It is becoming a more common breeder in the east.

Period of Occurrence: Transients are most numerous from late April to mid-May and in late July and early August; extreme dates are 4 April and 15 October (however, birds have left the breeding areas months earlier!).

Breeding: The Cliff Swallow typically nests colonially on a vertical surface with an overhang, usually a cliff face, a bridge, or under the eaves of a building. Some colonies may number several thousand individuals; rarely a pair will nest singly or in a Barn Swallow colony. In some areas nesting has been encouraged by nailing a narrow, unpainted board under the eaves of a building. The nest, gourd-shaped with the entrance at the end of the neck, is constructed with mud and rootlets and lined with grass, rootlets, and feathers. Old nests are frequently used in successive years. Nest building requires about two weeks, and a colony is a very busy place, with streams of swallows gathering mud and carrying it to their nests. The clutch is three to six, usually four or five, creamy white eggs spotted with brown. The incubation period is 12 to 15 days, the nestling period is about 24 days, and the species is single brooded in Kansas. Most clutches are completed between late May and mid-June. Nests are sometimes forcibly appropriated by House Sparrows.

Habits and Habitat: Alfred Gross (*in* Bent 1942) presents an interesting history of the Cliff Swallow in North America in the eighteenth and nineteenth centuries. It is very erratic in distribution and breeding in central and western Kansas and merits further study. Its breeding distribution is limited by nest sites and by the proper type and consistency of mud. As a result, colonies may move frequently from site to site or even nest at unexpected times. For example, near Hays, more than 100 birds suddenly appeared on 6 July, a month after birds usually begin nesting, and rapidly began carrying mud to a large culvert. They departed several days later, leaving strips of mud and a quarter-finished nest! At a large colony at Elkader, Logan County, nest building continued over a period of weeks as new birds arrived and joined the periphery of the colony. When the young of the major part of the colony fledged, the late arrivals deserted their nests and left with the earlier nesters. Unusual nest sites reported by Bent included nests placed among the sticks of a Great Blue Heron's nest and on a cliff above a Prairie Falcon's nest and plastered under large branches of pine trees.

Breeding birds depart soon after the young are fledged, often by mid-July. Most sightings after late August are from the larger reservoirs in eastern Kansas. Our birds winter in South America; one banded at Elkader was found in Argentina. This is the species widely heralded to return, on a given date, to San Juan Capistrano — more a media tale than a biological fact. Occasionally birds arrive early and die in their nests as a result of an unseasonal period of cold weather, as in northern Illinois in June 1887 (Bent 1942).

Field Marks: At all ages the buffy rump and dark rufous throat are distinctive. Adults have a conspicuous white or buffy forehead, but this is darker, often brown, in juveniles. In flight the Cliff Swallow glides, on flattened wings, more than other swallows. The call is described as a harsh "chur" or a nasal "nyew."

Food: The Cliff Swallow feeds almost entirely on flying insects, including beetles, true bugs, ants, wasps, moths, grasshoppers, and small dragonflies. It also takes spiders and rarely a few berries.

Remarks: The Cave Swallow (*Hirundo fulva* Vieillot) continues to expand its range in south-central Texas, where it is apparently replacing Barn Swallows nesting in culverts. Individuals wander, and the Cave Swallow may eventually visit Kansas. It resembles the Cliff Swallow but has a buffy throat and dark forehead — but remember that Cliff Swallows in juvenile plumage have dark foreheads too!

A Barn Swallow (*Hirundo rustica*). Photograph by Bob Gress.

Barn Swallow
Hirundo rustica Linnaeus

Status: The Barn Swallow is a common transient and summer resident statewide but is local in the far west.

Period of Occurrence: It is most numerous from mid-April through mid-October; first spring arrivals are around 5 April in most years; extreme dates are 13 March and 25 November. Winter records are suspect and need verification.

Breeding: Most nesting in Kansas today is on horizontal beams or upright walls of man-made structures such as barns or bridges and in road-side culverts. In the latter the Barn Swallow is sometimes colonial, with nests spaced as closely as three feet or less. The nest is a cup or a half-cone (when supported on one side) constructed of mud and rootlets lined with rootlets and feathers. The clutch is three to seven, usually four or five, white eggs spotted with brown. The incubation period is 13 to 15 days; the nestling period is 16 to 24 days. Both sexes build, but most incubation is by the female. It is double brooded in Kansas: peak periods for first and second clutches in eastern Kansas are late May and early July, respectively. As with many species, these peaks are later in western Kansas — early June and mid-July respectively. Early arrivals to a site take over any surviving nests, refurbishing them if necessary. Anthony (1969) found that these nests had a higher success rate than new nests.

Habits and Habitat: The Barn Swallow is one of the most familiar and best-loved species in Kansas. It has a very large range that includes most of the Old World; our birds winter in South America. It has a very swift and highly maneuverable flight, with less gliding than other swallows. Most feeding is by sweeping low over grassland or water courses. The Barn Swallow is a day migrant and can often be seen traveling in loose flocks that dart about but maintain an overall constant direction. In fall it congregates in huge flocks at favorable feeding and roosting areas such as Cheyenne Bottoms and our larger reservoirs. It mobs such predators as cats and hawks and defends its nest by calling loudly and flying at the intruder.

Originally swallows nested on cliff faces, caves, and rock ledges, often near water. Populations increased greatly with the arrival of Europeans and their structures, and more recently the range of this species expanded again with the construction of interstate highways across the prairies. Now swallows nest in roadside culverts and feed over nearby farm ponds and prairies. R. Lohoefener (1977) found that swallows nesting colonially had a lower success rate than did birds nesting singly, probably because the increased activity at a colony attracted predators and molesters. Lohoefener also found significant disruption of Barn Swallow colonies when Cliff Swallows arrived later and began nesting. Most mortality at single nests was due to high temperatures and interference by House Sparrows. Both the Barn Swallow and the Cliff Swallow have inadvertently aided in the expansion of House Sparrows, which now occupy swallow nests in otherwise inhospitable areas.

Banding in west-central Kansas showed that adults have a very high rate of fidelity to successful nest sites and return year after year, whereas immatures disperse widely and rarely return to their natal site. This presumably ensures continued success at proven breeding sites while providing a surplus that finds new areas or replaces local mortality.

Field Marks: This is our only species with a deeply forked tail; it is metallic blue above and rufous to pure white below.

Food: Food of this species is entirely flying insects, including grasshoppers, flies, true bugs, beetles, moths, and small dragonflies.

A Steller's Jay (*Cyanocitta stelleri*). Photograph by Bob Gress.

CROWS, RAVENS, AND JAYS (FAMILY CORIVDAE)
Steller's Jay
Cyanocitta stelleri (Gmelin)

Status: The Steller's Jay is a casual winter visitant in western Kansas and a vagrant in eastern Kansas. There are two specimens from Morton County, one from Riley County, and one from Douglas County. Most of the recent records are from Morton County.

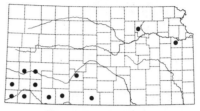

Period of Occurrence: The Steller's Jay has been recorded from September to May, with most records falling within the November-December limits. The dates of extreme occurrence are 11 September and 5 May. This jay is sporadic in its occurrence and has been recorded only in 1916, 1934, 1953–54, 1964, 1973, 1978, and 1989.

Habits and Habitat: This spectacular jay may occur in wooded areas along the Cimarron River in Morton County. In 1989, it was found inhabiting the cottonwood trees along the river and was also found in shelterbelts with redcedar. In 1989 at Hugoton, Stevens County, and in Satanta, Haskell County, they fed at feeders. Steller's Jays are sometimes found in the company of Blue Jays. This jay like all jays is noisy when disturbed.

Field Marks: The Stellar's Jay is similar in size and shape to the Blue Jay but is darker in coloration and holds the crest more erect.

Food: The Steller's Jay feeds upon both vegetable and animal matter, the latter mainly insects. Small mammals, eggs, and sometimes carrion are also included in the diet.

A Blue Jay (*Cyanocitta cristata*). Photograph by Frank S. Shipley.

Blue Jay
Cyanocitta cristata (Linnaeus)

Status: The Blue Jay is a common transient and summer resident statewide. In the winter it occurs mainly in the eastern part of the state, with small numbers in the west.

Period of Occurrence: This jay occurs throughout the year.

Breeding: There are nesting records sufficient to show that this jay breeds throughout the state. The nest is usually placed in trees and is constructed of twigs and bark, with leaves and fine roots lining the interior. In Kansas the usual number of eggs is four. The eggs are light blue with dark spots. Most of the nesting records for the state are in May, but there are April and July records. The incubation period is 17–18 days. The young fledge in about 17 days. They may raise two broods in Kansas.

Habits and Habitat: This bright bird can be found in almost any town in Kansas during the summer. In the winter it frequents bird feeders and makes a bright splash of color in an otherwise dull environment.

The Blue Jay's noisy "jay, jay, jay" call is a familiar sound to most. You can be sure when it's calling its loudest that there are would-be predators in the area. It will frequently spot danger and will be the first to alert other birds in the area. Although most of us are familiar with the "jay" call note of the Blue Jay, few are familiar with the other sounds it makes. Strange sounds in the trees will frequently lead a bird-watcher to look for an exciting new species only to find the sounds coming from a Blue Jay.

Although the Blue Jay is frequently said to destroy other birds' nests, it probably does no great harm to bird populations. We frequently take common birds for granted and don't take time to look at them closely to appreciate their beauty. The Blue Jay is such a bird that bears closer inspection. The blending of the blues, blacks, and whites is most attractive.

Blue Jays migrate south in large flocks in the fall, with upward of 150 birds in a group being reported. Movements of groups have been observed over vast expanses of grassland, far from trees.

Field Marks: The Blue Jay in Kansas needs little describing to anyone. It makes itself well known even to the most unobserving.

Food: Blue Jays are mainly vegetarians. They eat a variety of seed types including sunflowers; they are particularly fond of pecans and may decimate a crop. They do eat bird eggs and occasionally baby birds or small mammals.

A Scrub Jay (*Aphelocoma coerulescens*). Photograph by Bob Gress.

Scrub Jay
Aphelocoma coerulescens (Bosc)

Status: The Scrub Jay is an irregular, low-density visitant to the southwest corner of the state and casual to those counties bordering the Arkansas River. It has been recorded as far east as Cowley and Barton counties.

Period of Occurrence: Almost all of the Scrub Jay records are from fall and winter. Dates of extreme occurrence are 16 September and 14 May.

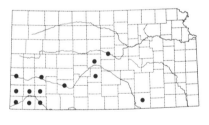

Habits and Habitat: In southwest and western Kansas the Scrub Jay can be found along wooded river valleys such as the Cimarron and Arkansas River valleys and in towns. It occasionally comes to bird feeders. In Morton County, it has been found in Elkhart and along the river north of town. In 1989 it fed at feeders in the Cimarron Grasslands, Morton

County, and at Satanta, Haskell County. Although it is a jay, it can be very quiet and secretive and may go unnoticed.

Field Marks: The Scrub Jay is slightly larger than a Blue Jay but has no crest, a longer tail, pale brown back, and a streaked throat that is lighter than the breast.

Food: The Scrub Jay feeds primarily upon acorns and pinyon pine nuts. If these foods are in short supply it may wander in search of other types of seeds. It occasionally eats bird eggs and young.

A Gray-breasted Jay (*Aphelocoma ultramarina*). Photograph by Dale and Marian Zimmerman.

Gray-breasted Jay
Aphelocoma ultramarina (Bonaparte)

Status: The Gray-breasted Jay is a vagrant to Kansas. There is one acceptable record, a specimen taken near Mt. Jesus, Clark County, March 1906. The specimen was identified by L. L. Dyche. Although the present whereabouts of the specimen is unknown, measurements published seem to leave little doubt as to its identification. The usual range of this species is western Texas to Arizona and south into Mexico.

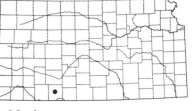

A Pinyon Jay (*Gymnorhinus cyanocephalus*). Photograph by Dale and Marian Zimmerman.

Pinyon Jay
Gymnorhinus cyanocephalus Wied

Status: The Pinyon Jay is an irregular winter visitant in western Kansas and casual elsewhere. It can be found in large flocks in its normal range, but most sightings in Kansas are of single birds. However, Scott Seltman recorded a flock of 100+ birds in Morton County on 12 September 1982.

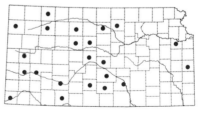

Period of Occurrence: The Pinyon Jay has been recorded every month of the year in Kansas except June. However, most records are for the winter months. The dates of extreme occurrence are 31 July to 7 May.

Habits and Habitat: In Kansas the Pinyon Jay is usually found along the Cimarron River in Morton County. Most of the other records are of birds found in towns, frequently at feeders. A Pinyon Jay was sighted on 31 July 1966 at a feeder in Kingman County. R. Lohoefener has had up to a dozen at his feeder in Decatur County. One individual at a feeder in Pratt, Pratt County, was present from 23 October to 15 March. This species is known for its nomadic wandering, possibly in search of a food supply when its normal sources fail.

Although this "blue crow" is called a jay, it may be more closely allied to the crows.

Field Marks: The Pinyon Jay is a uniformly light blue colored bird with no distinctive markings. The bill is more crow size than in the Blue Jay.

Food: The Pinyon Jay feeds primarily on the nuts of the pinyon pine. When this source fails the birds may have to seek other sources of vegetable matter. This jay has been known to eat insects, particularly in the breeding season. Occasionally, it resorts to eating bird eggs and young.

A Clark's Nutcracker (*Nucifraga columbiana*). Photograph by Bob Gress.

Clark's Nutcracker
Nucifraga columbiana (Wilson)

Status: The Clark's Nutcracker is a casual visitor. Although this is a species from the mountains of the western United States, the Kansas records are scattered throughout the state.

Period of Occurrence: This nutcracker occurs in Kansas primarily in the fall, winter, and spring months. There was a notable irruption during the fall and winter of 1972–73. The dates of extreme occurrence are 13 August and 7 May.

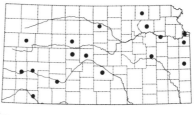

Habits and Habitat: The Clark's Nutcracker was named after the famous explorer Capt. William Clark, who was the first one to mention the nutcracker, although he erroneously identified it as a "new species of woodpecker." This is not surprising if one observes its woodpeckerlike flight.

In Kansas, this species does not seem to prefer any particular habitat and has been seen in cities as well as countryside as long as there are trees available.

Field Marks: The Clark's Nutcracker is larger than a Blue Jay and has gray and white plumage. The bill is heavier than a jay's.

Food: The Clark's Nutcracker is primarily a vegetarian, preferring pinyon nuts and other types of pine and fir seeds. It has been known to take eggs and young birds of other species. During the breeding season, it will consume insects.

A Black-billed Magpie (*Pica pica*). Photograph by Allen Cruickshank for the Cornell Laboratory of Ornithology.

Black-billed Magpie
Pica pica (Linnaeus)

Status: The Black-billed Magpie is a common resident in the western part of Kansas, east at least to Comanche, Stafford, Barton, and Republic counties. It is of casual occurrence farther east in fall and winter.

Periods of Occurrence: In western Kansas the magpie is a year-round resident. It has occurred in the east in the summer, but most records from the east are post-breeding wanderers.

Breeding: The Black-billed Magpie breeds throughout the western half of Kansas. Magpie breeding records extend from 11 April through 20 June, with most nesting occurring around 15 May (Johnston 1964b). The nest is a bulky structure composed of large sticks with a mud cup lined with softer material. It is placed in a sturdy tree usually about 10 to 12 feet high. Although clutch-size data are not available from Kansas, records from other states indicate that most nests contain from four to seven eggs, with five being an average. The eggs are greenish gray with dark spotting. Incubation of the eggs is done by the female and lasts for approximately 18 days. The naked young grow rapidly and depart the nest in approximately four weeks. The fledged young continue to be fed by the adults for several days after leaving the nest.

Habits and Habitat: This beautiful member of the crow family is a familiar sight in the western part of the state. It usually occurs in small flocks during the nonbreeding season. Although nesting in trees, it frequently is seen feeding on the ground. If unmolested, Black-billed Magpies can become fairly tame and allow you to closely approach them. However, most magpies are very wary and fly at the first sign of people.

Many states formerly considered the magpie a nuisance and placed a bounty on it. Although it was never killed in large numbers in Kansas, it was not so fortunate in other states. Poison bait was frequently placed for the coyote and to prevent the magpie from eating the bait, poison grain was spread first to control the magpie. In 1921–22 in Umatilla County, Oregon, it was estimated that 5,000 magpies were poisoned in just a few months (Kalmbach 1927). The species now has the full protection of federal law and can no longer be shot or poisoned.

Field Marks: The magpie's large size, oily green plumage with contrasting white, and long tail serve to identify it. There are no other birds in the state with this combination.

Food: The Black-billed Magpie, like many of the members of this family, is opportunistic and will eat most anything that is available. Some of the more common foods are carrion (especially road kills), dung, and insects. Insects are the primary food of this species, with carrion being second. Grain is eaten but usually when other food is unavailable (Bent 1946).

An American Crow (*Corvus brachyrhynchos*). Photograph by Bob Gress.

American Crow
Corvus brachyrhynchos Brehm

Status: The American Crow is a common resident statewide. It is an abundant migrant and winter resident in the central part of Kansas, especially in Stafford, McPherson, Harvey, and Sedgwick counties.

Period of Occurrence: This crow occurs in all months of the year. The resident population is probably augmented by migrants from further north.

Breeding: The American Crow breeds throughout the state, with breeding densities greater in the eastern half of Kansas. Nest building begins in early spring, and the eggs are laid from 10 March to 31 May.

Nests are frequently built in cities as well as in the countryside. Because of their quiet nature during the breeding season, the nesting birds may go unobserved until the young hatch and start begging for food. The average number of eggs is four. After an incubation period of approximately 18 days, the eggs hatch and the young are fed in the nest for about 36 days. Even after the young leave the nest, they are tended by the parents for several weeks.

Habits and Habitat: The American Crow is a very successful species. It is able to exploit its environment to its best use whether in town or country. Like many of the crow family, it can become quite tame if left alone. Thompson regularly observed crows coming in to feed on garbage that was discarded near a house. In towns they frequent lawns and open parks.

Crows have been considered a nuisance by some. They have been slaughtered by the thousands but are exceedingly successful in sustaining their numbers. Many years ago it was not uncommon for "hunters" to find winter roosting trees of crows. While the crows were away during the day, the "hunters" placed dynamite in the tree. When the crows returned and had settled for the night, the dynamite was detonated, killing thousands of crows, not to mention the trees. In recent years, crows have become a problem during the winter in Wichita. Thousands seek the shelter of the warmer city and quickly become a public nuisance. Driving them out of residential sections into the parks has been fairly successful. Despite their being a nuisance, it is amazing how many crows will cram into a small area! The crows usually start dispersing to the countryside or migrating back north in early March.

Over the years, crows may have received a bum rap for their destructive ways. Bent (1946) tells of a letter he had from a Mr. Horsfall. Horsfall had planted corn and asparagus but was not getting any harvest from an area where he daily saw the crows feeding. Assuming the crows to be the culprits, he shot them. The stomachs of a number of birds were analyzed and found to contain cutworm heads and black beetles. He visited the field the next day about the time crows usually showed up and found great numbers of cutworms burrowing for shelter for the day. He repented from his previous conclusion and welcomed the crows back. They promptly ate the cutworms, allowing Mr. Horsfall to harvest his crop, and they all lived congenially together for ever after!

Crow hunting using calls and decoys (usually an owl) was once a popular sport. The mobbing behavior of crows is well known as is their dislike for owls. If you hear a flock of crows calling, you can bet they have spotted an owl, snake, or some other predator.

The American Crow is now fully protected by law. The Kansas Department of Wildlife recently set a hunting season and except in unusual circumstances where the birds have become a public nuisance, it is unlawful to shoot them outside of this open season.

Field Marks: See Chihuahuan Raven.

Food: The American Crow is omnivorous and will eat nearly anything. The U.S. Biological Survey identified nearly 650 different items in the food eaten by 2,118 crows (Bent 1946). Crows are frequently seen along roads early in the morning eating animals killed by cars.

Fish Crow
Corvus ossifragus Wilson

Status: The Fish Crow has recently been added to the list of Kansas birds. The first reported sighting was from Linn County, 30 September 1984. All other sightings have been made in Cherokee County along the Spring River, in the spring and summer of 1989 and 1990. On 27 July 1990, 15 were found at a roost on the Spring River near Galena. In the summer of 1991, a nesting pair was observed in a Great Blue Heron rookery in Cherokee County. It should remain on the hypothetical list until a specimen has been collected for positive identification.

Chihuahuan Raven
Corvus cryptoleucus Couch

Status: The Chihuahuan Raven appears to be an uncommon summer resident in the extreme southwestern part of the state and rare elsewhere in the west. It is a rare winter resident in the west. In January 1984 large numbers of ravens wintered in Liberal, Seward County. They were feeding at the local garbage dump. That dump has since been closed, and the ravens 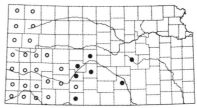 no longer occur. Their numbers may be declining. They occasionally wander eastward in the winter. A raven was accidentally shot in Wichita, Sedgwick County, in December 1989 by health officials trying to move crows out of residential areas. Because it was such a "large crow," it was mounted and later identified as a Chihuahuan Raven. This is the only verified record from so far east in Kansas.

Period of Occurrence: The Chihuahuan Raven has been recorded every month of the year. However, recent indications are that it is a rare winter resident.

Breeding: The Chihuahuan Raven's breeding range formerly encompassed the western part of Kansas along the Colorado border eastward to at least Ford, Kearny, Finney, and Gray counties. Although it was thought to be absent from Kansas, research by Marvin Schwilling and H. B. Tordoff found it to be common in the two western tiers of counties. The stick nests were placed in isolated trees and on windmills. They often contained pieces of barbed wire. There is little known of the breeding season. Clutch size in Kansas has not been determined, but in other states it is three to eight with an average of 4.7 (Johnsgard 1979). In Kansas the eggs are probably laid from late March to early May. Incubation time is 21 days. After hatching the young remain in the nest approximately four weeks before fledging. The adults tend the young for some time after they leave the nest.

Habits and Habitat: This raven is the largest member of the crow family still found in Kansas. In the summertime it is usually found in the far western part of the state. It does not require trees but may be found nesting in an isolated tree on the prairie. It can be quickly told from a crow by its croaking call. More information is needed about its habits in Kansas.

Field Marks: Four species of crows occur in Kansas. This may cause confusion in identification. The American Crow is much smaller than the
two ravens and generally has a "caw caw" call note, although young birds
may make noises totally unlike the adults. The recent occurrence of
the Fish Crow complicates crow identification in southeastern Kansas.
The Fish Crow is smaller than the American Crow but can only be safely
identified by knowledgeable birdwatchers. The Chihuahuan Raven is
the only likely raven species to be found in Kansas. In the hand the
nape feathers have white bases (hence its former name White-necked
Raven), but this is not a reliable field mark and is rarely observed in
the field. This species also has pointed feathers on the neck below the
large bill. The Common Raven has not been reported from the state
since 1916.

Food: Little is known about the food habits of the Chihuahuan Raven
in Kansas. It has been seen at garbage dumps in Seward County. It is
probably an opportunist and will eat carrion or vegetable matter as it
is available.

A Common Raven (*Corvus corax*). Photograph by Gerald J. Wiens.

Common Raven
Corvus corax Linnaeus

Status: The Common Raven is probably extirpated from the state. When buffalo were common in the state so was this raven, but it dis-appeared with the buffalo. This species is easily confused with the White-necked Raven, and there-fore all sight records of this species are suspect. There is but one spec-imen, and it was taken on 8 November 1916 in Jewell County.

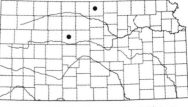

Allen (1872) recorded it as being common in Ellis County in 1871, but few other references are available.

A Black-capped Chickadee (*Parus atricapillus*). Photograph by Bob Gress.

TITMICE AND CHICKADEES (FAMILY PARIDAE)
Black-capped Chickadee
Parus atricapillus Linnaeus

Status: The Black-capped Chickadee is a common resident except in the southern tier of counties and in the extreme western part of the state. A bird of riparian habitat and forested cities, it becomes increasingly uncommon westward in the state. There seems to be little seasonal movement, and most birds are probably sedentary.

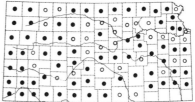

Period of Occurrence: The Black-capped Chickadee is a year-round resident.

Breeding: Since the Black-capped Chickadee is a resident, it probably breeds in all counties where it occurs. Johnston (1964b) listed 51 breeding records from March through June. He found that 64 percent of all eggs are laid between 11 April and 30 April. The usual clutch size is five eggs. Nests are placed in holes in trees or in nest boxes erected for either chickadees or wrens. The incubation period is 12 or 13 days, with the young leaving the nest in about 16 days. Both parents help to rear the young and continue to feed the young for several weeks after they leave the nest.

Habits and Habitat: The Black-capped Chickadee is primarily a bird of the woodlands and wooded cities. It is a common and welcome bird at winter feeders and can become tame and confiding. Banders have often trapped and banded chickadees only to find that they return to the baited trap for dinner, seemingly knowing that they will be released once again. It is one of the first birds to alert other birds in the area to a predator. The call note, "chicka, dee, dee, dee," is probably recognizable by most of the people who hear it.

An early nester, it is one of the first birds in the spring to start singing and nest building. However, unlike the call that gives it its name, the song is a two-note whistle, the first note being higher than the second. Chickadees will frequently use wren nesting boxes if available and to their liking.

Field Marks: See Carolina Chickadee.

Food: The Black-capped Chickadee is primarily an insect eater but takes seeds in the winter when insects are scarce. However, even in summer it will frequent feeders. Chickadees are easily lured to a feeder with sunflower seeds or sunflower hearts. They also will be attracted to other seeds but seem to prefer the former.

A Carolina Chickadee (*Parus carolinensis*). Photograph by Gerald J. Wiens.

Carolina Chickadee
Parus carolinensis Audubon

Status: The Carolina Chickadee is common in the southern tier of counties westward to Seward County. The western and northern limits are not precisely known except for Cowley and Sumner counties. There are reports from farther north, but owing to the similarity and intergradation with the Black-capped Chickadee, their validity is in doubt.

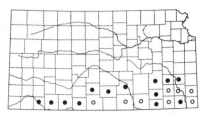

Period of Occurrence: The Carolina Chickadee is a year-round resident and does not migrate.

Breeding: There are few breeding records for Kansas, but since the Carolina Chickadee is a common resident there is no doubt of its breeding status. As far as is known, the breeding behavior is identical to that of the Black-capped Chickadee with which it interbreeds in Cowley County and other counties where their ranges meet. In Kansas there is no known hiatus in the ranges. Johnsgard (1979) states that they have a clutch size of seven. The incubation period is 13 days. The young leave the nest 17 days later and are tended by the parents for several weeks.

Habits and Habitat: The Carolina Chickadee is a bird of more moist forests than the Black-capped Chickadee. In Kansas it is found in cities and along streams and other wooded areas. In the southern counties, it replaces the Black-capped Chickadee at feeders. The Carolina Chickadee is an early nester and is one of the first birds to sing and court the female in the spring. Its four-note song is a cheerful start for the day. The Carolina Chickadee has the "chicka, dee, dee" call of the Black-capped but at a slightly different pitch and faster.

Field Marks: Distinguishing the Black-capped Chickadee from the Carolina Chickadee in the field can be difficult for the amateur in the area where the two overlap. Black-capped Chickadees in fresh fall plumage have white on the edges of the secondaries. This looks like a white streak on the top of the wings. This white is absent in Carolina Chickadees and in worn plumage of the Black-capped. In areas of intergradation, call notes may not be reliable. In Cowley County and southern Butler County, individual chickadees have been observed singing both songs, often one right after the other. Some birds sing a three-note song, unlike the song of either species. The area of intergradation in Cowley County is approximately seven miles wide, and specimens are intermediate in size between the two species.

Food: The food habits are similar to those of the Black-capped Chickadee.

A Mountain Chickadee (*Parus gambeli*). Photograph by Dale and Marian Zimmerman.

Mountain Chickadee
Parus gambeli Ridgway

Status: The Mountain Chickadee is a rare winter visitor to the southwestern corner of the state. It was first recorded from Finney County in 1951 by Marvin Schwilling. The most recent records are primarily from Morton County, where it is recorded with some regularity. The 1989–90 occurrence found it moving somewhat farther east and north than usual with records

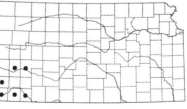

from Kearny, Finney, and Seward counties along both the Arkansas and Cimarron rivers.

Period of Occurrence: This chickadee occurs primarily in the winter months, with most records falling in December (possibly due to in-

creased observers). The Mountain Chickadee's earliest arrival date is
21 October, with some birds remaining until 5 May.

Habits and Habitat: In Kansas the Mountain Chickadee occurs in woodlands along the Cimarron and Arkansas rivers and in towns, particularly Elkhart, Morton County. In Kansas it is frequently found in small
flocks of three to 10 birds. The bird is usually detected by its noticeably different chickadee call.

Field Marks: The white superciliary stripe distinguishes the Mountain
Chickadee from the Black-capped Chickadee, which is occasionally
found in the same area.

Food: The food habits of the Mountain Chickadee are probably similar to those of other chickadees in Kansas.

A Tufted Titmouse (*Parus bicolor*). Photograph by Bob Gress.

Tufted Titmouse
Parus bicolor Linnaeus

Status: The Tufted Titmouse is a common resident in eastern Kansas, becoming progressively less common westward in the state. It is rare or absent in the western half of Kansas, with records only from Clark and Finney counties.

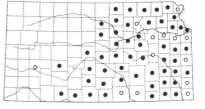

Period of Occurrence: The Tufted Titmouse is a resident of Kansas and occurs throughout the year.

Breeding: Since this titmouse does not migrate and does not seem to wander much after the breeding season, it is probably safe to assume that where it occurs, it breeds. The Tufted Titmouse, like other parids, starts breeding in late March. Johnston (1964b) states that most clutches are laid from 11 April to 30 April. The clutch size in Kansas averages about five eggs. The eggs are laid in a nesting cavity in a tree and are incubated for about 13 days. After hatching the young are fed by both parents. The young fledge in about 17 days and are tended for several more weeks by the parents.

Habits and Habitat: The Tufted Titmouse is a woodland bird and occurs along streams, in woodlots, and in cities with trees old enough to have nesting cavities. It readily comes to feeders that tempt it with sunflower seeds. Like other titmice, it is vociferous when disturbed and quickly alerts other animals to intruders.

Although the Tufted Titmouse is a small bird, the bite it can inflict is painful, as any bird bander will attest. The Tufted Titmouse begins courtship late in February, and its "peter, peter, peter" call can be heard for a considerable distance. It is inquisitive and does not hesitate to come and investigate any disturbance in its territory. It is easily called in by making squeaking calls on the back of your hand or "pishing."

Field Marks: The plain gray color with salmon-colored sides, along with an erect crest, make this titmouse easy to identify.

Food: The Tufted Titmouse is a regular visitor to bird feeders, where it takes sunflower seeds. However, Bent (1946) lists about 67 percent of its food intake as animal and 33 percent as vegetable. In the winter it frequently eats acorns, which it is able to open with its strong beak.

A Bushtit (*Psaltriparus minimus*). Photograph by Dale and Marian Zimmerman.

BUSHTITS (FAMILY AEGITHALIDAE)
Bushtit
Psaltriparus minimus (Townsend)

Status: The Bushtit is a casual winter resident in Morton County and a vagrant in Ellis County. The Ellis County record was a flock of four netted at Hays on 16 November 1968. There have been several sightings since 1976 in Morton County and in Hamilton County in December 1987.

Period of Occurrence: The extreme dates of occurrence are 14 September through 31 December.

Habits and Habitat: Most of the records of the Bushtit in Kansas are from

Elkhart, Morton County. Bushtits have been seen foraging around homes in town. There are some observations from the Cimarron River north of Elkhart and along the Arkanasas River in Hamilton County. They are constantly on 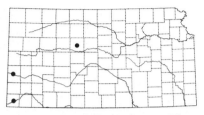 the move and difficult to observe for more than a few minutes. They generally tend to congregate in small flocks, but in Kansas single birds may be found.

Food: The Bushtit's food habits in Kansas are unknown, but elsewhere it tends to feed primarily on insects. Some vegetable matter is taken when insects are unavailable (Bent 1946).

A Red-breasted Nuthatch (*Sitta canadensis*). Photograph by Bob Gress.

NUTHATCHES (FAMILY SITTIDAE)
Red-breasted Nuthatch
Sitta canadensis Linnaeus

Status: The Red-breasted Nuthatch is a common to uncommon transient and winter resident throughout the state. It may be a casual nesting species.

Period of Occurrence: The Red-breasted Nuthatch most often occurs in fall and winter but has been recorded in the summertime. The dates of normal occurrence are 12 August to 11 May, with the dates of extreme occurrence 7 July to 18 June.

Breeding: Although the Red-breasted Nuthatch is a coniferous forest species, it has nested in the state in Geary, Sedgwick, and possibly Cowley counties. The Cowley County record was a June observation of birds carrying food, but the nest could not be located. The nest in Geary County also could not be found, but an adult bird was seen feeding three juveniles (Shane and LaShelle 1974). The Sedgwick County record was of birds nesting in a pine log made into a wren house (Gress 1982). Initially the nuthatches could not enter, so the house was taken down and the hole enlarged. The nesting pair carried pine resin and spread it around the entrance. This was removed by the observer, who thought it came from the log. He later left it on after finding that the birds were carrying it in from other pine trees. Look for the Red-breasted Nuthatch during May and June in cemeteries or other areas with stands of pines and redcedars.

Habits and Habitat: The Red-breasted Nuthatch occurs in Kansas primarily in areas that contain extensive stands of conifers. This habitat requirement makes it a fairly easy bird to find in fall and winter. Although fairly regular in the state, in some winters it is not to be found. The call note is an unmistakable "yank" with the tonal quality of a plugged-up nasal passage. Red-breasted Nuthatches are inquisitive birds and can easily be lured to within two or three feet of the observer. Once they become agitated they attract other nuthatches in the area with their call notes.

Field Marks: The Red-breasted Nuthatch's gray back, reddish buff belly, black line through the eye, and nuthatchlike behavior will help to identify it.

Food: The Red-breasted Nuthatch feeds on seeds in the winter, particularly those of conifers. At bird feeders it is especially fond of shelled sunflower seeds or peanuts. The birds frequently take the sunflower seeds and fly to a cache and quickly return for more.

A White-breasted Nuthatch (*Sitta carolinensis*). Photograph by Bob Gress.

White-breasted Nuthatch
Sitta carolinensis Latham

Status: The White-breasted Nuthatch is an uncommon medium-density resident and winter visitant in the east and becomes less common in the west, especially during the summer.

Period of Occurrence: This nuthatch is a year-round resident, with numbers in winter augmented by migrants.

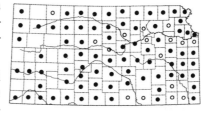

Breeding: The White-breasted Nuthatch breeds primarily in the eastern half of Kansas. The breeding status in the west is not well known, but it may breed throughout the state in suitable habitat. Actual nest records for the state are scarce because of the difficulty in getting to the nests, which are usually in natural cavities or old woodpecker excavations 15 feet or higher. They have been known to use birdhouses. The nest is usually lined, and the female will lay from five to 10 eggs in March or April. Incubation takes about 12 days, with fledging in two weeks.

Habits and Habitat: The White-breasted Nuthatch, like other nuthatches, goes down the tree head first carefully searching the bark for insects or vegetable matter. Like the Red-breasted Nuthatch, it readily comes to feeders, where it dines on sunflower seeds and occasionally on suet. The White-breasted Nuthatch is not adverse to feeding on the ground, where it probes about leaves and bark looking for insects and seeds. Although not a secretive bird, you usually find it first from its call note in well-forested cities and in woodland. It is one of the few birds found in deep forest in the winter. The call is unmistakably a nuthatch "yank" but does not have the nasal qualities of the Red-breasted Nuthatch.

Field Marks: The white breast and black cap separate it from the other nuthatches in Kansas.

Food: The White-breasted Nuthatch feeds on seeds of acorns, sunflowers, nuts, or other types of seeds that it can open.

Pygmy Nuthatch
Sitta pygmaea Vigors

Status: The Pygmy Nuthatch is a vagrant. It has been recorded in Ford, Geary, Linn, Morton, Saline, and Sedgwick counties. The first record was on 23 November 1961 at Sim Park in Wichita, where Carl Holmes and others observed a flock of 10 birds through 13 January 1962. Most records have been of only one to two birds. The Linn County record was possibly the 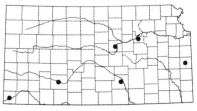 Brown-headed Nuthatch (*Sitta pusilla*) (Schwilling 1956). There are two specimen records.

Period of Occurrence: This nuthatch has been recorded from 21 September through 13 January and 30 March through 13 May.

Breeding: The Pygmy Nuthatch is not known to breed in the state.

Habits and Habitat: The Pygmy Nuthatch is generally found in conifers. The flock in Sim Park, Sedgwick County, was associated with Scotch pine. Look for this species in cemeteries or other concentrations of conifers, primarily in the western part of the state.

Field Marks: This nuthatch can be easily distinguished from the other two Kansas nuthatches by the absence of the conspicuous black caps of the white-breasted and red-breasted species.

Food: The Pygmy Nuthatch's primary food appears to be insect matter with a smaller amount of vegetable matter (Bent 1948).

A Brown Creeper (*Certhia americana*). Photograph by O. S. Pettingill for the Cornell Laboratory of Ornithology.

CREEPERS (FAMILY CERTHIIDAE)
Brown Creeper
Certhia americana Bonaparte

Status: The Brown Creeper is an uncommon transient and winter resident.

Period of Occurrence: This creeper usually occurs from late October to mid-April, with extreme dates of 4 May and 3 September.

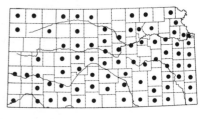

Habits and Habitat: The Brown Creeper is one of the smallest of Kansas birds. It spends most of its time foraging for food on tree trunks and limbs. After carefully scrutinizing a nearby tree, it flies to the base and carefully works its way to the top, repeating the pattern over and over. It is frequently heard before it is seen — that is, if your hearing is tuned to high pitch frequencies. The plumage blends very well with the bark of the trees, making it difficult to see until it moves. One might confuse it with the nuthatch, but the creeper goes up the tree, whereas nuthatches forage going down the tree, usually headfirst. In the winter creepers roost behind loose bark on a tree.

Field Marks: The creeper is a tiny bird, brown on the back, faintly streaked with pale gray, and white beneath.

Food: The Brown Creeper feeds on insects and some vegetable matter. Thompson has had it come to the feeder in winter for pieces of sunflower seed.

A Rock Wren (*Salpinctes obsoletus*). Photograph by Bob Gress.

WRENS (FAMILY TROGLODYTIDAE)
Rock Wren
Salpinctes obsoletus (Say)

Status: The Rock Wren is a common summer resident in suitable habitat in the western half of the state. It is a casual migrant in the east and a casual winter resident in the west.

Period of Occurrence: This wren arrives back in the state about 10 April and departs by 20 September. The dates of extreme occurrence are 17 March and 2 January.

Breeding: The Rock Wren breeds throughout the western half of Kansas east to at least Cloud and Washington counties in the north and Co-

manche County in the south. Although it has not been recorded
nesting in Barber County, there is
little doubt that it does since the
habitat is identical to Comanche
County. The nests are placed in
holes on rocky slopes or cliffs. The

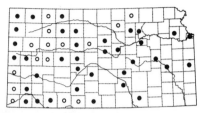

entrance to the nest is almost always paved with stones or other odds
and ends. Bent (1948) lists one nest in which the paving consisted of
"one safety pin, 2 pieces of wire, 2 pieces of a pair of scissors, 10 pieces
of zinc from old batteries, 2 fish hooks, 2 pieces of glass, 1 piece of leather,
4 copper tacks, 2 pieces of limestone, 4 pieces of plaster from the walls
of the house, 12 pieces of shingles, 9 bits of abalone shells, 20 bits of
mussel shells, 106 rusty nails, 227 bits of flat rusty iron, 492 small granite stones (very regular in size), and 769 bones of rabbits, fish, and birds,
as well as the usual nesting material." Rock Wrens lay five eggs in a nest
constructed of twigs and grasses, usually lined with hair or wool. The
eggs are white with some brown spotting. The eggs hatch in 14 days,
and the young fledge in another 14 days. They may produce two
broods a year.

Habits and Habitat: The Rock Wren prefers rocky outcrops and eroded
areas with rocks in generally arid environments. In Kansas they are common summer residents in the west where their habitat requirements
are met, as at Point of Rocks, Morton County. Florence Bailey (*in* Bent
1948) probably put it best when she said: "*Salpinctes!* To the worker in
the arid regions of the west this name calls up most grateful memo-
ries. On the windblown rocky stretches where you seem in a bleak world
of granite or lava with only rock, rock, everywhere, suddenly, there on
a stone before you, stands this jolly little wren, looking up at you with
a bob and a shy, friendly glance." The eastern records are usually from
the same type of habitat. They might be looked for along riprap at the
large reservoirs in eastern Kansas. Observations in Cowley County have
been on dry slopes of rocky hills.

Food: The Rock Wren eats mainly insects and spiders.

A Carolina Wren (*Thryothorus ludovicianus*). Photograph by Gerald J. Wiens.

Carolina Wren
Thryothorus ludovicianus (Latham)

Status: The Carolina Wren is a common resident of the eastern half but rare in the western part of the state. The range expands and contracts depending upon the severity of the winters.

Period of Occurrence: This wren is a resident throughout the year. However, records from western Kansas may only be seasonal movements from the east.

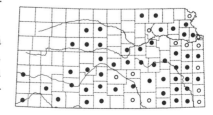

Breeding: The Carolina Wren breeds west to at least Rice and Sumner counties and north to Riley and Doniphan. The breeding range retracts from the more northerly areas after particularly hard winters with significant accumulations of snow. These wrens do not seem to be noticeably affected by cold, but snow is devastating to the populations and they may take years to recover.

The nests are placed in crevices in banks, stumps, forest edges, wood piles, and many man-made structures. One pair nested on top of an old mop sitting in the corner of a shed. Another pair was noted nesting on a window ledge concealed by a flower pot in front. They seem to be found nesting in cities more often than in the past.

The four to five white eggs with brown spotting around the large end are incubated for 12 to 14 days. The young remain in the nest for 13 to 14 days. The parents raise two broods a year and sometimes three.

Habits and Habitat: The Carolina Wren is mainly an inhabitant of the eastern forest of Kansas. Unlike most birds, it sings its loud song, which can be rendered "tea-kettle, tea-kettle, tea-kettle," 12 months out of the year, although more heartily in late winter and early spring. What a delight to go out on a clear, cold winter day and hear such a beautiful song. Look for it around brushy riverine habitat or man-made brush piles. Know the song for that is the best way to find it. In western Kansas it strives for the same type of habitat, but the wren is rare in that area.

Field Marks: This is the largest of the wrens in Kansas. Its large size, the reddish brown coloration above and buff below, and its white eye stripe should aid in its identification.

Food: The Carolina Wren feeds on insects.

A Bewick's Wren (*Thryomanes bewickii*). Photograph by Roger Boyd.

Bewick's Wren
Thryomanes bewickii (Audubon)

Status: The Bewick's Wren is a common migrant and rare summer resident throughout the state. It is an uncommon winter resident at least in the the south but probably withdraws from the more northerly areas in winter.

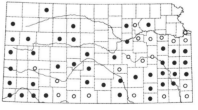

Period of Occurrence: The exact dates are hard to determine since this species remains throughout the year. However, numbers seem to increase in early April, decrease by mid-May, and then increase again by September. Most migrants have moved on south by mid-October.

Breeding: The Bewick's Wren breeds mainly in the eastern half of Kansas. In the west it breeds north at least to Finney and Ford counties. This wren seems to utilize a variety of areas to nest in. It rarely uses wren houses in Kansas, possibly due to the aggressive behavior of the House Wren with which it must compete. In Cowley County it has used the end of a pipe blocking a road and a pipe being used as a fence post. It also nests in crevices and other man-made structures.

The five white eggs with dark spots at the larger end are laid beginning about 15 April. The incubation period is 14 days. The young leave the nest in about 14 more days. They are usually double brooded, with the second clutch being laid about 15 June.

Habits and Habitat: The Bewick's Wren is generally found in and around brush piles in the winter. It is sometimes seen in town if enough protection can be found from winter winds. In the summertime it breeds in towns, farmsteads, and in woodland areas. The woodland does not have to be extensive if a good nesting site is found.

This wren is one of the better songsters in the wren family. Its song is much more varied and melodic than the monotonous House Wren song.

Field Marks: This wren is smaller than a Carolina Wren and larger than a House Wren. It has a longer tail than either of them, and it is tipped with white. There is a conspicuous white line above the eye.

Food: The Bewick's Wren is insectivorous.

A House Wren (*Troglodytes aedon*). Photograph by David A. Rintoul.

House Wren
Troglodytes aedon Vieillot

Status: The House Wren is a common summer resident throughout the state. It may be a casual winter resident, but most winter records are suspect because of the wintering of other wrens for which it could be mistaken.

Period of Occurrence: This small wren arrives around 15 April and departs by 18 September. The earliest date of arrival is 4 March and the latest departure 5 November. There are several records for late December.

Breeding: The House Wren breeds throughout the state, primarily in man-made wren houses. It is much sought after for a yard bird because of its cheerful, if rather monotonous, song. The nest is a simple one made of somewhat coarse sticks lined with grasses and other soft materials. The six eggs, like other wren eggs, are white covered with reddish brown dots. The incubation period is 12 to 15 days. The young leave the nest in about 15 days. The House Wren is double brooded.

Male House Wrens typically pick out several nest sites, and the female can take her choice. The male may pick out another female for his second breeding and occasionally has two females laying and brooding at the same time. Frequently, the same pair will return to the same locality the next spring.

Habits and Habitat: The House Wren is a ubiquitous summer bird in Kansas. You are rarely out of earshot of the song. Because of its courtship and breeding habits, it has a longer song period than most summering birds. Nest boxes are used to attract this wren to our yards. Why the wren selects one house over another is a mystery. Thompson had one box that had been out for five years with no nesting activity. The nesting box was moved and was an instant hit with the male, but alas the fickle female, after careful examination, went elsewhere.

House Wrens are exceedingly tolerant of human activity. However, in one case a tape recording was played in an attempt to draw the male closer to an Australian observer. The male came in, took one listen to this horrendously loud wren song, decided it must be bigger than he, and took his mate and abandoned the bird house and all the babies.

Field Marks: This is one of the smaller of the wrens that inhabits Kansas. It can be confused only with the Winter Wren, but their migration periods only briefly overlap. The Winter Wren rarely comes into cities.

Food: The House Wren is insectivorous.

Winter Wren
Troglodytes troglodytes (Linnaeus)

Status: The Winter Wren is a rare winter resident, perhaps more common in the east than in the west.

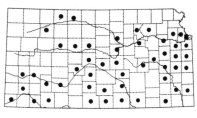

Period of Occurrence: The normal fall arrival time in Kansas of the Winter Wren is 15 October, with a spring departure on about 15 March. The spring data are scanty, and we need many more observations before we can be sure of the date of spring departure. The dates of extreme occurrence are 9 September and 26 April.

Habits and Habitat: The Winter Wren is normally found in woodland with dense undergrowth or brush. It is very secretive and scurries for cover at the first sign of danger. If you remain quiet, it will slowly come back out to see if the coast is clear.

Field Marks: This is one of the smallest North American birds. Its dark brown coloration and short tail help to distinguish it among the other wrens.

Food: The Winter Wren is insectivorous.

A Sedge Wren *(Cistothorus platensis)*. Photograph by Lang Elliott for the Cornell Laboratory of Ornithology.

Sedge Wren
Cistothorus platensis (Latham)

Status: The Sedge Wren is an uncommon transient and irregular, local, summer resident in the east. It is rare in the central part and casual in western Kansas. It is a casual winter resident.

Period of Occurrence: The spring arrival occurs about 20 April and the fall departure around 15 October. Data are lacking for definitive dates.

The date of earliest spring arrival is 15 April and the last fall date is 22 December.

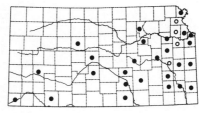

Breeding: The Sedge Wren has been recorded breeding in four counties. Most of our information on nesting comes from Schwilling (1982). He found many singing males on 7 August 1980 at Muscotah Marsh in Atchison County. Schwilling and others returned to the marsh on 10 August and found 15 territorial males and several dummy nests. Dan LaShelle reported nesting activity at Perry Reservoir, Jefferson County, that same year. One nest observed on 7 September contained six eggs. Zimmerman and others have observed nesting behavior in Geary and Riley counties since 1974 along waterways in tallgrass prairie but have not found actual nests except for the dummy nests built by the male. Males may build several dummy nests that are never used for raising young.

The present information suggests that this species probably nests in wet meadows and marshes in northeast Kansas in late August and September. They are probably overlooked since in late August most observers are looking for return migrants, not nesting species.

The nest is placed about one to three feet high in dense vegetation over land or water. It is a round nest about four inches around with a side entrance. The inside is lined with soft hair or hairlike materials. The clutch size is large for such a small bird, with the average about six eggs. The eggs are white with with no markings. The incubation period is 12 to 14 days. The young fledge in about 13 days. They are reportedly double brooded.

Habits and Habitat: The Sedge Wren is found in wet meadows, cattail marshes (said to be one of the least favorite of its haunts), and tall-grass prairie waterways. There is little known about the species in Kansas, and most of that information was given under breeding.

Field Marks: This is a diminutive wren that is difficult to observe. If you get a good look at it look for the streaked crown and absence of a white line over the eye and absence of the black back patch.

Food: These wrens are mainly insectivorous.

A Marsh Wren (*Cistothorus palustris*). Photograph by Dale and Marian Zimmerman.

Marsh Wren
Cistothorus palustris (Wilson)

Status: The Marsh Wren is an uncommon transient, rare summer resident, and rare but regular winter resident.

Period of Occurrence: This wren has occurred every month out of the year, and it is hard to determine just when the spring arrival occurs because of wintering birds. It appears that they arrive around 15 April and depart by 15 October.

Breeding: This species has been recorded breeding in only three counties. Look for it nesting in cattail marshes or other marshes with emer-

gent vegetation such as bulrushes.
The nests are placed in the vegetation about three feet high. The
nests are large, domed structures
about seven inches across. A side
opening is used for an entrance.
They are made of grasses and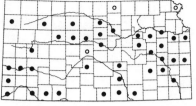
lined with cattail down. Marsh Wrens usually lay about five eggs, which
are cinnamon with darker spots. The incubation period is 13 days, and
the young leave the nest after 15 days or so. They are double brooded.

Habits and Habitat: The Marsh Wren is elusive and difficult to observe.
Frequently, all you see is a flash as it pops up on a cattail and immediately dives for cover. In wintertime they are usually found in cattails
but are even more difficult to find than in the breeding season. We
have found that a tape recording in the winter may be helpful in getting them to show themselves, although they don't always react to it.

Field Marks: Any wren found in wet marshes in Kansas is likely to be
this species. If you see it in a drier part of a marsh it can be distinguished
from the Sedge Wren by the blackish, unstreaked crown, the white line
over the eye, and the black upper back streaked with white.

Food: The Marsh Wren is insectivorous.

A Golden-crowned Kinglet (*Regulus satrapa*). Photograph by David A. Rintoul.

KINGLETS AND GNATCATCHERS
(FAMILY MUSCICAPIDAE, SUBFAMILY SILVIINAE)
Golden-crowned Kinglet
Regulus satrapa Lichtenstein

Status: The Golden-crowned Kinglet is a common transient and an uncommon winter resident in the east. In western Kansas its status is irregular, with some years having higher numbers of migrants than others. It is rare in the west in winter.

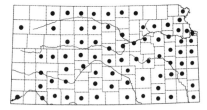

Period of Occurrence: The normal arrival time is 6 October, and it remains until 22 April. The dates of extreme occurrence are 26 September and 1 May.

Habits and Habitat: The kinglets are some of the smallest birds in Kansas. One wonders how such a small creature could survive the rigors of winter but survive it does. The kinglets are very curious, and when you make pishing calls, they may come down within inches of your face to see what the racket is all about. Only when you entice them to close range can you really see the brilliant crest that gives them their name. In winter they usually are found in small groups of two to 10 birds in conifers or redcedars. They frequently are heard before they are seen — that is, if your hearing is quite good. The call note is uttered at a high frequency that may be difficult to detect at a distance.

Field Marks: Kinglets constantly flick their wings, a field mark that helps to distinguish them from warblers. The Golden-crowned Kinglet can be told from the Ruby-crowned by the markings on the head. The ruby streak on the Ruby-crowned Kinglet is not normally visible.

Food: The Golden-crowned Kinglet's food consists almost entirely of animal matter, particularly insects and spiders.

A Ruby-crowned Kinglet (*Regulus calendula*). Photograph by H. R. Comstock for the Cornell Laboratory of Ornithology.

Ruby-crowned Kinglet
Regulus calendula (Linnaeus)

Status: The Ruby-crowned Kinglet is a common transient throughout the state. It is rare in the winter, occurring chiefly in the south-central and southeastern part of the state.

Period of Occurrence: Arrival in the fall occurs about 12 September, with the fall departure around 25 November. The spring migration begins around 21 March, with most birds gone from the area by 21 May. The dates of extreme occurrence are 19 August and 6 June.

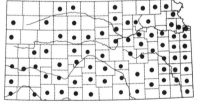

Habits and Habitat: Like the Golden-crowned Kinglet, this kinglet is a tiny bird that is found in areas of town and country with conifers or redcedars. Its curiosity seems insatiable, as it will come down and look at you from every angle if you disturb it. Ruby-crowned Kinglets may be small birds, but they have a loud song that is out of proportion to their size. They have a high frequency call note that is difficult to hear at a distance unless your hearing is keen.

Field Marks: Unlike the Golden-crowned Kinglet in which the crown color is quite evident, the Ruby-crown must flare the crest for the bright red stripe of feathers to appear. The crest is absent in the female.

Food: The Ruby-crowned tends to eat more vegetable matter than does the Golden-crowned Kinglet. However, the mainstay of the diet is animal matter (Bent 1949).

A Blue-gray Gnatcatcher (*Polioptila caerulea*). Photograph by John S. Dunning for the Cornell Laboratory of Ornithology.

Blue-gray Gnatcatcher
Polioptila caerulea (Linnaeus)

Status: The Blue-gray Gnatcatcher is a common transient and summer resident in the east. It is uncommon to rare in the western half of Kansas, with its breeding status there uncertain.

Period of Occurrence: The average arrival date is 30 March; it departs in fall around 23 September. The extreme dates are 12 March to 28 November.

Breeding: There are nesting records as far west as Barber and Stafford counties. It undoubtedly nests farther west along the Cimarron and Arkansas rivers where the habitat is suitable. It has been recorded in Finney, Phillips, and Ford counties in summer, but nesting was not observed. The nest is small and placed high in a fork or on the limb of a tree. It is an elaborate nest using plant materials held together by spiderwebs and other insect-type silks. The eggs are laid about 10 May with an average clutch size of five (Johnston 1964b). The incubation period is 14 days, and the young fledge in 12 days. There are too few nesting records from Kansas to indicate that two broods are reared. However, in other states they are frequently double brooded (Johnsgard 1979).

Habits and Habitat: The Blue-gray Gnatcatcher is another of the smallest birds in Kansas. The birds frequently return to the state in the spring before the leaves have begun to emerge. Like the kinglets to which they are related, they are curious and will come quickly to a disturbance in their territory. Their prime habitat in eastern Kansas is wooded streams. In the central to western part of the state they may be found in scrub forest as well as in cottonwoods along the streams.

Field Marks: The extremely small size of this gnatcatcher and the slate gray coloration will help to identify it.

Food: The Blue-gray Gnatcatcher feeds entirely on animal matter, particularly insects (Bent 1949).

An Eastern Bluebird (*Sialia sialis*). Photograph by Gerald J. Wiens.

THRUSHES (FAMILY MUSCICAPIDAE, SUBFAMILY TURDINAE)
Eastern Bluebird
Sialia sialis (Linnaeus)

Status: The Eastern Bluebird is a locally common resident in eastern and central Kansas. It is an uncommon, local summer resident in the west and is casual there in winter.

Period of Occurrence: The Eastern Bluebird is seen regularly all year in the east and chiefly from mid-March through October in western Kansas.

Breeding: The male may feed the female during courtship and up until the young hatch. The pair bond often persists throughout the year. The nest is placed in a natural tree cavity, old woodpecker hole, or a man-made bird box, usually within three to 20 feet of the ground. Nest building is by both sexes. The nest is a loose cup of plant stems and grasses lined with finer grasses. The clutch is three to six, usually four or five, pale blue, unspotted eggs. The incubation period is 12 to 16 days; the nestling period is 17 or 18 days, and there are usually two, sometimes three (in east), broods per year. Only the female incubates. First clutches are usually completed in late April; second clutches by early June. Young of the first brood sometimes help feed the young of later broods. In western Kansas second broods may succumb to very high temperatures during June and early July.

Habits and Habitat: The Eastern Bluebird is a beautiful and gentle species that appears a favorite of all who observe it. It is partial to areas of edge habitat, such as open deciduous woods, orchards, farmsteads, parks, and shelterbelts. In western Kansas it usually occurs in riparian areas. It occurs in small flocks, often family groups, much of the year. When perched it has a hunched or "round-shouldered" appearance. It is a permanent resident in the east, and westward a few overwinter during most years. However, occasional severe winters often decimate local populations. In winter birds roost in sheltered places such as buildings and bird boxes, sometimes numerous birds in one box. The call is a soft, plaintive "che-weee"; the song a warble sometimes expressed as "tru-a-lly, tru-a-lly!"

Bluebirds face strong competition from House Sparrows and European Starlings for nest sites and have responded in many areas to the construction of "bluebird trails" — lines of boxes placed in brushy fields and along roadsides from which competitors are excluded. This practice has been used since at least the early 1930s. To be most successful such boxes should have a one and one-half inch opening and should be placed in the open seven to 14 feet above ground. Boxes should face south or east, preferably with a tree limb or other perch in view of the entrance. L. P. Dittemore installed and cared for more than 500 nest boxes in Shawnee County during the late 1960s, and bluebirds increased noticeably during that period ("Woods" 1976).

Field Marks: The Eastern Bluebird can be confused only with the Western Bluebird, which is of doubtful occurrence in the state. Look for a solid blue back (with gray-edged feathers in fall and winter) and reddish brown throat.

Food: The chief food of this species is insects, especially grasshoppers, beetles, and caterpillars; some spiders, snails, earthworms, and similar terrestrial invertebrates; and rarely vertebrates such as small lizards and frogs. It also eats large quantities of fruit and berries, especially during winter. Fruits include pokeweed, Virginia creeper, and redcedar. In some areas bluebirds visit feeding stations for mealworms, suet, and peanut butter.

Western Bluebird
Sialia mexicana Swainson

Status: The Western Bluebird is possibly a vagrant in Kansas, but no specimen or confirming photo has yet been obtained.

Period of Occurrence: There are about a dozen sight records (none confirmed) between 7 October and 14 May and 4 and 5 July from Comanche, Cowley, Decatur, Geary, Hamilton, Meade, Morton, Russell, Sedgwick, and Sherman counties. The most convincing is a report of two in the Goodland cemetery, Sherman County, 4 March 1974, but the photos by John Palmquist are inconclusive.

Habits and Habitat: The Western Bluebird summers in open woodland and about farms and ranches and moves into the foothills and plains in late fall, at which time a few may reach Kansas. The Western Bluebird travels in small flocks and is very similar to the Eastern Bluebird in habits.

Field Marks: This bluebird is very similar to the Eastern Bluebird in color, but the male can be distinguished by its blue throat and rusty upper back, both of which are veiled by gray feather edgings in fall; the female by its gray throat and belly. In some positions and in poor light male Easterns may appear to have blue throats; if in doubt follow the bird and observe it from different angles and in different lights.

A Mountain Bluebird (*Sialia currucoides*). Photograph by Bob Gress.

Mountain Bluebird
Sialia currucoides (Bechstein)

Status: The Mountain Bluebird is an uncommon transient and winter resident in the west and is less common eastward to Cloud and Cowley counties. It is casual elsewhere and may breed occasionally in the far west.

Period of Occurrence: Most reports are between mid-October and early April; extreme dates are 6 October and 5 May. There are also records between 5 and 20 June from Ellis, Finney, Hamilton, and Wallace counties.

Breeding: The only evidence for breeding in Kansas is a full-grown juvenile collected in Hamilton County on 20 June 1911 and four fledged young seen by Marvin Schwilling in Wallace County on 8 June 1986. Although there are no breeding records for eastern Colorado, sporadic nesting in extreme western Kansas is possible, and nest boxes placed in sheltered ravines might 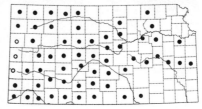 be used. The nest is placed in a natural tree cavity, bird box, or rock crevice in late April or early May. Both the nests and eggs are very similar to those of the Eastern Bluebird.

Habits and Habitat: Mountain Bluebirds usually occur in small flocks that feed in sparsely wooded areas or open fields. This species is sometimes common in western Kansas in winter and occurs more often in large flocks than does the Eastern. In winter its presence is often determined by the availability of such foods as juniper berries. Feeding is usually in open country and in typical bluebird fashion — dropping to the ground from a low perch to capture prey, then flying to another low perch to eat it. It may also sally out after flying insects, flycatcher fashion. During winter it is less vocal than the Eastern Bluebird, being limited to a low "terr."

Field Marks: Males are pale cerulean blue but in fall and early winter have grayish tips to most feathers. Females and immatures are gray with only a tinge of blue in wings and tail and lack any of the brown seen in comparably plumaged Eastern Bluebirds.

Food: Food of the Mountain Bluebird is primarily insects, especially beetles, ants, true bugs, grasshoppers, and caterpillars. It also eats a considerable amount of fruit, especially in winter, including hackberries, redcedar berries, and wild grapes.

A Townsend's Solitaire (*Myadestes townsendi*). Photograph by Dale and Marian Zimmerman.

Townsend's Solitaire
Myadestes townsendi (Audubon)

Status: The Townsend's Solitaire is an uncommon winter resident in western Kansas and occurs casually elsewhere.

Period of Occurrence: It is most common between October and March, with extreme dates of 17 September and 28 April and a straggler to 15 May.

Habits and Habitat: In winter birds move down mountain slopes and

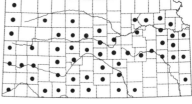

eastward across the plains, usually along watercourses. The Townsend's Solitaire usually occurs singly; on occasion several may be seen in the same general area but not as a discrete flock. While in Kansas solitaires occur most frequently near fruit-bearing trees and shrubs such as junipers. Parks, dooryards, and cemeteries are good places to look for the species. An individual often remains in the vicinity of a particular tree until the available food is exhausted or until it is displaced by another bird. Following an early spring blizzard in Hays, a robin spent most of two days persistently driving a solitaire from one of the few junipers still bearing fruit. Many observers have commented that solitaires resemble flycatchers, especially when perching in a tall tree and flying out to catch flying insects. It also feeds near the ground in bluebird fashion and from the ground, where it may run about briefly like a robin. In late winter males occasionally deliver their loud, brilliant, and unmistakable song. It is a typical thrush song consisting of a series of loud, prolonged warbles and flutelike notes.

Field Marks: The Townsend's Solitaire is sometimes confused with a mockingbird, but its dark underparts, white eye ring, and buffy (not white) patches in the wings are distinctive, as is its very different behavior.

Food: The food of this species includes a variety of insects, occasional spiders, earthworms, and a variety of wild and ornamental fruits and berries.

A Veery (*Catharus fuscescens*). Photograph by Bill Dyer for the Cornell Laboratory of Ornithology.

Veery
Catharus fuscescens (Stephens)

Status: The Veery is a low-density transient statewide and is probably more common than records indicate.

Period of Occurrence: It is most common during May and September; extreme spring dates are 28 April and 2 June; fall extremes are 27 August and 28 September. Specimens have been taken from 5 to 29 May and 4 to 28 September.

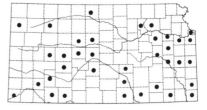

Habits and Habitat: Despite early published reports there is no evidence that the species has ever nested in Kansas. During migration it can occur in any wooded habitat, especially in riparian areas where it mingles with other *Catharus* thrushes. Most Kansas specimens and sight records are from spring. Much of its food is obtained by searching among leaves on the ground and flipping over leaves under woody vegetation.

It also gleans insects from foliage and trunks of trees, usually within a few feet of the ground. The song, heard occasionally in spring, is a whistled series of falling notes, each fainter than the previous one and sometimes interpreted as "veer, veer, veer, veer."

Field Marks: It can usually be distinguished from similar thrushes by its uniformly colored upperparts and very faint spotting on the breast. The call is described as "phew," falling in pitch.

Food: The Veery's food is about half invertebrates, including beetles, caterpillars, spiders, sow bugs, snails, and earthworms, and half wild berries and fruits, including elderberries, dogwood, wild cherries, and grapes.

A Gray-cheeked Thrush (*Catharus minimus*). Photograph by Dorothy Crumb for the Cornell Laboratory of Ornithology.

Gray-cheeked Thrush
Catharus minimus (Lafresnaye)

Status: The Gray-cheeked Thrush is a low-density transient, especially in the east in spring. Fall records need confirmation; many sightings are erroneous.

Period of Occurrence: This species is most common during the first three weeks of May. Dates of specimens are 25 April to 20 May and 10 to 27 June (all June specimens are from the southwest). The ear-

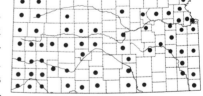

liest spring sighting is 24 April. Mid-April dates probably represent Hermit Thrushes. There are no fall specimens; fall sight records from 9 September to 24 October are from Harvey, Johnson, Lyon, and Shawnee counties.

Habits and Habitat: During migration the Gray-cheeked Thrush occupies deciduous woods and riparian habitats where it occurs primarily in the undergrowth together with other *Catharus*. It is usually seen on or near the ground, flying up to a perch when disturbed, and it is often difficult to get a good clear view. Like other thrushes, however, it may approach the viewer in response to a squeak or an approximation of its call. At times birds appear in the open on lawns or at bird baths and identification is easy. Banding studies in west-central Kansas and in Johnson County showed it to be the second most common *Catharus,* after the Swainson's, during spring migration. The song, occasionally heard in spring, resembles that of a Veery, but each successive note moves up the scale, not down. It is considered the champion migrant among North American thrushes, with some individuals moving from Alaska to Peru. It has recently extended its breeding range into northeast Asia.

Field Marks: This species differs from the very similar Swainson's Thrush in its gray rather than buffy cheeks and lack of distinct eye ring. It can easily be confused with the duller races of the Hermit Thrush, some of which do not have strongly contrasting reddish tails. The common call is described as "queep" (much lower than a Swainson's Thrush) or an abrupt "peep."

Food: The Gray-cheeked Thrush's food is chiefly invertebrates such as beetles, ants, caterpillars, spiders, sow bugs, and earthworms, but it eats a considerable amount of wild berries and fruit, especially in fall.

A Swainson's Thrush (*Catharus ustulatus*). Photograph by Bill Dyer for the Cornell Laboratory of Ornithology.

Swainson's Thrush
Catharus ustulatus (Nuttall)

Status: The Swainson's Thrush is a common to abundant transient statewide.

Period of Occurrence: This thrush is most common during May and from mid-September to mid-October. Specimens have been taken 24 April to 11 June and 10 September to 7 October. Extreme dates (sight records) are 3 April to 11 June and 1 September to 30 October, with stragglers to 5 November. Sightings after mid-October should be verified; July and August records need confirmation.

Habits and Habitat: This is by far the most common *Catharus* in Kansas. In Ellis County, banding showed that it outnumbered the Gray-cheeked Thrush, Veery, and Hermit Thrush by ratios of 65 to 5 to 3 to 1, respectively. The Swainson's Thrush frequently appears in yards and gardens, usually in the morning or evening, and may actually be common during the peak of migration and during "fallouts" caused by inclement weather. As one walks through wooded habitat, the typical sighting is of a single bird that flies up from the undergrowth, perches momentarily on an open branch, usually in shade, then flies forward to a new perch on or near the ground. At such times the bird is usually silent or gives a sharp "whit" or "whip." It feeds chiefly on the ground but may feed high in trees and is considered more arboreal than the other thrushes. On its wintering grounds this species spends considerable time in trees eating fruit.

The song is frequently heard in morning or evening and on overcast days. It is a complicated series of notes resembling the song of a Wood Thrush but less robust and softer. Bent (1949) interpreted it as "whip-poor-will-a-will-a-will-e-see-zee-zee," spiraling upward at the end.

Field Marks: The Swainson's Thrush is distinctly thrushlike in shape and behavior, with buffy cheeks and distinct buffy eye ring; also the call, a sharp "whit," is distinctive. It migrates at night, frequently uttering a sharp "queep" to mark its passage.

Food: This species eats a variety of invertebrates, including beetles, ants, caterpillars, flies, spiders, and snails, and both domestic and wild fruits and berries, including cherries, elderberries, mulberries, and blackberries. Considerable fruit may be taken in fall and winter.

A Hermit Thrush *(Catharus guttatus)*. Photograph by J. Robert Woodward for the Cornell Laboratory of Ornithology.

Hermit Thrush
Catharus guttatus (Pallas)

Status: The Hermit Thrush is an uncommon transient in both the east and west but is rare in central Kansas. It probably winters regularly in eastern Kansas but is casual west-ward.

Period of Occurrence: The Hermit Thrush is most common from mid-April to mid-May and from late September to early November. Specimen records are 28

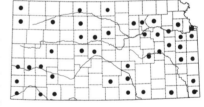

March to 22 May and 27 September to 28 November. Extreme dates for presumed transients are 11 and 23 March to 29 May and 20 September to 28 November. Stragglers or wintering birds have been reported in the east from 12 December to 9 February. Mid-summer records, June–August, are suspect.

Habits and Habitat: The Hermit Thrush shows an interesting hiatus in range in Kansas. It is an uncommon transient in deciduous forests of eastern Kansas and in the riparian growth of the far west but is the rarest of the four *Catharus* migrating through Ellis County. It is the only

Catharus likely to be seen in Kansas after mid-October. In winter it inhabits the floor and undergrowth of deciduous forests, occasionally visiting a yard or feeding station. It feeds on the ground like a robin — several hops, a pause, then additional hops but usually under cover. It flips over leaves rather than scratching like a sparrow. Its song, a remarkable series of "ethereal" flutelike and bell-like notes and the finest by any Kansas bird, regrettably is rarely, if ever, heard in Kansas. Some authors have called it the "American Nightingale."

Field Marks: Individuals of most populations have a reddish brown tail that contrasts with the olive brown back and well-defined breast spots. Some western birds, however, are more uniform in color and are easily confused in color with either the Veery or the Gray-cheeked Thrush. The call is a low "chuck." Upon alighting, a Hermit Thrush frequently raises its tail abruptly and then drops it slowly.

Food: The Hermit Thrush eats insects such as beetles, ants, caterpillars, true bugs, and other invertebrates, including spiders, sow bugs, and earthworms. Even salamanders and other small vertebrates are occasionally taken. It eats a great deal of fruit, especially in fall and winter, including pokeweed, wild grape, and elderberries.

A Wood Thrush (*Hylocichla mustelina*). Photograph by Gerald J. Wiens.

Wood Thrush
Hylocichla mustelina (Gmelin)

Status: The Wood Thrush is now an uncommon transient and summer resident in the east and appears to be decreasing in numbers. It is a casual transient west to Rawlins and Edwards counties. It presently breeds west to Cloud, Saline, and probably Sumner counties. It formerly nested westward to Decatur (1900) and (perhaps) Barber counties, but reports of nesting in Ellis County were in error.

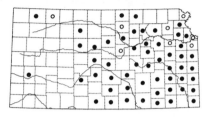

Period of Occurrence: It is most common from late April through September, with extreme dates of 1 April and 29 October.

Breeding: Pair formation is completed soon after females return. The nest is a compact structure of plants stems, leaves, and grass with a mud cup lined with rootlets and placed in a crotch or the fork of a horizontal branch, usually within 10 feet of the ground. The well-concealed nest is built by the female in about a week. The clutch is two to five, usually three or four, pale blue or bluish green unmarked eggs. The incubation period is 13 days; the nestling period is 12 to 14 days. It is often double brooded in extreme eastern Kansas. Incubation is by the female alone, usually with the male stationed nearby. Most clutches are complete in early June.

Habits and Habitat: The Wood Thrush prefers deciduous woods with a dense understory of saplings, dogwoods, or similar shrubs and usually with running water nearby. It usually feeds from the ground but also gleans food from foliage. The song is a series of loud, bell-like notes uttered at a deliberate pace and sometimes interpreted as "ee-oh-lee," "ee-oh-lay." Its calls include a "pip-pip-pip" and a low "quirt."

The Wood Thrush apparently had a wider range in Kansas at the turn of the century. Wolfe (1961), discussing the period 1908 through 1915, called it an "uncommon summer resident" with one or more nests nearly every year along Prairie Dog or Sappa creeks in Decatur County. At that time water tables were higher, and area streams had flowing water and shrubby undergrowth beneath taller trees. It is interesting that Rising (1974) found one on nearby Beaver Creek in Rawlins County on 12 June 1966. Smock (Seibel 1978) considered it a "common" summer resident in and around Arkansas City from at least 1900 to 1919. Recently one or more has summered, and perhaps bred, in

Cowley and eastern Sumner counties. However, a review of original notes shows that reports of nesting in Ellis County (Imler 1937) were in error. Wooster in his field notes called the Brown Thrasher the "Brown Thrush," and later this was attributed to the Wood Thrush. J. A. Allen considered it "exceedingly common" near Topeka in 1871, but it is now a "rare transient and summer resident" there ("Woods" 1976).

Field Marks: The russet head of the Wood Thrush and the large, round spots on the breast are distinctive. It is sometimes confused with the Brown Thrasher, a long-tailed species with streaked breast, yellow eye, and *very* different behavior.

Food: This species eats such invertebrates as beetles, ants, caterpillars, moths, true bugs, spiders, snails, and earthworms and also a variety of berries, including dogwood, Virginia creeper, pokeberries, and mulberries.

An American Robin (*Turdus migratorius*). Photograph by Gerald J. Wiens.

American Robin
Turdus migratorius Linnaeus

Status: The American Robin is a common transient and summer resident statewide. The size of the wintering population varies with food supply and weather conditions.

Period of Occurrence: It is present all year. Transients and summer residents are present from at least early March through mid-October.

Breeding: The nest is placed in a fork or on a horizontal branch of a tree or shrub, on a rock ledge, or on a ledge of a man-made structure, often a porch or outbuilding. The nest is a deep cup of plant stems, grass, bits of cloth, string, and so on, with a distinct mud cup and lined with fine grasses. The male assists in the nest building chiefly by bringing nesting materials. The clutch is three to five, usually four, bluish green ("robin's egg blue") unmarked eggs. First clutches are usually complete by 20 April. The incubation period is 12 to 14 days; the nestling period 14 to 16 days. Incubation is almost entirely by the female. The American Robin is two brooded in Kansas, and multiple renesting attempts are frequent.

Pairs usually remain intact for the second brood, but typically a new nest is built. Eggs have been reported through 21 June with few young fledged after mid-July.

It is probably not surprising that unusual nesting events would be recorded for such a common and confiding species. Calvin Cink (1975) found a robin's nest containing both robin and Mourning Dove eggs and being incubated by the dove. Ten days later one robin egg had hatched and the second was pipping, but unfortunately the next day the nest and contents were destroyed. At no time did he see an American Robin near the nest. Even more remarkable was a report by Raney (1939) of a robin and a Mourning Dove that shared the same nest for two consecutive years. The two species shared incubation duties and each fed its own young after they hatched. Neither nesting was successful, and by the third year the tree had been cut. There are also several cases of unsuccessful winter nesting by robins in the northeastern United States.

Habits and Habitat: This is undoubtedly one of the best-known and most-popular species in Kansas. Although the media frequently tout the "first robin of spring" in late February or early March, in most years at least a few birds have overwintered. These "first" arrivals are conspicuously different — they are males, in very bright plumage and with different habits — they keep their distance from one another! Within a few weeks they are singing and establishing territories, and as the females arrive nesting begins. American Robins have increased greatly in numbers since the arrival of Europeans, who provided increased habitat in the form of plantings on farms and ranches and in towns. Previously this species had been restricted to open riparian woods and woodland edge. One of its most familiar habits is its means of feeding by running a short distance over a lawn or similar open area, pausing with cocked head, and eventually pulling up an earthworm or other prey from the ground. Incidentally, Heppner (1965) has established that earthworms are seen, not heard, in their burrows. It also feeds on fruit and may be a local pest in cherry orchards or in strawberry beds. Another familiar sight is of plump, short-tailed, speckled-breasted juveniles hopping about on a lawn, not yet ready to fly, while the parents loudly harass a cat or other potential predator. By mid-August flocks of young robins appear in parks and on lawns; by early winter robins are congregating at forsythia, mock orange, hackberry, and juniper bushes and eventually strip the shrubs of all food. Occasionally birds will become "intoxicated" by eating too many frozen crabapples and fly and hop about drunkenly. The size and distribution of winter populations is undoubtedly dependent to a great extent on the local fruit supply, but weather and snow cover are also important. The song has been described as "cheer-up, cheer, cheer, cheer-up." A common call is "teet-teet, tut-tut." Although average life expectancy is low, one banded wild bird lived 11 years, eight months (Kennard 1975), and a captive exceeded 15 years of age.

Food: The American Robin eats a variety of invertebrates and fruit. Invertebrates include beetles, grasshoppers, cicadas, true bugs, snails, and great numbers of earthworms. The fruit includes domestic and wild cherries, grapes, and fruit of mulberry, pokeweed, chinaberry, and juniper. It has also been recorded eating occasional small vertebrates, including tiny fish and small snakes. At feeding stations robins have been observed eating bread and sunflower "hearts."

A Varied Thrush (*Ixoreus naevius*). Photograph by Dale and Marian Zimmerman.

Varied Thrush
Ixoreus naevius (Gmelin)

Status: The Varied Thrush is a casual winter visitor statewide.

Period of Occurrence: There are two specimen records (Barton and Finney counties) and at least nine sight records during the period 17 October to May.

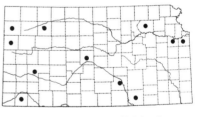

Habits and Habitat: In its normal range, conifer forests of the Pacific Northwest into Alaska, the Varied Thrush inhabits dense, moist stands of firs. In winter it moves down slope, and some individuals wander eastward, a few to eastern Canada and the northeastern United States. Most Kansas records have been at feeding stations or in riparian growth near open water. The Barton County specimen was a road kill found in Great Bend by Scott Seltman. The Varied Thrush is very similar to the American Robin in habits. Some of the Kansas sightings were reported to birders as "funny-colored" robins. This species forages on the ground under vegetation and is usually silent in winter.

Field Marks: The color pattern of this species is unmistakable; the orange eye stripe, black breast band, and reddish wing patterns are distinctive for the male; females and immatures are paler in color but have the same pattern.

Food: In summer the Varied Thrush eats both insects and other invertebrates and an appreciable amount of fruit. Fruit is a larger part of the winter diet.

A Gray Catbird (*Dumetella carolinensis*). Photograph by Lang Elliott for the Cornell Laboratory of Ornithology.

Thrashers (Family Mimidae)
Gray Catbird
Dumetella carolinensis (Linnaeus)

Status: The Gray Catbird is a common transient and summer resident in eastern and central sections and is rare and local in the far west.

Period of Occurrence: The Gray Catbird is most common from early May to late September. The usual extreme dates are 20 April and 24 October, with stragglers (usually at feeders) into January. One was in Hays, Ellis County, from 2 January through 4 February, and there are a few sightings during March in eastern Kansas.

Breeding: The nest is usually placed in dense vegetation, often a tangle of vines or dense shrub within seven feet of the ground, and is usually well concealed. It is a bulky cup constructed of small twigs, plant stems, leaves, and strips of bark and lined with rootlets. The male brings nesting material, but the female does most of the nest building, completing the nest in 5 to 6 days. The clutch is three to five, usually four, deep greenish blue, unmarked eggs, darker than those of a robin. The incubation period is 12 or 13 days, the nestling period 10 to 15 days. Most clutches are completed in late May or early June. It is single brooded, and incubation is by the female alone. Bent (1948) describes several instances in which catbirds fed the young of cardinals and flickers.

Habits and Habitat: Favored habitats in Kansas include dense riparian thickets and brushy roadsides near woods. The catbird prefers denser cover than either the mockingbird or Brown Thrasher and therefore is less familiar to most Kansans. Even when nesting in a back yard the Gray Catbird tends to call and sing from a tangle of bushes. However, it is a curious bird and can frequently be enticed to approach the observer by "squeaking" or by an imitation of its call. Its best-known call is a catlike "meeeaaah." The song is rather attractive, similar to that of a Northern Mockingbird but less complex and with less repetition of succeeding phrases. Some individuals are accomplished mimics, imitating numerous local species and such sounds of its environment as the croakings of frogs and cackling of domestic hens. Much of its feeding is on the ground, where it flips leaves and probes the surface for insects; it also gleans insects and fruit from twigs and leaves.

Field Marks: No other Kansas bird is dark gray with a black crown and brown under-tail coverts.

Food: The Gray Catbird's food is about half insects, including grasshoppers, beetles, caterpillars, true bugs, and moths. It also eats such invertebrates as spiders and millipedes and a variety of fruits and berries, including mulberries and pokeweeds. Bent (1948) reported the occasional taking of small vertebrates such as tiny fishes. At feeding stations it has been reported to eat bread, cheese, milk, peanuts, and boiled potatoes (Terres 1980).

A Northern Mockingbird (*Mimus polyglottos*). Photograph by Bob Gress.

Northern Mockingbird
Mimus polyglottos (Linnaeus)

Status: The Northern Mockingbird is probably resident in the extreme east. It is a common transient and summer resident elsewhere, becoming uncommon and local in the northwest. It is less common and irregular in winter in central and southwestern Kansas.

Period of Occurrence: This species is most common from mid-April to early October but is probably resident in the east. In central and western Kansas most individuals leave during the winter months.

Breeding: Courtship involves song and the carrying of nesting material to potential sites by the male. The nest is usually placed in a dense shrub or vine, less often in a tree fork, within 10 feet of the ground. The nest is bulky, with a low base of twigs and weed stems; an inner layer of plant stems, grass, and leaves; and a cup lined with fine rootlets. The clutch is three to five, usually four, bluish or greenish eggs heavily blotched with dark brown. The incubation period is 12 or 13 days, the nestling period 10 to 12 days. Most clutches are completed in early June. It may be double brooded in eastern Kansas. Both sexes build the nest, but incubation is by the female. In southeastern Kansas it nests chiefly near homes, but in southwestern Kansas it is primarily a riparian species in summer.

Habits and Habitat: At one time the mockingbird was a popular cage-bird. It has benefited by the presence of Europeans and in the last century has extended its range considerably. It is a conspicuous and popular species where it occurs regularly, but some insensitive persons resent being awakened by a male singing all night or before dawn. The song is a musical but highly varied series of phrases, each repeated three or more times before continuing to the next. It also includes a wide variety of mimicked calls of other species and varied sounds from the environment. Terres (1980) states that mockers have mimicked the songs of at least 39 species and the calls of 50 as well as the barking of dogs and similar nonavian sounds. Singing is usually from a high perch, but there is also a flight song in which the wing patches flash conspicuously. Its calls include a variety of harsh, grating calls such as "chair" or "tchack."

Mockers are very aggressive in defense of territory and especially the nest, regularly harassing cats, dogs, snakes, and larger birds. Males have an interesting display in which they face each other at the boundary of their territories and hop rapidly sideways like bantams. Another display is "wing flashing," in which the bird lifts and opens both wings and flicks them several times to show the white patches. Hailman (1960) concluded that this display is used to flush insects from the ground or grass. It is also used by adults as a display against predators and by immatures when they first encounter an unfamiliar object. During winter individuals may set up feeding territories around a dependable food source. A hand-reared bird lived just over 15 years.

Field Marks: The Northern Mockingbird is sometimes confused with a shrike but is larger and slimmer and lacks the black mask. The white wing patches are very distinctive in flight. Immatures have the breast faintly spotted with gray.

Food: The food of this species is about half insects, especially grasshoppers, beetles, and caterpillars, and various invertebrates such as snails and spiders. It also eats a variety of wild berries and fruits, especially in winter, including pokeberries, redcedar, poison ivy, hackberries, and mulberries. It has also been observed to eat small vertebrates such as lizards and small snakes. In some areas Northern Mockingbirds visit feeders for bread, suet, and fruit.

A Sage Thrasher (*Oreoscoptes montanus*). Photograph by David A. Rintoul.

Sage Thrasher
Oreoscoptes montanus (Townsend)

Status: The Sage Thrasher is a casual visitor to southwestern Kansas and is a vagrant elsewhere. It may have nested in Morton County in 1963.

Period of Occurrence: Most records are between 20 September and 1 November, with additional reports to 23 April and (once) 17 July.

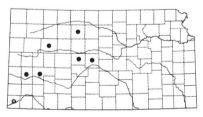

Breeding: The only evidence of breeding is of a family seen and one of three juveniles collected northeast of Elkhart, Morton County, on 17 July 1963. The nest is typically a bulky cup of twigs, plant stems, and bark, lined with rootlets and hair and well hidden in a shrub (often sagebrush) within three feet of the ground. The clutch is four to seven, usually four or five, blue or greenish blue eggs with large brown spots. The incubation period is 14 to 17 days, and both sexes incubate. It is usually single brooded. When approaching the nest adults typically alight some distance away and then approach it very secretively.

Habits and Habitat: The Sage Thrasher is a characteristic species of sand-sage grassland but in fall or winter may also occur in windbreaks and barnyards. It is usually shy and difficult to approach during the summer but is much tamer during the nonbreeding season. It feeds on the ground, robin-fashion, probing the ground and flipping debris for food. Its song has been compared favorably with that of the Northern Mockingbird. It also has an erratic flight song followed, upon alighting, by a raising and fluttering of the wings. The alarm call is a "chuck, chuck."

Field Marks: This small, short-tailed thrasher with its short straight bill looks like a pale thrush but with a streaked breast and yellow eyes.

Food: The Sage Thrasher's food includes a variety of insects, such as grasshoppers, beetles, and caterpillars, and other small invertebrates and a variety of wild berries.

A Brown Thrasher (*Toxostoma rufum*). Photograph by Bob Gress.

Brown Thrasher
Toxostoma rufum (Linnaeus)

Status: The Brown Thrasher is a common transient and summer resident statewide and is casual in winter.

Period of Occurrence: This thrasher is most common from mid-April through early October; extreme dates are 1 April and 27 October, with frequent stragglers to 21 January. There are mid-winter sightings (29 January through 11 February) from Decatur, Ellis, and Shawnee counties.

Breeding: The nest is placed in a tree crotch or in a thick shrub or vine, usually within seven feet of the ground. In some areas ground nesting is common. The nest is bulky, having a base of loose, thorny twigs and a deep cup of smaller twigs, weed stems, leaves, and fine bark lined with rootlets. The clutch is two to five, usually three or four, bluish white or pinkish white eggs thickly dotted with brown spots and dots. The incubation period is 12 to 14 days, the nestling period 10 to 13 days. Both sexes build the nest and share incubation. Most clutches are completed in mid-May. This species is apparently single brooded in Kansas.

Habits and Habitat: The Brown Thrasher nests in various types of edge habitat from isolated riparian thickets to towns, dooryards, and parks. When not singing it is usually inconspicuous, but in towns it often feeds on lawns with robins and grackles. In spring it is a persistent singer; it perches in the top of a tall tree, from which it delivers a series of doubled phrases with a definite cadence. Listeners have described the song in numerous ways. Ely's favorite is "plant-a-seed, plant-a-seed, bury-it, bury-it, cover-it-up, cover-it-up, let-it-grow, let-it-grow, pull-it-up, pull-it-up, eat-it, eat-it, yum-yum." After pair formation is completed the male also sings a very faint song when near the female. Although some individuals become very adept at mimicking songs and calls of local species, most individuals do so rarely. The call is a loud smacking "spuck."

Some adults are very aggressive in defense of their nests (especially with young), scolding very loudly, flying at the intruder, and sometimes making contact. This thrasher usually feeds on the ground, where it probes plant debris and flips leaves in search of prey. It usually occurs singly in winter, but a flock of 12 was reported from Decatur County on 25 December 1977.

Field Marks: With its long tail, streaked breast, and yellow eye, the Brown Thrasher is unlike any other Kansas species. However, it has often been called the "brown thrush," a term then confused with the *very* different Wood Thrush.

Food: The Brown Thrasher eats a variety of insects, including beetles and caterpillars; other small invertebrates; and rarely vertebrates such as small lizards, snakes, salamanders, and frogs. It also eats a variety of berries and fruits, especially in winter.

A Curve-billed Thrasher (*Toxostoma curvirostre*). Photograph by David A. Rintoul.

Curve-billed Thrasher
Toxostoma curvirostre (Swainson)

Status: The Curve-billed Thrasher is a casual visitor and occasional (local) summer resident in the southwest, where it is apparently resident some years. It is vagrant to casual elsewhere in the state north and east to Norton, Riley, and Cowley counties.

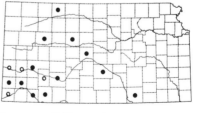

Period of Occurrence: The Curve-billed Thrasher has been reported during all months in the south-west. Most sightings elsewhere are between 2 November and 23 April but with single sightings on 22 May (Barton County) and 24 June (Norton County). One wintered in Hays, Ellis County, 8 December 1975 through 17 April 1976.

Breeding: Breeding has been reported from Hamilton, Gray, Kearny, and Morton counties. Nest building began by mid-April; in *each* case the nest was in a cholla cactus — a plant occurring very locally and in very low density in southwestern Kansas. All nests have been constructed of thorny twigs, lined with grass and rootlets, and placed within seven feet of the ground. The clutch is two to four, usually three, bluish green eggs with very fine brown speckling. The incubation period is 13 days, the nestling period 14 to 18 days. This species is apparently double brooded in Kansas, with clutches completed in late May and late June. Both sexes incubate. Pairs frequently return to the same immediate territory in successive years and build new nests each year.

Habits and Habitat: In summer the Curve-billed Thrasher is restricted to arid parts of the southwest, usually in sand-sage grassland and usually near a cholla cactus. In winter birds wander and have been reported in barnyards, windbreaks, cemeteries, brushy ravines, and even in dooryards. The distribution of records suggests that it moves eastward along major rivers. It spends much of its time on the ground, where it both runs and hops. Its flight is rapid, usually of short duration and typically near the ground or low vegetation. It feeds on the ground, probing with its beak and tossing debris aside in search for food. It also takes fruit from cacti and shrubs. The calls include a sharp whistled "whit-wheet" and several harsh, scolding, wrenlike calls. The song is a series of clear melodious phrases delivered from the top of a tall bush or low tree.

Field Marks: The Curve-billed Thrasher is easily distinguished from the Brown Thrasher by its dull gray plumage, conspicuously longer, curved bill, and faintly spotted breast. At close range the orange eye is apparent. Immatures have shorter, straight bills and are less streaked below.

Food: The food of this species is insects and small invertebrates and a considerable amount of fruit and berries, especially in winter.

An American Pipit (*Anthus rubescens*). Photograph by Dale and Marian Zimmerman.

PIPITS (FAMILY MOTACILLIDAE)
American Pipit
Anthus rubescens (Tunstall)

Status: The American Pipit is an uncommon spring and fall transient throughout the state. It is an occasional winter resident.

Period of Occurrence: The American Pipit generally arrives mid-March and departs around 30 April. Fall occurrence begins around 6 September and lasts through 7 November. Dates of extreme spring occurrence are 15 February to 14 May with one record from 9 July. Sightings in fall have occurred until 30 December.

Habits and Habitat: Until 1989, the American Pipit was known as the Water Pipit. They are now considered separate species. Nevertheless the American Pipit does seem to prefer moist areas around lake shores, ponds, areas of short grass, and recently plowed fields. The birds frequently can be seen around drainage ditches, water seeps, or river bars. Like most of the pipits, they feed on the ground, running quickly to catch an insect before it escapes. The American Pipit does some tail wagging. Bent (1950) states, "Observers differ as to the amount of tail wagging and when it occurs, but the pipit belongs to the wagtail family and must indulge in a certain amount of it." Several observers have reported the tail wagging to be up and down; others report it to be side to side. The flight of this pipit is undulating, and its white, outer tail feathers only show in flight.

Field Marks: See Sprague's Pipit.

Food: The American Pipit feeds primarily on animal material, particularly insects. It only occasionally will take vegetable matter.

Sprague's Pipit
Anthus spragueii (Audubon)

Status: The Sprague's Pipit is an uncommon transient in the Flint Hills to west-central Kansas and is rare elsewhere. It is a casual winter resident.

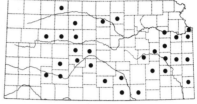

Period of Occurrence: The Sprague's Pipit arrives in spring around the end of March, with most records falling from 30 March to 27 April. The fall passage begins about 23 September and continues until about 25 October. The dates of extreme spring occurrence are 24 March to 10 May and in fall 5 September to 20 December. There is a specimen record for Cowley County on 20 January.

Habits and Habitat: This pipit is found primarily in short-grass prairie or heavily grazed tall-grass prairie. In the Flint Hills it is found in areas that are either grazed down to two to three inches or in areas where it is so eroded that tall grasses do not grow well. When disturbed the Sprague's Pipit usually takes off, giving its call note during its undulating flight. It usually flies only a short distance before suddenly dropping to the ground. It is adept at camouflaging itself and can be very difficult to see if it sits tight. Sometimes this species will sneak away in the grass rather than fly. Birds may occasionally be found along gravel roads next to grass. They are always found as singles in dispersed flocks.

Field Marks: The American Pipit and the Sprague's Pipit usually do not occupy the same habitat; the former is found in more open areas. Thompson did find a Sprague's feeding close to Americans along a drainage ditch and has seen them in pastureland around ponds where Americans had been found. The American Pipit has a plain back, whereas the Sprague's has a streaked back. They both possess white outer tail feathers.

Food: The Sprague's Pipit is primarily an insect eater but may take seeds as a supplement (Bent 1950).

A Bohemian Waxwing (*Bombycilla garrulus*). Photograph by Calvin L. Cink.

WAXWINGS (FAMILY BOMBYCILLIDAE)
Bohemian Waxwing
Bombycilla garrulus (Linnaeus)

Status: The Bohemian Waxwing is an irregular winter visitant. In some years it may be quite common as far south as the southern tier of counties. There have been no large influxes in the past 20 years.

Period of Occurrence: Although the Bohemian Waxwing has been recorded as early as 4 November, most records are from 25 November through

mid-March. The latest date of
spring occurrence is 16 April.
There are few dated records.

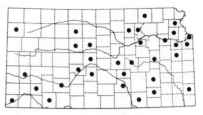

Habits and Habitat: The Bohemian
Waxwing is found primarily in
areas that have redcedar trees,
such as cemeteries and shelter
belts. They usually flock, although in 1989 there was a lone bird in Morton County. The flocks are usually small, but there was a flock of 85 in
Topeka on 26 February 1962. They may associate with flocks of Cedar
Waxwings. Bent (1950) describes this waxwing as "a well dressed gen-
tleman in feathers, a Beau Brummel among birds." They are a roving
species in winter, and you never know when they might show up in your
area.

Field Marks: One of the most beautiful birds, with soft plumage of subtle grays and browns, a band of white across the wings, chestnut under-
tail coverts, and a black chin. It can be told from the Cedar Waxwing
by its larger size and chestnut under-tail coverts.

Food: The Bohemian Waxwing feeds primarily on berries but has been
observed on the breeding grounds to be an expert flycatcher (Bent
1950).

A Cedar Waxwing (*Bombycilla cedrorum*). Photograph by Bob Gress.

Cedar Waxwing
Bombycilla cedrorum Vieillot

Status: The Cedar Waxwing is a common transient and winter resident statewide. It is a rare breeding bird, mainly in the northeastern part of the state.

Period of Occurrence: This waxwing occurs most months of the year as a nonbreeding bird. Flocks may be found into late May or even June without denoting breeding. Although it is hard to pinpoint exact dates, most birds probably arrive around 10 September and depart by 15 May. There are heavy influxes in the southward migration, a thinning in December, and northward movements from the south again in March and April.

Breeding: Johnston (1964b) stated, "This waxwing is a rare, local, and highly irregular summer resident in northeastern Kansas, in woodland and forest edge habitats. The known nesting stations are in Wyandotte and Shawnee counties." Thompson found an adult with young in juvenile plumage in Cowley County in mid-August, and they were assumed to have been reared in the area. Steve Fretwell had a nest in Riley County

on 3 June 1979. Bob Wood and Ken Brunson saw an adult carrying
nesting material in Osage County on 6 June 1979. Little is known
about clutch size in Kansas, but elsewhere the Cedar Waxwing has four
or five eggs. The nest is usually placed around 10 feet high in deciduous woodlands (Johnsgard 1979).

Habits and Habitat: Although called Cedar Waxwings, they are by no
means confined to redcedars and may be found in most any kind of
woodland where there is an ample food supply. They are often heard
before they are seen, but the very high frequency call may be hard to
hear if you have high pitch problems with your ears. They seem to prefer redcedar berries in the fall and winter and in the spring can be found
eating pyracantha berries or small crab apples. There are many stories about waxwings sitting in a line on a branch with the first bird passing the berry to the next up and down the line. Why this peculiar
behavior occurs is not known. Sometimes the waxwings can become
intoxicated from the fermenting berries. Sometimes they may be poisoned, as happened in Wichita in 1990 where several birds were found
dead underneath a soapberry where they had been feeding on the fruit.
The soapberry is not listed as a poisonous species, and the birds may
have been poisoned from some other cause (Gress, pers. comm.).

Field Marks: See Bohemian Waxwing.

Food: The Cedar Waxwing feeds primarily on fruits but is known to take
insects during the breeding season. The birds seem to eat most any
fruit that they can swallow.

A Northern Shrike (*Lanius excubitor*). Photograph by Southgate Hoyt for the Cornell Laboratory of Ornithology.

SHRIKES (FAMILY LANIIDAE)
Northern Shrike
Lanius excubitor Linnaeus

Status: The Northern Shrike is a rare, irregular winter visitor, primarily in the western third of the state.

Period of Occurrence: The Northern Shrike has been recorded from 5 October to 5 April. There is one report for 8 September.

Habits and Habitat: The Northern Shrike seems to prefer open country, where it can be found perching on lone trees, other vegetation, and telephone or power lines. These lofty perches enable it to spot its prey, which it swoops down on. The Northern Shrike may then fly back to its perch to consume its meal.

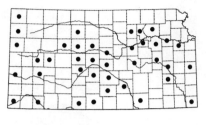

Field Marks: See Loggerhead Shrike.

Food: This shrike will attack anything that it thinks it can kill, including snakes, birds, mice, and insects.

A Loggerhead Shrike (*Lanius ludovicianus*). Photograph by Bob Gress.

Loggerhead Shrike
Lanius ludovicianus Linnaeus

Status: The Loggerhead Shrike is a common transient and summer resident throughout the state. It is rare in winter, found chiefly in the southern and eastern parts of the state.

Period of Occurrence: Although Loggerhead Shrikes are present in some parts of the state all year, the majority of them return to Kansas in early March and depart by the end of November.

Breeding: The Loggerhead Shrike breeds throughout the state in open areas with scrub vegetation or small groves of trees. The nests are placed from six to 10 feet high. Johnston (1964b) lists 57 breeding records from 1 April to 30 June, with most nests being found around 15 April. The clutch size averages five eggs. The incubation period is

16 days, and the young fledge in 17 days. The adults continue to hunt and feed the young for a few days after fledging.

Habits and Habitat: The Loggerhead Shrike is a bird of open areas interspersed with trees and shrubs. The birds are usually found either in the tops of dead trees or on power or telephone lines from which they watch for prey. Unlike many of our passerine birds, the shrike is well equipped to hunt insects, small rodents, and small birds. The hooked bill and sharp claws can inflict a painful wound. Thompson watched a Loggerhead Shrike attack a European Starling in Morton County. Alas, the starling escaped after a five-minute battle. Shrikes occasionally impale their prey upon thorns or barbwire, using these as "pantries." Impaling is probably only used when food is plentiful. When food is scarce it is usually eaten immediately.

Field Marks: Because of their similarity, Loggerhead and Northern shrikes may be difficult for the amateur to distinguish. The Northern Shrike differs in having a more narrow face mask, grayer coloration, fine barring on the breast, and a more strongly hooked bill. Immature Northerns may appear quite brown.

Food: The Loggerhead Shrike feeds on large insects, which are probably the bulk of the diet, small mammals, and small birds. Other animal matter is probably utilized as it is available.

A European Starling (*Sturnus vulgaris*). Photograph by Gerald J. Wiens.

STARLINGS (FAMILY STURNIDAE)
European Starling
Sturnus vulgaris Linnaeus

Status: The European Starling is an introduced species. It is a common, sometimes abundant, resident of the state.

Period of Occurrence: This starling is a resident species and is found throughout the year.

Breeding: The European Starling breeds throughout the state but is more common in the central part and east than in the west. Star-lings first arrived in Kansas in 1926 near Arkansas City, Cowley County.

They were considered common in Wichita, Sedgwick County, by 1933, they gradually worked their way westward, and were noted in Ellsworth County by 1938. These birds were first recorded breeding in Kansas in the early 1930s and were well established by 1935 or 1936 (Johnston 1964b). They were slow to colonize the southwestern corner and were apparently not present there until the late 1950s or early 1960s. Breeding has been recorded from 1 March to 30 June. The nest is placed in a cavity in a tree or in a martin house or any other type of hole the bird can find. Because of this habit of using cavities for nests, the European Starling has displaced many of the native birds.

One of the reasons starlings are so successful is that they are double brooded — that is, they raise two sets of young per year. The average date for the first clutch is 15 April and the second 5 June. The usual clutch size is five eggs. The incubation period is around 12 days, with the young fledging about 21 days later.

Habits and Habitat: The starling occurs in almost every type of habitat that occurs in Kansas except deep woods. After raising their young, starlings often congregate in large flocks that can devastate grain fields or native fruits that other birds depend upon. They have become a nuisance at cattle feedlots in the fall. Within the last 10 years, starlings have learned to eat redcedar berries and can wipe an area clean in a matter of days before moving on, leaving little food for waxwings and other fruit-eating birds. On the good side of starlings, they do eat enormous quantities of insects during the breeding season.

Although starlings are aggressive, Thompson has seen them driven out of Purple Martin colonies, sometimes falling to the ground with one or two martins flogging them. Sometimes reducing the height of a martin house is enough to discourage starlings from entering.

Field Marks: Most people can easily identify an adult European Starling. However, the young in juvenile plumage look like anything but an adult and are often confusing to the amateur. They are brown all over, but the back is darker than the belly.

Food: The starling is omnivorous and eats insects, grain, and other types of vegetable matter. Its varied diet probably is one of the secrets of its success.

A White-eyed Vireo (*Vireo griseus*). Photograph by Bob Gress.

VIREOS (FAMILY VIREONIDAE)
White-eyed Vireo
Vireo griseus (Boddaert)

Status: The White-eyed Vireo is an uncommon transient and uncommon summer resident in the eastern fourth of the state, becoming increasingly rarer farther west and north.

Period of Occurrence: This vireo arrives in Kansas around 15 April and departs around 14 October. The periods of extreme occurrence are 9 April and 7 November.

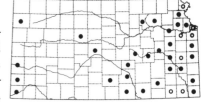

Breeding: There are few actual breeding records for the state, although the White-eyed Vireo is present all summer in the east. There are breeding records from as far west as Montgomery County, although this species probably breeds at least to Cowley County in some years. The nest is usually placed in shrubs or low trees about three feet high. It is a suspended cuplike nest held together by spider webs. Johnston (1964b) lists 10 breeding records from 10 May to 30 June, with an average clutch size of four eggs. The incubation period is 14 days, with fledging occurring approximately 15 days later. The Brown-headed Cowbird is a serious parasite of this species as it is of all vireos. Much more information is needed on the breeding distribution of this species in Kansas.

Habits and Habitat: The White-eyed Vireo prefers dense thickets in riparian woodlands. This type of habitat confines it to the extreme eastern part of Kansas during the breeding season. In migration it occurs rarely west to the Colorado border and is usually encountered along wooded streams. This vireo is curious and can easily be called in to the observer with a squeaking noise. It is said to be a good mimic (Bent 1950).

Field Marks: This is a small vireo, bright olive green above and tinged with yellow on the sides of its white underparts. The space in front of the eye is yellow, and the iris is a conspicuous white, unlike any other vireo in Kansas.

Food: The White-eyed Vireo feeds in Kansas primarily on insects but probably relies heavily on vegetable matter in the winter (Bent 1950).

Bell's Vireo
Vireo bellii Audubon

Status: The Bell's Vireo is a common transient and summer resident in the eastern half of Kansas, becoming less common in the west.

Period of Occurrence: The spring arrival of the Bell's Vireo is around 30 April; it departs in fall by 15 September. The dates of extreme occurrence are 14 April and 29 September.

Breeding: The breeding areas of Bell's Vireos are confined to riparian thickets and second-growth scrub. They are frequently found nesting in second-growth osage orange that was cut off but not bulldozed. Other favorite nesting sites are dogwood, coralberry, willow, locust, plum, and other shrubby vegetation. In central Kansas, roughleaf dogwood in a fence row is sure to produce this vireo.

The nest is suspended in the fork of a tree, usually placed from one to five feet high. The nests are intricately woven and a thing of beauty. The four eggs are laid from 1 May to 20 July, with most eggs being laid around 25 May. Incubation takes about 14 days, and the young fledge in 11 days. The Brown-headed Cowbird is a serious parasite and may be causing a reduction in numbers of Bell's Vireos.

Habits and Habitat: The smallest of the Kansas vireos, the Bell's Vireo is confined to scrub vegetation in Kansas. If the vegetation gets much over eight to 10 feet, the birds abandon the area and go to locations where the vegetation is short and dense. They are confiding birds early in the nesting season and can easily be squeaked up for the observer to get a better look. After the nesting season is over, they become retiring and difficult to observe.

Field Marks: One of our smallest vireos with no conspicuous field marks. It is a gray and olive bird with yellowish sides and one to two white wing bars.

Food: The Bell's Vireo feeds almost exclusively on insects.

Black-capped Vireo
Vireo atricapillus Woodhouse

Status: The Black-capped Vireo, once a summer resident of the Red Hills in the south-central part of Kansas, is now a vagrant to the state if it occurs here at all. Sight records from Manhattan, Riley County (1953), and Halstead, Harvey County (1951), are hypothetical (Tordoff, 1956).

Period of Occurrence: The birds apparently arrived in April and departed in August, but actual arrival and departure dates are lacking.

Breeding: There are confirmed nesting records only from Comanche County. Purported nesting in Cowley and Hodgeman counties is assumed to be in error as are sight records from Doniphan and Gray counties (Graber 1957). These records date back to the biological surveys, although the Hodgeman County record is reportedly based on a set of eggs in the Baylor University egg collection. We have not examined these eggs, but they are undoubtedly misidentified since Hodgeman County does not have the habitat, nor had it in the past, that would support the nesting of this species. Goss (1891) collected three pairs in southeastern Comanche County, 7 May to 18 May 1885, and found a nest under construction on 11 May 1885. He considered these vireos to be quite common. They might still breed in Comanche County if it were not for the Brown-headed Cowbird, which is a heavy parasite on this species.

Habits and Habitat: In Kansas the Black-capped Vireo was confined to the gypsum hills in the south-central part of the state. In this area scrub oak and other short, shrubby materials supplied the nesting habitat that it likes. This habitat is still available in the area, but cowbird parasitism has probably extirpated it from the state.

Field Marks: A conspicuous black and white head pattern in the male, with the female a little duller, is diagnostic for this vireo. No other vireo in the state approaches this pattern.

Food: It is presumed that this vireo consumed mostly insects.

A Solitary Vireo (*Vireo solitarius*). Photograph by Mike Hopiak for the Cornell Laboratory of Ornithology.

Solitary Vireo
Vireo solitarius (Wilson)

Status: The Solitary Vireo is a common transient in the east and rare in the west. Most records from western Kansas are from the fall.

Period of Occurrence: This vireo usually arrives about 24 April and departs 20 May, with an extreme occurrence of 3 June. The earliest fall arrival is 9 August, but most Solitary Vireos pass through Kansas from 29 August to 22 Oc-

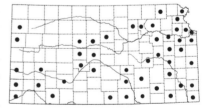

tober, with some stragglers to 11 November. There is one record of a straggler in Cowley County on 13 December.

Breeding: There is one egg from Decatur County in the Field Museum of Natural History. It was reportedly taken on 16 June 1912 by G. Love.

It was listed as being the gray race *plumbeus*. We have not examined this egg, and its validity is in doubt.

Habits and Habitat: The elegant Solitary Vireo is a woodland species and occurs in woodlots of a few acres or less into heavy forest. It is occasionally found in stands of exotic conifers. It was once called the Blue-headed Vireo, but since the western races are mostly gray, this was a poor name. The gray western race does occasionally occur in Kansas, chiefly in the southwest, and can look quite different than its "blue-headed" cousin from the east.

Field Marks: This vireo appears in Kansas in two forms: a bluish-headed form with yellow sides and white spectacles and a gray form with faintly yellow sides. The latter may eventually be reclassified into a separate species.

Food: Like other vireos, this one feeds mainly on insects.

A Yellow-throated Vireo (*Vireo flavifrons*). Photograph by Mike Hopiak for the Cornell Laboratory of Ornithology.

Yellow-throated Vireo
Vireo flavifrons Vieillot

Status: The Yellow-throated Vireo is an uncommon transient and summer resident in the extreme eastern part of Kansas at least as far west as Shawnee and Woodson counties. This vireo is a casual transient in the western part of the state, with records from Morton and Hamilton counties.

Period of Occurrence: This vireo arrives in eastern Kansas around 24 April and remains until 6 September. The extreme dates are 12 April and 10 October. More data are needed on arrival and departure times.

Breeding: Although the Yellow-throated Vireo breeds in Kansas, there are few nesting records. Johnston (1964b) listed no actual records but did mention Shawnee and Woodson counties. Thompson has found this vireo breeding in Douglas and Linn counties. Each nest observed was about 25 to 30 feet above the ground in deciduous forest. Much more data are needed on breeding distribution, habitat, and clutch size for Kansas.

Johnsgard (1979) lists the clutch size as four eggs, with incubation lasting 14 days and young fledging in 15 days.

Habits and Habitat: The Yellow-throated Vireo is a bird of deciduous forests, mainly in the eastern fourth of Kansas. In western Kansas it is usually found in woodland along river courses. Little is known about this beautiful vireo's habits in Kansas.

Field Marks: The Yellow-throated Vireo is the largest vireo in Kansas and the only one with a bright yellow throat.

Food: The Yellow-throated Vireo is an insect eater.

A Warbling Vireo (*Vireo gilvus*). Photograph by Dale and Marian Zimmerman.

Warbling Vireo
Vireo gilvus (Vieillot)

Status: The Warbling Vireo is a common transient and summer resident throughout the state.

Period of Occurrence: The spring arrival begins around 20 April, with fall departure around 10 September. The extreme dates are 6 April and 8 October.

Breeding: The Warbling Vireo breeds throughout the state in woodland

and towns. The nest is suspended from the fork of a tree or shrub. Egg laying can begin as early as 1 May, with four eggs laid. However, most eggs are laid around 5 June (Johnston 1964b). Incubation takes 12 days, with fledging occurring 14 days after hatching. Because of the height of most of the Warbling Vireo nests, little is known of the breeding habits of this species in Kansas. It is commonly parasitized by the Brown-headed Cowbird.

Habits and Habitat: This vireo's song is a common voice in the woodlands and cities of Kansas. It is an incessant singer, often to the point of monotony. The Warbling Vireo is more of an edge bird of woodlands and does not penetrate deeply into the interior of dense eastern forest. It is common in riparian woodlands. City trees seem to give the woodland edge effect and are consequently utilized fairly heavily by this species. Although the nest is usually placed high, a nest in Winfield, Cowley County, was in a grape arbor barely seven feet above the ground.

It is of interest that of the six recoveries of banded Warbling Vireos, two were banded in Kansas at the same banding locality (Winfield) and recovered in Guatemala and El Salvador.

Field Marks: The best field mark of the Warbling Vireo is its absence of field marks. Its uniformity in color and song are good combinations with which to identify it. Bird watchers should take caution, however, as this species can sometimes be *very* yellow and be mistaken for a Philadelphia Vireo if the other field characters of the Philadelphia are missed.

Food: The Warbling Vireo is primarily an insect eater.

Philadelphia Vireo
Vireo philadelphicus (Cassin)

Status: The Philadelphia Vireo is an uncommon transient in the east and a rare transient in the west.

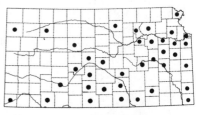

Period of Occurrence: The dates of occurrence for this species are not well documented. The earliest date of record is 24 April, with departure for the breeding grounds by 30 May. The autumnal arrival is around 2 September, with the latest fall record being 17 October. There should be close scrutiny of all April and August dates because of possible confusion with the Warbling Vireo.

Habits and Habitat: The Philadelphia Vireo is usually found along woodland edges and in towns with mature trees. It is a fairly nondescript bird and does not sing much in migration. This probably causes us to overlook it. It may be more common than records would indicate, as it has been taken in the fall several times at tower kills at the WIBW-TV tower near Topeka.

Field Marks: This vireo looks very much like a Warbling Vireo with a yellower breast and more indistinct eye line. See comments under Yellow-throated Vireo.

Food: This vireo, like the others in the family, is an insect eater.

A Red-eyed Vireo (*Vireo olivaceus*). Photograph by Mike Hopiak for the Cornell Laboratory of Ornithology.

Red-eyed Vireo
Vireo olivaceus (Linnaeus)

Status: The Red-eyed Vireo is an uncommon transient and summer resident in the east. In the west it is regular but an uncommon transient.

Period of Occurrence: This vireo arrives around 24 April and departs in the fall around 18 October, with an extreme fall departure of 6 November. In the western part of Kansas, where it does not commonly breed, it departs in spring by 5 June. The autumnal arrival in the west is around 9 August; departure is by 30 September. There are scattered summer records for the western half of Kansas.

Breeding: The Red-eyed Vireo breeds in woodlands in the eastern half of Kansas. The western limits of breeding are uncertain but extend at least to Rooks and Decatur counties in the north and to Sumner

County in the south. It undoubtedly breeds in the denser riparian woodlands of the west, but there are no records. The suspended nest is usually placed from five to 10 feet above the ground, but nests as high as
60 feet and and as low as two feet have been recorded (Bent 1950). A
clutch of four eggs is usually laid in late May to late July. Incubation
lasts 12 days, and the young fledge in 12.

Habits and Habitat: The Red-eyed Vireo is found in riparian woodlands, where it remains to breed in the summer, at least in the eastern
part of Kansas. On a hot summer afternoon, it usually is the only bird
singing. The height from which it sings and its olive-green coloration
make it a difficult bird to observe. The song is a rather monotonous
one of four short phrases and usually is repeated over and over. This
fortunately gives the observer plenty of time to locate it in the dense
leaves. Bent (1950) states, "No other of our birds sings so persistently
all day long, and because his long-continued series of utterances, given
in short, emphatic phrases, going on for hours, calls to mind a lengthy
sermon, he has won the title 'Preacher.'"

Field Marks: This vireo has a gray crown, bordered by black lines, the
black line through the eye, and white underparts. The red iris can only
be seen at short range.

Food: We turn to Bent (1950) once again to give some idea of the prodi-
gious appetite of a young bird. "His entire menu for the first day consisted of: 40 blue-bottle flies; 30 elderberries; 25 grasshoppers; a tent
full of tent caterpillars, of which he ate at least 15; 5 moths; 2 daddy-
long-legs; 1 dragon fly; 1 young locust; 1 inch-worm; 1 spider; 1 bee;
1 butterfly — a total of 123 distinct items." Some vegetable matter is
taken, particularly berries.

A Blue-winged Warbler (*Vermivora pinus*). Photograph by John S. Dunning for the Cornell Laboratory of Ornithology.

WOOD WARBLERS (FAMILY EMBERIZIDAE, SUBFAMILY PARULINAE)
Blue-winged Warbler
Vermivora pinus (Linnaeus)

Status: The Blue-winged Warbler is a very rare transient in eastern Kansas and a casual visitor elsewhere.

Period of Occurrence: Most sightings have been in early to mid-May. Specimen records are from 1 May to 2 June and 10 August to 4 September and 10 October. Sight records, some dubious, extend these dates to 18 April and 18 September.

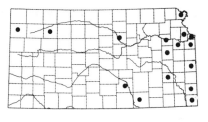

Breeding: There are no fully documented accounts of breeding in Kansas, although both Goss (1891) and Snow (1903) considered it a "rare summer resident." However, Shirling (1920), in a 1916 survey of the breeding birds of Swope Park in Kansas City, Missouri, reported 17 singing males of this species, so it may have bred in nearby Kansas. It was not breeding in Swope Park in 1973 (Branan and Burdick 1981).

Mick McHugh reports that it currently breeds in Missouri within 50 miles of Kansas City and in southwestern Missouri within 35 miles of the Kansas border.

Habits and Habitat: The Blue-winged Warbler breeds in the central and northeastern United States in woodland edge and brushy fields and thickets, often near water. While migrating through Kansas it occurs in similar areas and in parks and residential areas. Except when singing it stays near the ground and is a ground nester. Its behavior is slow and deliberate, reminding one of a vireo. The song is a two-note lisping buzz, sometimes interpreted as "zee-bee," which is delivered repeatedly from the open top of a low tree.

The Blue-winged Warbler interbreeds with the closely related Golden-winged Warbler where the two ranges overlap, producing two very distinct hybrids and numerous intermediate types. The first generation produces the "Brewster's Warbler," a combination of dominant traits that resembles a Golden-winged without the black throat and cheek but having a black streak through the eye. Much rarer is the expression of recessive traits, the "Lawrence's Warbler," which is essentially a Blue-winged with black throat and cheek. Hybrids generally mate with one or the other of the two parental types rather than with other hybrids. For details of this interesting phenomenon, see Parkes (1951). There are excellent illustrations in Farrand (1983). The Blue-winged Warbler has also hybridized with the Kentucky and Mourning warblers, the former producing the "Cincinnati Warbler" painted by Audubon.

Field Marks: Both sexes are largely yellow with bluish gray wings crossed by two white wing bars and with a dark streak through the eye. Immatures are duller and greener above and have wing bars.

Food: This species eats small beetles, ants, caterpillars and spiders.

Golden-winged Warbler
Vermivora chrysoptera (Linnaeus)

Status: The Golden-winged Warbler is a rare spring transient in eastern Kansas and is casual westward. There are very few fall records.

Period of Occurrence: This species has been reported in the east from 28 April to 28 May and 8 September to 23 October. In the central and western parts of the state, records are from 17 April to 26 May and 9 to 17 September. It was common in Johnson County during spring 1972.

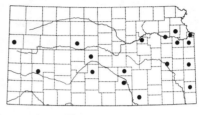

Habits and Habitat: In its breeding range (the northeastern United States and adjacent Canada) the Golden-winged Warbler occurs in deciduous woods, especially second growth, and in overgrown pastures. Transients through Kansas also use various riparian habitats and especially parks and residential areas. Early arrivals often feed high in leafless trees and actively search terminal buds for insects, vaguely resembling chickadees in both habits and appearance. The song is a buzzy series of notes, with the first note highest, sometimes interpreted as "zee, bz, bz, bz." As mentioned in the previous account, it hybridizes readily with the Blue-winged Warbler, and its breeding range is gradually shrinking as a result of replacement by that species.

Field Marks: The male has a black throat and mask and at first glance may remind one of a chickadee. However, it also has a yellow crown and a broad yellow wing patch (actually overlapping wing bars). The female is similar, with gray replacing the black. Immatures resemble the female but with an olive tinge above and a greenish tinge below.

Food: The Golden-winged Warbler eats small invertebrates, especially caterpillars and spiders.

A Tennessee Warbler (*Vermivora peregrina*). Photograph by B. D. Cottrille for the Cornell Laboratory of Ornithology.

Tennessee Warbler
Vermivora peregrina (Wilson)

Status: In spring the Tennessee Warbler is a common transient in the east and uncommon in the west. In fall it is uncommon in the east and rare in the west.

Period of Occurrence: Specimen records are from 23 April to 9 June and 20 September to 22 October with a straggler on 30 November. Sight records are 18 April to 9 June and 29 August to 24 October (and possibly 16 November) in the east; 23 April to 30 May and 1 September to 30 November in the west. It is most common in the east during the first half of May and the last half of October; in the west 15 to 25 May and 10 to 25 September. The Tennessee Warbler is easily overlooked when not singing, and being a treetop species, it is easily confused with similar species, especially in fall. Extreme dates, especially in fall, need verification.

Habits and Habitat: The Tennessee Warbler breeds primarily in conifer and mixed forests in Canada and Alaska, nesting on the ground, often in bogs. In Kansas it feeds primarily in treetops, usually within foliage, but fortunately is an active, persistent singer with a distinctive song. Bent (1953) described the loud, staccato song as "wi-chip, wi-chip, wi-chip, wi-chip, chip, chip, chip, chip, chip," speeding up at the end. Once one becomes familiar with the song, the Tennessee Warbler becomes surprisingly common for a brief period during spring. At Hays, 60 were banded on 20 and 21 May 1967. The fall migration is largely east of Kansas.

Field Marks: The color pattern is similar to that of a Vireo, but the Tennessee Warbler differs dramatically in more active behavior and its slender, pointed beak. In spring males are completely white below with a gray crown, a white line over the eye, and a dark line through the eye. Females are duller and more yellowish above, and immatures have much more yellow, sometimes extending through the under-tail coverts. It lacks wing bars in all plumages.

Food: The Tennessee Warbler eats beetles, small grasshoppers, aphids, caterpillars, and spiders and has been observed to pierce grapes for juice and to eat seeds of sumac and berries of poison ivy. It has been reported to eat bananas, suet, and peanut butter at feeding stations. On the wintering grounds it regularly joins local species in feeding on nectar in the tops of tall forest trees. At such times the face may become stained a bright orange color, and the bird appears to be an exotic species.

An Orange-crowned Warbler (*Vermivora celata*). Photograph by Dale and Marian Zimmerman.

Orange-crowned Warbler
Vermivora celata (Say)

Status: The Orange-crowned Warbler is a common transient in the west and usually less common in the east. It is casual in winter, chiefly in the east.

Period of Occurrence: It is most common from late April through early May and from mid-September to mid-October. Specimen records are from 13 April to 20 May and 7 September to 19 October. Extreme dates for sight records are 29 March to 24 May and 28 August to 31 October. Stragglers have been reported from eight counties (at least 14 records) to mid-December and exceptionally to 7 (Riley County) and 25 February (Cowley County).

Habits and Habitat: The Orange-crowned Warbler breeds in the forested regions of Canada and Alaska and south in the mountains of the western United States. There it prefers the second-growth vegetation of cleared and burned areas and nests on the ground. During migration it occurs in all types of shrubby or woody vegetation and nearby weed patches. It feeds at all elevations from near ground level in weed patches to high in trees, where it feeds chiefly at the tips of branches and within the canopy. Early in spring it is conspicuous as it feeds actively, often with Yellow-rumped Warblers, among developing buds and flowers of tall deciduous trees. The song has been described as a "colorless trill" weakening near the end and is similar to the spring song of the Yellow-rumped Warbler. The call is a sharp, distinctive "chip."

Field Marks: This is a nondescript, unmarked, olive green warbler with pale yellowish underparts. There is considerable individual variation in brightness of color; all have yellow under-tail coverts. Most individuals have a yellow eyebrow or partial eye ring and faint dusky streaking on the breast. The orange crown is rarely visible except in the hand.

Food: The Orange-crowned Warbler's food is chiefly insects, including true bugs, beetles, leafhoppers, caterpillars, and flies, and spiders. In winter it adds berries and may visit feeders for suet and peanut butter.

A Nashville Warbler (*Vermivora ruficapilla*). Photograph by Dale and Marian Zimmerman.

Nashville Warbler
Vermivora ruficapilla (Wilson)

Status: The Nashville Warbler is a common transient statewide.

Period of Occurrence: The Nashville Warbler is most numerous from late April to mid-May and from September through mid-October. Specimen records are from 25 April to 20 May and 24 August to 12 October; sight records extend these dates to 12 April and 27 May and 9 August and 30 October. 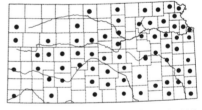 Stragglers have been reported to 11 November, but winter records (15 December to 15 February) need confirmation. One in Johnson County, 7 January to 15 February 1983, was photographed and verified (Mick McHugh, pers. comm.).

Habits and Habitat: This species breeds in second-growth deciduous or mixed forests of the northern United States and Canada, preferring to nest on the ground in brushy areas. It feeds at all elevations from ground level in weed patches (chiefly in fall) and bushes to tall trees, but chiefly at low to moderate elevations. It prefers the interior parts of leafy trees and is usually heard before it is seen. The Nashville Warbler often occurs in mixed flocks with other warblers. Its song is similar to that of a Tennessee Warbler and has been described as "see-it, see-it, see-it, ti-ti-ti-ti-ti," becoming more rapid at the end.

Field Marks: Males in spring are unmistakable, with contrasting gray head, yellow underparts, and conspicuous white eye ring. Females, males in fall, and immatures are paler, with less contrast, and present a grayer or browner overall pattern. Some immatures have pale yellowish wing bars.

Food: The food of this species is almost entirely insects such as caterpillars, leafhoppers, and aphids as well as spiders gleaned from twigs, buds, and leaf surfaces.

A Virginia's Warbler (*Vermivora virginiae*). Photograph by Dale and Marian Zimmerman.

Virginia's Warbler
Vermivora virginiae (Baird)

Status: The Virginia's Warbler is probably a rare spring transient in the southwest and possibly a vagrant elsewhere.

Period of Occurrence: Specimen records are from Morton County (6 and 8 May 1950) and Finney County (7 May 1964). There are additional sight records from Morton County (4 to 10 May 1950; 20 September 1986), one  from Johnson County, 14 May 1972, by Mary Louise Myers, and an unconfirmed report from Haskell County.

Habits and Habitat: The Virginia's Warbler breeds in scrubby brushland, in pinyon-juniper forest, and under open pines in the central Rockies and southwestern United States. It nests on the ground. This is a very shy species that feeds near the ground, often in dense vegetation, making it very difficult to observe. It twitches its tail frequently.

Field Marks: The male resembles a very pale (gray) Nashville Warbler with the yellow underparts limited to breast and under-tail coverts. It is gray above with a conspicuous eye ring and yellow rump. The female has reduced yellow; the immature is olive brown rather than gray above.

Food: The diet of this species includes caterpillars.

A Northern Parula (*Parula americana*). Photograph by Bill Dyer for the Cornell Laboratory of Ornithology.

Northern Parula
Parula americana (Linnaeus)

Status: The Northern Parula is an uncommon transient and summer resident in eastern Kansas and a rare transient in the central and west. Nests are extremely difficult to find, but recent observations suggest that the species is a more common breeder than formerly thought. It probably breeds locally west to Sumner and Riley counties.

Period of Occurrence: The Northern Parula usually arrives in mid-April and is most numerous during late April and May; extreme dates in the east are 1 April and 9 October. In the central part of the state and the west, reports are from 9 April to 23 May (once to 3 June, Morton County). The only fall record from western Kansas is 23 August.

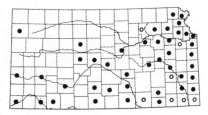

Breeding: Shirling (1920) reported 32 males during a June 1916 survey of the breeding birds of Swope Park, Kansas City, Missouri, and Branan and Burdick (1981) counted 11 in that location in 1973, suggesting that the species nests in nearby counties of Kansas. In the eastern United States nests are typically placed in festoons of Old-man's Beard Lichen (*Usnea*) or Spanish Moss (*Tillandsia*). In Kansas the nest is usually placed in a hanging cluster of leaves or other debris on a horizontal branch. Ed and Jean Schulenberg watched a pair completing a nest in a thick clump of dead leaves, about 10 feet above ground in an oak tree, in Cherokee County on 2 May 1980 (Schwilling, Schulenberg, and Schulenberg 1981). The nest is constructed of grass and plant tendrils and lined with plant down and hair. The clutch is three to seven, usually four or five, creamy white eggs spotted and dotted with brown. The incubation period is 12 days, and incubation is by the female alone.

Habits and Habitat: During migration this species may occur in any wooded habitat from deciduous woods to tree-lined city streets, but during the breeding season it is restricted to riparian situations. When feeding it hops or crawls along branches and twigs gleaning insects and is rather deliberate in its movements. It occurs most often in treetops, especially when singing and during the breeding season, but may occur at lower elevations. The song is a characteristic ascending buzzing trill with a very abrupt ending, sometimes interpreted as "zeeeeeee-yip!"

Field Marks: The Northern Parula was once appropriately known as the Blue Yellow-backed Warbler. The male is bluish gray above with yellow throat and breast crossed by black and rufous bands; it has two white wing bars and a partial white eye ring. The female is duller and lacks the breast bands; immatures are even duller.

Food: The Northern Parula's food is entirely small invertebrates, including small beetles, caterpillars, ants, wasps, scale insects, and spiders.

A Yellow Warbler (*Dendroica petechia*). Photograph by David A. Rintoul.

Yellow Warbler
Dendroica petechia (Linnaeus)

Status: The Yellow Warbler is a common transient statewide. It presently breeds in the east and very locally westward. Its presence in summer is spotty, and the species is perhaps much less common and widespread than formerly.

Period of Occurrence: It is most numerous from late April to mid-May and from late August through mid-September; extreme dates are 11 April and 14 October. Most migration is about 20 April to 26 May and 20 August to 25 September. Stragglers have been reported to 11

June, and migrants return by 23 July (Ellis County). There are also numerous midsummer records of nonbreeding birds. Early winter reports are probably brightly plumaged Orange-crowned Warblers.

Breeding: Courtship involves both singing and sexual pursuit. The nest is usually built in the crotch of a shrub or in an upright fork of a tree within 10 feet of the ground. It is a beautiful compact cup of milkweed fibers, dogbane bark, grass, and plant down lined with felted plant down, hair, and very fine grasses. The clutch is three to six, usually four or five, grayish or bluish white eggs with brown and gray markings, chiefly at the larger end. The incubation period is 11 or 12 days; the nestling period is nine to 12 days. Nest building and incubation are by the female alone. This species is commonly parasitized by the cowbird and often responds by building a new nest over the parasitized one. Bent (1953) reported up to six stories with a cowbird egg buried in each story. Parasitism by cowbirds may very well be one of the factors limiting the present breeding distribution of the Yellow Warbler in Kansas.

Habits and Habitat: In parts of the eastern United States the Yellow Warbler is a familiar dooryard bird. In some areas it may be so abundant as to be considered colonial. This is probably the wood warbler most familiar to Kansans because of its brilliant color and its occurrence in shade trees and shrubby parks and gardens. During the breeding season, however, it is most common in riparian situations and prefers willows and cottonwoods. Its breeding status in much of Kansas is unclear. It presently breeds very locally, usually near water, and more data are needed. Early reports of widespread breeding may indicate a wider distribution than at present or merely the presence of nonbreeding birds during mid-summer. A definite decline in numbers has been reported for Shawnee County ("Woods" 1976). The song is a series of three or four notes often interpreted as "sweet, sweet, sweetie-o-sweet." Godfrey (1979) reported one male uttering 3,240 songs in one day during the height of the breeding season. On its wintering grounds (Mexico to northern South America) individuals maintain winter territories in forest edge, brushy fields, and patios in towns.

Field Marks: Individuals of both sexes are largely yellow, brighter on the head and underparts, though some immatures of the northwestern races are dull olive green. Males have striking chestnut stripes on the underparts, and both sexes have yellow wing bars. This is our only warbler with yellow tail spots (both sexes). The dark eyes of adults contrast sharply against the yellow face.

Food: The Yellow Warbler eats small invertebrates including caterpillars, beetles, small moths, aphids, grasshoppers, and spiders.

Chestnut-sided Warbler
Dendroica pensylvanica (Linnaeus)

Status: Rare transient in east; casual in west.

Period of Occurrence: The Chestnut-sided Warbler is most frequently recorded during May and from mid-September to mid-October. Extreme dates are 27 April to 26 May (once to 10 June) and 17 August to 15 October. A published nesting record (Lowther 1977) was later found to be in error (Jenkinson 1984).

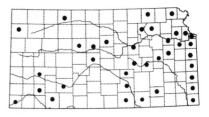

Habits and Habitat: According to Terres (1980) this was a very rare species during the early nineteenth century but became one of the most abundant wood warblers in the northeastern quarter of the United States and Canada following the clearing of the original forests. It prefers shrubbery in clearings of second-growth forests and in brushy fields, nesting in low shrubs. Most of its feeding is within seven feet of the ground. The Chestnut-sided Warbler gleans insects in typical warbler fashion and also flutters near foliage to snatch insects from exposed surfaces. Males sing from within or from the tops of small shrubs and low trees. The song is a loud series of phrases long ago described as "I wish, I wish, I wish to see Miss Beecher"; it is similar to that of the Yellow Warbler. Near Dodge City on 11 October 1970 one arrived with a mixed flock of warblers just after the first snow of the winter!

Field Marks: In all plumages adults are white below with two yellow wing bars and a yellowish crown. The male has a broad chestnut streak on the flanks; this is greatly reduced in the female. The immature is pure white below with a pale greenish, unstriped back and a white eye ring.

Food: This species feeds primarily on small arthropods, especially beetles, small moths, small grasshoppers, and spiders, and also eats a few fruits and seeds.

Magnolia Warbler
Dendroica magnolia (Wilson)

Status: The Magnolia Warbler is an uncommon transient in the east and rare or casual in the west.

Period of Occurrence: The Magnolia Warbler is most common during mid-May and from mid- to late September. Extreme dates are 26 April to 6 June (singing male, Johnson County) and 3 September to 6 October. A singing male 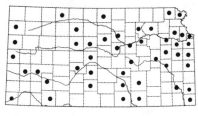 observed in Ellis County on 25 June 1968 was very unusual. A 15 April report (Meade County) is unverified, and a 14 December report from Saline County was almost certainly a Yellow-rumped Warbler.

Habits and Habitat: This species breeds in low conifer and mixed woods in southern Canada and the northeastern United States, where it prefers the edges of clearings. It nests in low shrubs or conifer saplings. During migration it occurs in all types of woody habitats from riparian growth to shrubbery in dooryards. It is a very active species, hopping around with drooping wings and partly spread tail, usually at low elevations. It has a variety of songs — a frequent one has been described as "wisha, wisha, wisha, witsy," rising at the end. On its wintering grounds, from southern Mexico to Costa Rica, it is very common in disturbed habitats such as forest edge and brushy fields.

Field Marks: The Magnolia Warbler is sometimes confused with the *very* different Yellow-rumped Warbler. The striking male is unmistakable with its conspicuous wing bars, yellow breast and rump, and white tail bands. Females are much duller; immatures have a contrasting gray band across the yellow breast.

Food: The Magnolia Warbler is largely insectivorous, eating beetles, leafhoppers, aphids, flies, caterpillars, and moths and also taking spiders.

A Cape May Warbler (*Dendroica tigrina*). Photograph by Dale and Marian Zimmerman.

Cape May Warbler
Dendroica tigrina (Gmelin)

Status: The Cape May Warbler is a rare transient, primarily in eastern Kansas. It occurs primarily in spring but is casual in winter.

Period of Occurrence: Sight records are 3 to 25 May and 31 August to 25 September and 18 October. There are four mid-winter records, one to 28 January, from Cowley and Douglas counties.

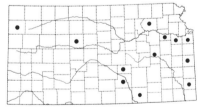

Habits and Habitat: This species breeds in mature, open spruce forests of Canada, building its nest in the very top of a tall tree. It may become very numerous locally in response to outbreaks of forest caterpillars. The song is a faint, high-pitched, slow, monotonous "zee-zee-zee-zee" on one pitch, usually delivered from the top of a tall tree. During migration the Cape May Warbler may be found in any woody vegetation, often high in trees such as oaks, where it gleans insects from flowers and opening buds. It also feeds by darting out at passing insects and by fluttering against vegetation. It is one of the warblers most likely to occur in Kansas in mid-winter.

Field Marks: In all plumages this species is yellow to olive gray above with dark streaking, white wing bars and tail spots, a yellow rump, and usually a yellow neck patch. The spring male is unmistakable with its orange cheek patch and heavily streaked back.

Food: The Cape May Warbler feeds primarily on such insects as beetles, flies, wasps, moths, and caterpillars and on spiders. It has also been seen to pierce grapes for their juice and to drink sap from the holes drilled by sapsuckers.

A Black-throated Blue Warbler (*Dendroica caerulescens*). Photograph by Bill Dyer for the Cornell Laboratory of Ornithology.

Black-throated Blue Warbler
Dendroica caerulescens (Gmelin)

Status: The Black-throated Blue Warbler is a rare transient statewide. All specimens and more than two-thirds of all sightings to date are from fall, usually between the third week of September and mid-October.

Period of Occurrence: Extreme dates (chiefly sight records) are 29 April to 20 May and 3 September to 23 October and 8 November.

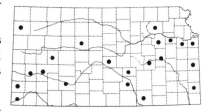

Habits and Habitat: This warbler breeds in dense undergrowth of mixed and conifer forests from southeastern Canada south through the Appalachians. It prefers second growth with shrub understory and usually nests in a laurel or rhododendron shrub or conifer sapling. It is noted for its unusually fearless behavior near the nest. It is an eastern species, wintering in the West Indies, and rarely reaches Kansas. At such times it may occur in any type of wooded area, usually at a low height and with other warblers. It is an active feeder, gleaning insects from twigs, snatching those flying nearby, or fluttering against foliage. The song is a slow, wheezy, slurred "zweeea, zweeea, zweeea, zweeet"; the call is a junco-like "smack."

Field Marks: The male is the only bird in Kansas to combine blue-gray upperparts and black cheek and throat. The female and immature are greenish, unstreaked, with a white line over the eye and partial eye ring. All plumages are unique among Kansas wood warblers in having a white patch (not bars) in the primaries.

Food: The Black-throated Blue Warbler is almost entirely insectivorous, taking moths, caterpillars, flies, beetles, and aphids. It also eats spiders and occasionally seeds and fruits.

A Yellow-rumped Warbler (*Dendroica coronata*). Photograph by Bob Gress.

Yellow-rumped Warbler
Dendroica coronata (Linnaeus)

Status: The Yellow-rumped Warbler is a common transient statewide. It winters occasionally, especially in the east.

Period of Occurrence: The "Myrtle"
Warbler is most regular and most
common from early April to early
May and during October. Varying
numbers linger into early winter
in some years, especially in the
east, and it has wintered at Marais
des Cygnes Refuge in Linn
County. It is rare in winter in the
west (to 18 February, Ellis County).
Extreme dates are 31 August to 21
May. There is an unconfirmed
record for Barton County on 30
July. "Audubon's" Warbler is an
uncommon transient in the far
west and a rare to casual transient

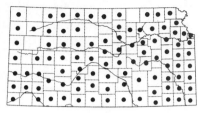

"Myrtle"

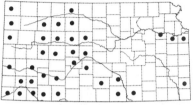

"Audubon's"

in the central and eastern portions of the state. It is most regular and
most common from mid-April to mid-May and from late September
to mid-October. Extreme dates are 11 September and 25 May, with stragglers to 16 June (Morton County). Intermediates between the two
forms are common.

Habits and Habitat: The species consists of two well-marked forms that
interbreed freely where their ranges overlap in southwestern Canada.
It breeds in coniferous forests of Alaska, Canada, and the western
United States, the widest breeding range of any wood warbler. It prefers
edges of clearings and places its nest on a horizontal branch at a moderate height. Godfrey (1979) considered it probably the most numerous wood warbler in Canada and noted that it has wintered
successfully as far north as Nova Scotia, near bayberry bushes. Its song
is a weak series of notes sometimes interpreted as "twee, twee, twee"
and similar to that of the Orange-crowned Warbler. The "Myrtle" form
was named for its fondness for wax myrtle and bayberries. It is a very
common migrant, occurring in any woody or shrubby habitat, including the vicinity of houses. It is a very early migrant, arriving before
leaves have emerged, and is often quite tame and very conspicuous. It
also occurs in flocks of sparrows and other nonwarblers. It feeds among
twigs, on tree trunks, even on the ground and at all heights. It usually
gleans but also darts out after passing insects and flutters against foliage. In late fall individuals also glean insects from nooks and cran-
nies of buildings, and in winter they may visit feeders. Wintering
concentrations along the Atlantic coast have been described as "awe-
some" by Kaufman (Farrand 1983).

Field Marks: The yellow rump is conspicuous in all plumages, suggesting the local common name of "butter butt." Males have a black breast with a yellow patch on the side near the bend of the wing. "Myrtles" have white throats; "Audubon's" have yellow throats and more white in the wings and tail. Females are duller and grayer, immatures even duller and browner. Intermediates with variable amounts of yellow occur, and some immature "Audubon's" lack the yellow throat. The yellow crown patch is often not visible on immature birds.

Food: The Yellow-rumped Warbler eats small arthropods, especially beetles, aphids, flies, moths, caterpillars, and spiders. Chiefly in winter, its diet includes large quantities of such berries as wax myrtle, bayberry, poison ivy, and redcedar. Less common items include grass seeds and (at feeders) sunflower "hearts," raisins, suet, and peanut butter. It also sips liquid from fruits, including fallen oranges, and sips maple tree sap.

Black-throated Gray Warbler
Dendroica nigrescens (Townsend)

Status: The Black-throated Gray Warbler is probably a rare spring migrant in the far west and occurs casually elsewhere.

Period of Occurrence: There are presently seven specimen records from Finney and Morton counties taken between 28 April and 13 May. There are additional sight records from western and north-central Kansas during the periods 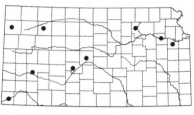 18 April to 17 May and 3 to 22 September. One was observed by over 30 birders during a Kansas Ornithological Society field trip to Cheyenne Bottoms on 2 May 1982.

Habits and Habitat: The Black-throated Gray Warbler breeds in fir forests (north) or deciduous scrub of mountain slopes (west) of the western United States and the southern Rockies. It prefers open pine or oak woods with considerable undergrowth and builds its nest on a horizontal branch at low to moderate heights. As a transient it occurs in deciduous growth, often riparian, usually at low to moderate heights. This warbler is usually shy and retiring and is deliberate in its actions. The song is described as "wee-zy, wee-zy, wee-zy wee-zy-weet" (Terres 1980).

Field Marks: The male has a black cheek like the Black-and-white Warbler but is gray above with fine black streakings and *very* different behavior. Females and immatures are grayer and lack the black throat. A yellow spot in front of the eye is rarely visible.

Food: The food of this warbler is said to be largely caterpillars but undoubtedly includes other groups of small insects and spiders.

A Townsend's Warbler (*Dendroica townsendi*). Photograph by Dale and Marian Zimmerman.

Townsend's Warbler
Dendroica townsendi (Townsend)

Status: The Townsend's Warbler is a rare transient in western Kansas and a vagrant in the east.

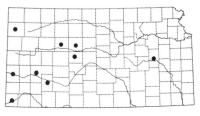

Period of Occurrence: Four specimens have been taken during the period 3 to 18 May and on 29 August from Ellis, Morton, and Trego counties, and there is a good photographic record from Rush County on 27 April. Additional sight records, 14 April to 20 May and 3 to 24 September, are from Gray, Hamilton, Lyon, and Sherman counties.

Habits and Habitat: This is the western counterpart of the Black-throated Green Warbler, which it closely resembles in behavior and song. The Townsend's Warbler breeds in coniferous forests from Alaska south into the Pacific Northwest, usually building in the top of a tall tree. On the breeding grounds it prefers tall treetops and moves rapidly while feeding. As a transient, however, it occupies a wider range of habitats, including deciduous riparian growth, and occurs at much lower heights.

It hybridizes with the Hermit Warbler where the two meet in Oregon and Washington.

Field Marks: In all plumages the dark cheek patch (black in males) outlined in yellow is diagnostic. The male has a black throat; females and immatures have yellow throats and upper breasts.

Food: The Townsend's Warbler feeds primarily on beetles, true bugs, leafhoppers, caterpillars, and spiders. At feeding stations it has been reported to eat peanut butter and cheese. It has also been observed taking spiders from under the eaves of buildings.

Hermit Warbler
Dendroica occidentalis (Townsend)

Status: The Hermit Warbler is a vagrant in Kansas.

Period of Occurrence: The only record for Kansas is one collected on the
Arkansas River near Holcomb,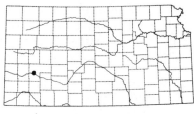
Finney County, on 7 May 1964 by
John A. Davis.

Habits and Habitat: This warbler
breeds in conifer forests of the
Coast Ranges and Sierra Nevada,
placing its nest on the horizontal
limb of a conifer at moderate height. During the breeding season it
spends most of the time in the very tops of tall trees and is very difficult to observe. However, it does feed nearer the ground in nearby deciduous vegetation. The only specimen taken in Kansas was feeding
in saltcedar (*Tamarix*). It flits about gleaning insects from branches,
trunks, and terminal twigs and at the tips of conifer needles, sometimes
hanging chickadee-fashion.

Field Marks: The Hermit Warbler is a gray and white warbler with wing
bars and an unmarked yellow head and black throat.

Food: The food of this species is small arthropods, including beetles,
caterpillars, flies, aphids, and spiders.

A Black-throated Green Warbler (*Dendroica virens*). Photograph by L. Page Brown for the Cornell Laboratory of Ornithology.

Black-throated Green Warbler
Dendroica virens (Gmelin)

Status: The Black-throated Green Warbler is an uncommon transient in eastern Kansas, becoming progressively less common westward. It is casual in winter.

Period of Occurrence: This species is most numerous from late April through May and from mid-September through mid-October. Extreme dates are 1 April and 26 May (one straggler to 11 June) 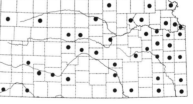 and 22 August to 11 November. One was observed in Cowley County from 16 December 1970 through 5 January 1971.

Habits and Habitat: The Black-throated Green Warbler breeds in conifer forests and deciduous woods from central and eastern Canada south through the Appalachians. The nest is placed in a crotch or on a horizontal branch from near ground level to high in a tree. The birds sing persistently from within foliage and in tall trees are often difficult to observe. The song has been interpreted as "pines, pines, murmuring pines" or "zee, zee, zee, za-zeet." This species is sometimes relatively tame during migration.

Field Marks: The solid yellow cheek and greenish crown are distinctive in all plumages. The black throat and breast so conspicuous in spring males are reduced in females and lacking in immatures.

Food: The Black-throated Green Warbler eats small arthropods, including beetles, flies, moths, and caterpillars, and occasionally eats berries of poison ivy.

A Blackburnian Warbler (*Dendroica fusca*). Photograph by W. A. Paff for the Cornell Laboratory of Ornithology.

Blackburnian Warbler
Dendroica fusca (Muller)

Status: The Blackburnian Warbler is an uncommon transient in the extreme eastern part of the state and rare in the west.

Period of Occurrence: The Blackburnian Warbler arrives around 3 May, and most birds have departed by 31 May, with an extreme spring departure of 2 June. The fall passage begins about 28 August and contin-

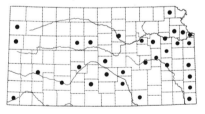

ues until 12 October. The latest date of southward movement is 21 October.

Habits and Habitat: In Kansas this beautiful warbler is a transient visitor that frequents dense riparian woodlands but is also frequently found in the heavily wooded parts of cities. Probably the best area for a birdwatcher to see this species would be the easternmost tier of counties in the state. Forbush (in Bent 1953) described a "fallout" in Massachusetts during which swarms of Blackburnians moved through treetops, low shrubs, and even grassy areas and plowed fields. It must have been an exciting experience! The Blackburnian Warbler winters primarily in northern South America.

Field Marks: The spring male is one of the most beautiful of warblers, with a black back, orange stripe in the crown and over the eye, and an orange throat and breast.

Food: The Blackburnian Warbler feeds primarily on insects.

A Yellow-throated Warbler (*Dendroica dominica*). Photograph by Wilson Bloomer for the Cornell Laboratory of Ornithology.

Yellow-throated Warbler
Dendroica dominica (Linnaeus)

Status: The Yellow-throated Warbler is a rare transient in the eastern-most tier of counties. It is a rare breeding bird in Cherokee County. It may also breed in Linn, Woodson, and Leavenworth counties, but actual nests have not been found.

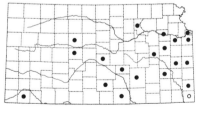

Period of Occurrence: This warbler has not been recorded very often in Kansas, and the dates of passage are poorly known. The earliest sight record is on 15 April. Resident birds have been seen until 3 July. The only later date is for Harvey County on 30 September. Records from the west are from 17 April to 26 May.

Breeding: The only area where the Yellow-throated Warbler nests regularly is Schermerhorn Park, Cherokee County. Marvin D. Schwilling and Ed and Jean Schulenberg (1981) found the first nest on 2 May 1980, and there were 11 to 14 birds present in the area. E. McHugh found the species in Linn County on 3 July 1976 but no nest. Scott Seltman found Yellow-throated Warblers in the same area on 16 June 1984. Goss (1891) found them at Neosho Falls, Woodson County, during the summer months but never succeeded in finding a nest.

The nest found in Cherokee County (Schwilling, Schulenberg, and Schulenberg 1981) was about 35 feet up in a sycamore tree. Nest material appeared to be thin grass, small fine pieces of bark, lichen, moss from an overhanging rocky ledge, and tent caterpillar webbing. Both birds assisted with the nest construction. Although the clutch size in Kansas is not known, it is presumed to be four eggs. The incubation period is 12 days, and the young leave the nest about 12 days later.

Habits and Habitat: Because of the name of this species, many casual birders still confuse it with the much more common and *very* different Common Yellowthroat, and all records should be verified. The Yellow-throated Warbler is confined mostly to riverine forests, particularly in southeastern Kansas. It prefers tall sycamores for nesting and foraging. It seems to be a regular nester at Schermerhorn Park, Cherokee County, the only reliable place to add it to one's state list. This warbler is slow and deliberate in its movements, creeping about on branches and trunks more often than flitting about. In this respect it resembles a Black-and-White Warbler and even reminded Bent of a Brown Creeper. Males may sing very persistently during the early part of the breeding season and are most easily found at that time.

Field Marks: The brilliant yellow throat and gray plumage serve to identify this species.

Food: This warbler is primarily an insect eater.

A Pine Warbler (*Dendroica pinus*). Photograph by Wilson Bloomer for the Cornell Laboratory of Ornithology.

Pine Warbler
Dendroica pinus (Wilson)

Status: The Pine Warbler is a casual transient in the extreme east and a vagrant elsewhere in the state.

Period of Occurrence: The Pine Warbler occurrence is sporadic, and consequently little can be said of its passage through Kansas. There are only two specimens (29 October 1964, Wyandotte County; 4 December 1980, Ellis County).

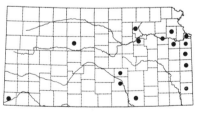

The species is often confused with other species. There are sight records from 11 April through 23 May and from 3 September through 29 January. The winter records are from feeding stations.

Habits and Habitat: The Pine Warbler is a hardy species, nesting early and wintering over much of its breeding range. Late fall stragglers through Kansas often visit dooryards and feeding stations. During migration it can occur in any wooded habitat. It feeds at any height in trees and shrubs, and in the east, during fall and winter, the Pine Warbler even feeds on the ground with bluebirds and sparrows. Early ornithologists called it the "Pine Creeping Warbler" because of its habit of feeding about the trunks of pines in nuthatch fashion. It also gleans insects from twigs and flies out after passing insects.

Field Marks: The male is yellow below, usually with distinct gray streaking, and is plain olive green above. The female is similar but duller. In all plumages two white wing bars and white tail spots are helpful field marks.

Food: The food of this warbler is small invertebrates, including spiders and insects. In winter it may rely upon seeds of grasses, dogwood, poison ivy, Virginia creeper, and wild grapes.

A Prairie Warbler (*Dendroica discolor*). Photograph by David A. Rintoul.

Prairie Warbler
Dendroica discolor (Vieillot)

Status: The Prairie Warbler is a rare transient and casual local summer resident in the eastern tier of counties. It is a vagrant elsewhere.

Period of Occurrence: There are sight records of the Prairie Warbler from 28 April through 23 September.

Breeding: The Prairie Warbler has bred in Cherokee, Johnson, and Wyandotte counties. A sighting on 10 July 1977 in Linn County by

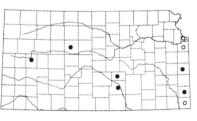

John Parrish may indicate that the species nests there also. However, there have been no breeding records since 1976 in Johnson or Wyandotte counties, where the first breeding for the state was recorded on 1 May 1941 by Harold Hedges. He had noted 13 singing males, and the species continued to breed in those two counties until at least 1953. A singing male in Morton County occupied a territory from 14 May to 2 July 1988, but no female was ever observed. The nest is built in scrub or brush and is placed one to 10 feet high. The clutch size is four, with an incubation period of about 12 days. The young fledge in approximately 14 days.

Habits and Habitat: These warblers are confined almost entirely to scrubland or vegetation that is not over 10 to 15 feet high. In Kansas they are rarely seen west of the breeding area. They are one of the rarest warblers to visit the state.

Field Marks: The breeding male is bright greenish yellow on the breast with greenish olive upperparts, two white wing bars, and white patches on the end of the outer tail feathers.

Food: The Prairie Warbler feeds primarily on insects.

A Palm Warbler (*Dendroica palmarum*). Photograph by Dale and Marian Zimmerman.

Palm Warbler
Dendroica palmarum (Gmelin)

Status: The Palm Warbler is a rare transient in the east and casual in the west. There are two early winter records through 30 December.

Period of Occurrence: This rare transient arrives in the spring about 20 April and departs for the northern breeding grounds by 17 May. The autumnal passage begins around 27 September and is finished by 29 October. There are winter records from 22 November into January in Elk and Morton counties.

Habits and Habitat: The Palm War-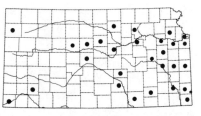
bler can be found in a variety of
habitats in Kansas, from deciduous
forest in the east to dikes of Cheyenne Bottoms in the central part.
Nowhere can you expect to find
it with regularity. Unlike most war-
blers that pass through Kansas, this one seems to prefer feeding in forest litter or around scrubby vegetation. The habit of bobbing the tail
helps to identify it.

Field Marks: The reddish brown crown and light yellow under-tail
coverts will help to identify it.

Food: The primary food of the Palm Warbler is insects, but it is known
to consume berries also (Bent 1950).

A Bay-breasted Warbler (*Dendroica castanea*). Photograph by L. Page Brown for the Cornell Laboratory of Ornithology.

Bay-breasted Warbler
Dendroica castanea (Wilson)

Status: The Bay-breasted Warbler is a rare transient in the east and casual in the west. There are few fall sightings, perhaps because of confusion with the Blackpoll Warbler.

Period of Occurrence: This warbler arrives around 1 May and departs by 20 May. The earliest date of spring arrival is 2 April, and the latest spring departure is 10 June. The fall passage begins around 23 September and finishes by 18 October. The extreme fall departure is 11 November.

Habits and Habitat: The Bay-breasted Warbler is an inhabitant of riparian woodland and is most commonly found in the eastern tier of counties. In the west it can appear wherever trees are found, for instance, in cities or shelter-belts.

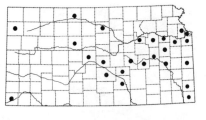

Field Marks: Although the spring male is unmistakable, the fall plumage male and female are easily confused with the Blackpoll Warbler and are only safely separable in the hand. Even in the hand they may be confused, and many a museum has specimens that are incorrectly identified.

Food: This warbler consumes primarily insects.

A Blackpoll Warbler (*Dendroica striata*). Photograph by B. D. Cottrille for the Cornell Laboratory of Ornithology.

Blackpoll Warbler
Dendroica striata (Forster)

Status: The Blackpoll Warbler is an uncommon spring transient throughout the state. It is a rare fall transient, and these records need careful verification.

Period of Occurrence: The spring passage of the Blackpoll Warbler is later than that of most warblers, with the first migrants usually showing up 8 May and departing by 18 May. The extreme dates for spring migration are 15 April and 11 June. Blackpoll Warblers return to the wintering grounds via the northeastern United States and miss Kansas and the central states. The few fall records that are substantiated mainly by specimens and banding records show a fall passage from 12 September to 29 September.

Habits and Habitat: The Blackpoll Warbler is a bird of riparian wood-land. It is one of the few warblers that have had their migrations thoroughly studied. They move northward slowly at first; by the time they reach Kansas, they may be covering several hundred miles a night until they reach the breeding grounds in the coniferous forests from Alaska to Laborador. They are thought to make the southern passage from the east coast directly over water to their wintering grounds in South America. They have the largest breeding area of any warbler except possibly that of the Yellow-rumped (Myrtle) Warbler.

Food: Like most warblers, the Blackpoll Warbler is an insect eater.

A Cerulean Warbler (*Dendroica cerulea*). Photograph by Bill Dyer for the Cornell Laboratory of Ornithology.

Cerulean Warbler
Dendroica cerulea (Wilson)

Status: The Cerulean Warbler is a rare transient and summer resident in the east and a casual transient in the west.

Period of Occurrence: This bluish gray warbler arrives in the eastern part of Kansas around 24 April, and most depart around 10 May. However, those that remain to nest probably do not depart until August, with the latest departure date on 13 September.

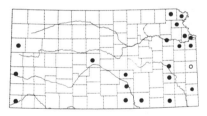

There are only two fall records on its southward passage to the wintering grounds in South America.

Breeding: Although the Cerulean Warbler had been suspected of nesting in the state, it was not until 26 May 1985 that a nest was actually found (Boyd 1986). The nest was located near the Marais des Cygnes Refuge in Linn County. It was placed about 40 feet high in a silver maple. The nest was successful, and the adults were seen feeding young on

19 June. Snow and Goss considered it a rare summer resident during the late nineteenth century, but the nearest specific evidence is of two birds collected by Goss in Woodson County on 30 July and 11 August.

Habits and Habitat: Cerulean Warblers had been seen in the Marais des Cygnes area of Linn County prior to the nest discovery and have been seen there in the years since the nest was discovered. Look for this warbler in mature, deciduous trees along rivers. In the western part of Kansas, if it is to be found, it will be in shelterbelts, along rivers, or in towns. It typically occurs in the canopy of the trees, making it very difficult to observe.

Field Marks: The bluish back, white breast with black streaking is diagnostic.

Food: Boyd (1986) observed the Cerulean Warbler adults feeding their young caterpillars and small unidentified arthropods.

A Black-and-White Warbler (*Mniotilta varia*). Photograph by Bob Gress.

Black-and-White Warbler
Mniotilta varia (Linnaeus)

Status: The Black-and-White Warbler is a common transient and an uncommon to rare summer resident in the east. It is an uncommon transient in the west.

Period of Occurrence: The spring arrival of the Black-and-White Warbler begins around 2 April and ends around 5 May. The earliest recorded spring arrival is on 18 March. There is an extreme spring

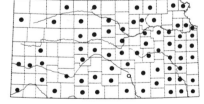

departure of 12 June, but that could have been a breeding bird and not a migrant. The fall passage begins around 10 September and is finished by 6 October. There is an extreme date of 10 August, but again this could have been a summer bird. The latest fall departure is 29 November, although there are four other November records.

Breeding: The breeding status of this warbler in Kansas is poorly understood. It has bred at least west to Sedgwick County, but most records are from the eastern third of the state. Although this is a species that spends its life in trees, the nest is placed on the ground. There are not enough records to make any statement on clutch size or other aspects of their breeding in Kansas, but elsewhere the clutch size is four to five eggs (Johnsgard 1979).

Habits and Habitat: The Black-and-White Warbler is a bird of woodlands and heavily wooded cities. Its behavior is similar to that of the Brown Creeper; birds "work" the branches and tree trunks gleaning insects from the bark. Because it does not particularly need leaves with accompanying insects to survive, it arrives earlier than most warblers. Its high-pitched song may be heard before the species is seen.

Field Marks: This warbler's black and white coloration, with the white stripe in the crown, and its creeperlike behavior serve to separate it from the Blackpoll Warbler.

Food: The food of this warbler is insects or other animal matter that it gleans from the bark of trees.

American Redstart
Setophaga ruticilla (Linnaeus)

Status: The American Redstart is a common transient in the eastern third of Kansas and an uncommon transient in the western two-thirds. There are breeding records west to a line from Republic County probably to Sumner County.

Period of Occurrence: The redstart arrives about 30 April, and most have departed northward by 15 May. The fall passage begins in late August and continues until 23 September. Dates of extreme occurrence are 22 April and 12 October. It is difficult to determine exact dates of spring departure and fall arrival because of breeding by this species in Kansas.

Breeding: The area in Kansas in which the American Redstart breeds is primarily the northeastern counties. The nest is placed in a tree from six to 30 feet high. Singing males are occasionally found in mid-summer in areas where they do not nest. The normal clutch size is four eggs, with an incubation period of approximately 12 days. The young fledge in approximately nine days. Like most warblers in Kansas, more information is needed on the breeding biology of this species.

Habits and Habitat: The American Redstart is found primarily in wet deciduous woodlands. In the western part of the state it may occur in shelterbelts as well as in riparian woodlands and cities. This warbler seems more "nervous" than other species of warblers and when disturbed constantly fans its tail and twists about on the limb.

Field Marks: The black-backed male with the bright orange sides and fanning tail should help to identify it. The female resembles the male but is duller.

Food: The American Redstart utilizes insects for food.

A Prothonotary Warbler (*Protonotaria citrea*). Photograph by L. Page Brown for the Cornell Laboratory of Ornithology.

Prothonotary Warbler
Protonotaria citrea (Boddaert)

Status: The Prothonotary Warbler is an uncommon migrant in the eastern third of the state and rare in the rest of the state. There are breeding records west to Sumner County.

Period of Occurrence: The Prothonotary Warbler arrives in Kansas about the third week of April. The earliest date of arrival is 15 April, with a fall departure of 10 September. The latest recorded date of fall departure is 10 October. A late date of 10 November was recorded for Kearny County but is unsubstantiated.

Breeding: This warbler usually breeds in areas that have swampy woodland. In Cowley County Prothonotary Warblers have been found along the Arkansas River, usually in areas that have been flooded and have water standing 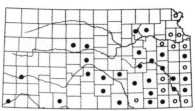 in the woods. They nest in holes or in stumps. The nest can range from five to 20 feet high. In Winfield, Cowley County, one nested in a wren house in town. In 1978, one nested in an old bluebird house that was in flooded timber. The nest contained seven eggs but was later destroyed (McHugh, pers. comm.). Goss (1891) found one nesting in a tin cup in a sawmill. Johnston (1964b) listed the clutch size at five, with most eggs being laid around 5 June. The incubation period is 12 days, with fledging in 10 days.

Habits and Habitat: The brightly colored "Golden Swamp-bird" is indeed a creature of great beauty. As the previous name might imply, this warbler inhabits swampy woodlands or river edges with dense stands of willow. Where does the name Prothonotary come from? Bagg and Eliot (1937) rightly commented, "What a name to saddle on the Golden Swamp-bird! Wrongly compounded in the first place, wrongly spelled, wrongly pronounced! We understand that Protonotarius is the title of papal officials whose robes are bright yellow, but why say 'First Notary' in mixed Greek and Latin, instead of Primonotarius?"

Field Marks: The large size, bright yellow head and breast, and absence of wing bars help to identify this species.

Food: The Prothonotary Warbler feeds on insects and other small arthropods.

A Worm-eating Warbler (*Helmitheros vermivorus*). Photograph by John S. Dunning for the Cornell Laboratory of Ornithology.

Worm-eating Warbler
Helmitheros vermivorus (Gmelin)

Status: The Worm-eating Warbler is a rare transient and possible summer resident in the extreme east and is casual in the rest of the state.

Period of Occurrence: The Worm-eating Warbler is rare enough in Kansas that most of the temporal occurrence records are of little value. The earliest spring arrival date is 9 April, with most arriving in late April or early May and de-

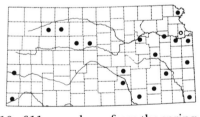

parting by 25 May. In Ellis County 10 of 11 records are from the spring migration. There are only a few fall records in the east, from 10 to 19 September, and only one in the west on 5 September.

Breeding: The only breeding records are those listed by Tordoff (1956). He states that Linsdale saw a singing bird on 11 July 1923 in Doniphan County and that Hilton reported a newly fledged young bird with an

adult at Fort Leavenworth, Leavenworth County, 7 June 1919. Johnston (1964b) ignored the Worm-eating Warbler as a possible breeding species. However, Shirling (Branan and Burdick 1981) found 21
males in Swope Park, Kansas City, Missouri, in June 1916, very close to
the Kansas line. It seems probable with that close proximity that they
also nested in Kansas at that time. The nest should be looked for in
dense cover. It is usually placed on the ground on a slope.

Habits and Habitat: The Worm-eating Warbler occurs in dense understory in deciduous woodland. In the west it may occur in shelterbelts
or any other habitat that comes close to matching its requirements. In
spring 1990, one was located in a shelterbelt in Elkhart, Morton County.
So rare is the species in the state that several members of the Kansas
Ornithological Society spent several hours observing it. Thompson netted three in Cowley County in April and May 1974. One was captured
each day for three successive days in the same net, each being caught
within two feet of the same spot in the net. They were banded and released. The species has not been seen in the area since that time.

Field Marks: This warbler could only be confused with the Ovenbird,
from which it differs in having a plain buff breast and in its much smaller
size.

Food: Although it is called a Worm-eating Warbler, its food is primarily insects.

Swainson's Warbler
Limnothlypis swainsonii (Audubon)

Status: The Swainson's Warbler is a vagrant in the extreme eastern part of the state. There are two specimen records: Cherokee County, 16 May 1965, found dead at a television tower; Johnson County, 11 May 1957. In addition there are three sightings in Johnson County by Mary Louise Myers: 23 May 1969; 4 May 1973; 13 May 1980.

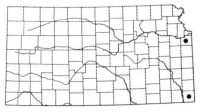

Habits and Habitat: The Swainson's Warbler should be looked for in dense thicket in river edge habitat.

Field Marks: This warbler is plainly colored with no distinctive field marks. The general coloration is brown above and whitish below.

Food: This warbler feeds primarily on insects.

An Ovenbird (*Seiurus aurocapillus*). Photograph by Mike Hopiak for the Cornell Laboratory of Ornithology.

Ovenbird
Seiurus aurocapillus (Linnaeus)

Status: The Ovenbird is a common transient and rare summer resident in the eastern third of the state. It is an uncommon transient in the rest.

Period of Occurrence: Most of the Ovenbirds arrive in Kansas the first week of May. The earliest spring arrival date is 19 April, with a spring departure around 26 May. The fall passage begins in mid-

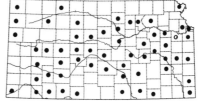

August and is completed by 6 October. The extreme date of fall departure is 23 October.

Breeding: There are few breeding records for this species from the state. Tordoff (1956) reported it nesting in Leavenworth County. Cink and Boyd (1982) provided the first tangible evidence of nesting. They observed an Ovenbird in 1978 in a Douglas County woodland. In the same woodland in 1979 they discovered 10 adults plus one nest with young. Another nest was found in the same area in 1980; it contained four eggs. The nest is placed upon the ground and is dome shaped, hence the name Ovenbird. Incubation takes approximately 12 days, with the young fledging in eight to 10 days.

Habits and Habitat: The Ovenbird is found primarily in deciduous forest in the east and along wooded rivers and in shelterbelts in the west. It spends much of its time on the ground or low in bushes, where it picks up insects. Its loud song will quickly draw your attention. You may have to work to find it, however, because the dense habitat in which it often occurs may obscure your view.

Field Marks: This warbler is one of the larger warblers. It has conspicuous black marking on the otherwise orange crown. The breast is white with black stripes.

Food: The Ovenbird feeds primarily on insects.

A Northern Waterthrush (*Seiurus noveboracensis*). Photograph by Mike Hopiak for the Cornell Laboratory of Ornithology.

Northern Waterthrush
Seiurus noveboracensis (Gmelin)

Status: The Northern Waterthrush is an uncommon migrant throughout the state.

Period of Occurrence: This ground-dwelling warbler arrives in Kansas about 1 May and departs for the breeding grounds by 20 May. The earliest date of spring arrival is 7 April, with a late spring departure of 2 June. The 2 June record could

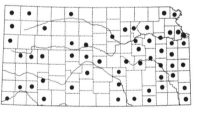

be that of a Louisiana Waterthrush, and all late dates need to be verified as to species. The fall passage begins in late August, with the earliest fall arrival on 22 August. Fall passage is completed by 15 September, with a late date of 10 October.

Habits and Habitat: The Northern Waterthrush, which is a warbler despite the name, is usually seen in riparian habitat, where it may be found feeding around pools of water. One was observed in Morton County in May 1990 feeding along a pool of water in an opening in a shelterbelt. While feeding it teeters and pumps the tail up and down. Once you have found birds of this species, they are fairly confiding and easy to observe.

Field Marks: The two waterthrushes can be difficult to distinguish from each other. The Northern is yellowish on the breast with streaking on the sides and on the throat. The Louisiana Waterthrush is white on the breast with streaking on the sides and a plain throat.

Food: The Northern Waterthrush feeds upon insects it picks up from the ground.

A Louisiana Waterthrush (*Seiurus motacilla*). Photograph by John S. Dunning for the Cornell Laboratory of Ornithology.

Louisiana Waterthrush
Seiurus motacilla (Vieillot)

Status: The Louisiana Waterthrush is an uncommon migrant and summer resident in the eastern third of the state. It is an uncommon to rare transient in the west.

Period of Occurrence: The Louisiana Waterthrush is one of the earliest spring warblers, arriving as early as 29 March. In the east, where it breeds, it departs about 26 August. In the western part of Kansas

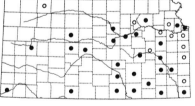

its spring arrival is much later, averaging 30 April with a last spring date of 10 June. The latest fall departure date is 8 September.

Breeding: The Louisiana Waterthrush breeds along fast flowing streams in hilly country in the eastern part of the state. Wolfe (1961) found a nest near Oberlin, Decatur County, in 1910, but at that time the creeks had running water and shrubby understory along the banks. The species probably does not now nest regularly west of the Flint Hills. Unlike most birds who set up breeding territories, this waterthrush establishes a territory that usually follows the river course. The nest is placed on the ground under an overhang on the bank close to water. The clutch size is usually around five eggs, with incubation taking 12 days. The young leave the nest in about 10 days.

Habits and Habitat: The Louisiana Waterthrush is found primarily along fast flowing rivers and creeks in the eastern part of the state. Birds are frequently seen feeding along the water's edge, where they pick up insects and other arthropods. They are rarely found away from water, and one of the best ways to see them is by going out in a canoe. Like the Northern Waterthrush, the Louisiana Waterthrush teeters the body and pumps the tail.

Field Marks: See Northern Waterthrush.

Food: This warbler feeds mainly upon insects.

A Kentucky Warbler (*Oporornis formosus*). Photograph by Calvin L. Cink.

Kentucky Warbler
Oporornis formosus (Wilson)

Status: The Kentucky Warbler is an uncommon migrant and local summer resident in the eastern third of Kansas and rare migrant in the rest of the state.

Period of Occurrence: This warbler arrives in the east around 25 April and departs in the fall near 10 September. In the western part of the state its spring arrival coincides with that in the east, but it

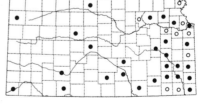

departs by 31 May. The earliest arrival date for the state is 2 April and the latest departure 13 October.

Breeding: The Kentucky Warbler breeds in hardwood forest east of the Flint Hills. It may breed sporadically to eastern Cowley County. The nest is usually placed on the ground or low in a shrub. The clutch size is four eggs. Incubation is completed in 12 days, and the young leave the nest in nine days.

Habits and Habitat: The Kentucky Warbler prefers oak-hickory forest, where it occupies the understory. It is rarely found west of this type of habitat. The Carolina Wren–like song of these birds is loud, making them easy to find in the dense thicket.

Field Marks: The olive green upperparts and bright yellow underparts, combined with the black markings on the crown and sides of the head and neck, are distinctive. A word of caution on the call of this bird: It can be mistaken for a Carolina Wren or vice versa.

Food: This warbler feeds upon insects.

Connecticut Warbler
Oporornis agilis (Wilson)

Status: The Connecticut Warbler is a casual migrant in eastern Kansas and a vagrant elsewhere.

Period of Occurrence: The records for this species in Kansas are too few to determine migration dates, as the bulk of the migration passes to the east of Kansas. The few available records suggest that it is a late spring migrant, passing through 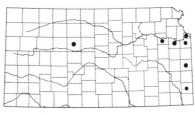 around 9 through 15 May. The specimens were taken on 23 September (Shawnee County) and 28 September (Ellis County). Records of birds singing in the spring are the most reliable records. Steve Crawford and Mark Corder had one respond to a tape recording of its song at Marais des Cygnes on 9 May. Fall plumage birds are difficult to distinguish from the Mourning Warbler, and the reports of Connecticut Warblers are open to question unless substantiated by a specimen or a bird that was netted and measured during banding operations.

Habits and Habitat: The Connecticut Warbler, like other members of the genus, is a skulker in dense understory or woodland edge and very difficult to see. However, it sometimes comes in to towns where there is sufficient cover to hide. Robert M. Mengel (pers. comm.) had an adult male singing in his yard in Lawrence, Douglas County, on about 15 May 1978.

Field Marks: The Connecticut Warbler, Mourning Warbler, and Mac-Gillvray's Warbler form a difficult complex for field identification. It is beyond the scope of this book to go into details. It suffices to say that any records of these three species identified by sight in the fall are suspect. The MacGillvray's Warbler in extreme western Kansas is the safest to call. The Connecticut Warbler and Mourning Warbler are almost impossible to separate unless held in the hand and measurements taken. Spring records are more valid, especially if the birds are singing.

Food: The Connecticut Warbler feeds upon insects.

A Mourning Warbler (*Oporornis philadelphia*). Photograph by H. R. Comstock for the Cornell Laboratory of Ornithology.

Mourning Warbler
Oporornis philadelphia (Wilson)

Status: The Mourning Warbler is a common transient in the eastern half of the state and an uncommon transient in the west.

Period of Occurrence: This warbler arrives in Kansas in spring about 15 May and departs for the breeding grounds about 25 May. The dates of extreme spring arrival and departure are 22 April and 3 June. The Mourning Warbler is the last

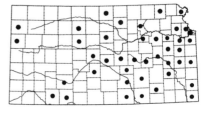

of the warblers to arrive in the spring, and when it does, you know the spring warbler migration is finished. It is one of the earliest fall migrants, arriving around 1 September, with passage nearly completed by 15 September. The extreme autumnal arrival and departure dates are 21 August and 26 October.

Habits and Habitat: The Mourning Warbler is an inhabitant of dense thickets and hence is easily missed in migration. Thompson, while conducting banding operations in Cowley County, banded 46 Mourning Warblers the first week of September. Although the Mourning Warbler appears to be more common in fall than spring, the above numbers suggest that far more birds pass through Kansas than observations indicate. They were common at some of the television tower kills in Topeka. The late passage in spring and early passage in fall of this species may also contribute to the lack of records, since observers may surmise that the spring migration is over or fall passage has not yet begun.

Field Marks: See the Connecticut Warbler.

Food: The Mourning Warbler is an insect eater.

A MacGillivray's Warbler (*Oporornis tolmiei*). Photograph by Dale and Marian Zimmerman.

MacGillivray's Warbler
Oporornis tolmiei (Townsend)

Status: The MacGillivray's Warbler is an uncommon transient in the western third of Kansas and a vagrant eastward in the state.

Period of Occurrence: MacGillivray's Warblers, like the other members of the genus, are late migrants in the spring and early in the fall. The spring arrival usually begins around 15 May and lasts until 25 May. The earliest date of spring oc-

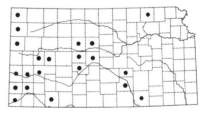

currence is 3 May, and the latest is 6 June. The fall passage begins 27 August, and most have passed southward by 10 September. The dates of extreme fall passage are 19 August and 8 October. There is one record on 2 December of an *Oporornis* from Ellis County.

Habits and Habitat: The MacGillivray's Warbler prefers dense undergrowth and may easily avoid detection. It does seem somewhat more confiding and therefore more easily observed than the Mourning Warbler, the species with which it may be easily confused. The only sure way to separate them in the fall is by measuring them. In Kansas, the

Cimarron River, Morton County, is probably the most consistent area of occurrence.

Field Marks: See the Connecticut Warbler.

Food: This warbler consumes primarily insects.

A Common Yellowthroat (*Geothlypis trichas*). Photograph by David A. Rintoul.

Common Yellowthroat
Geothlypis trichas (Linnaeus)

Status: The Common Yellowthroat is a common transient and summer resident in favorable habitat throughout the state.

Period of Occurrence: This black-masked warbler arrives in Kansas around 20 April and remains as a nesting species until 9 October. About 105 were killed on 30 September at the Topeka television tower. The dates of extreme occurrence are 4 April and 29 November. There are win-

ter records from 18 December to
7 January from Barton, Harvey,
and Linn counties.

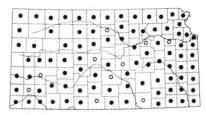

Breeding: The Common Yellowthroat is probably the most common breeding warbler in the state.
It nests primarily in marshes with
cattails and sedges. In larger marshes such as Cheyenne Bottoms
Wildlife Management Area, Quivira National Wildlife Refuge, and
Slate Creek Marsh, it is an abundant nester. Even small marshes of one
acre or less will sometimes have one or two breeding pairs.

The nest is placed about two feet high in cattails or sedges. The birds
lay an average of five eggs beginning around 1 June. The incubation
period is 12 days, and the young fledge in about eight days.

Habits and Habitat: The Common Yellowthroat is found primarily in
marshes during the breeding season and in dense thickets during migration. Their loud "witchity, witchity, witchity" call makes them easy
to detect but not necessarily easy to see. However, they are easily attracted to a "psst, psst, psst" call and will usually pop up on a cattail to
see what is causing the fuss.

Field Marks: This is one of the easiest male warblers to identify in
Kansas, with its black mask and yellow body. It is the only warbler in
the state found in cattails.

Food: This warbler feeds primarily on insects.

A Hooded Warbler (*Wilsonia citrina*). Photograph by W. A. Paff for the Cornell Laboratory of Ornithology.

Hooded Warbler
Wilsonia citrina (Boddaert)

Status: The Hooded Warbler is a rare migrant and casual summer resident in the extreme eastern part of the state. It is a casual migrant elsewhere.

Period of Occurrence: There are too few records of this species from Kansas to make any firm statements about migration times. However, available data suggest that the Hooded Warbler arrives 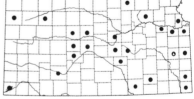 about the first week of May. The earliest arrival date is 20 April, and the latest fall date is 18 August. Outside of May, Kansas records are virtually nil. The three fall records are 18 to 30 August and 7 November.

Breeding: The Hooded Warbler breeds in Kansas in the extreme east. There are breeding records for Anderson and Leavenworth counties. It should be looked for breeding in areas of wet, mature hardwood forest. In the southern United States it is a bird of wooded swamps. The nest is placed up to six feet high, and four eggs are laid. The incubation period is 12 days, and the young fledge in eight days.

Habits and Habitat: The Hooded Warbler occurs generally in mature hardwood forest. It can be found in thickets during migration; during fall migration it can be secretive. Like some of the other warblers, the Hooded Warbler has a habit of fanning the tail, showing the white tail pattern.

Field Marks: The adult male is easily identified with its black hood and throat surrounding its bright yellow cheeks.

Food: The Hooded Warbler eats insects, which it obtains by flycatching or snatching them out of the air.

A Wilson's Warbler (*Wilsonia pusilla*). Photograph by Dale and Marian Zimmerman.

Wilson's Warbler
Wilsonia pusilla (Wilson)

Status: The Wilson's Warbler is a common transient in both the spring and the fall throughout the state.

Period of Occurrence: The Wilson's Warbler arrives in spring around 1 May and departs for the breeding grounds by 15 May. The extreme spring records are 7 April and 30 May. There is one unverified summer record of 26 June.

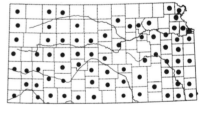

The autumnal arrival begins around 25 August, and passage continues until about 1 October. The extreme fall dates are 6 August and 20 October.

Habits and Habitat: This black-capped warbler occurs in dense undergrowth or sometimes in towns in shrubbery. It is occasionally seen feeding high in trees. It is a confiding species and easily squeaked to the observer by almost any strange sound you want to make. The black cap is distinctive in the spring but may be partially obscured in the fall.

Field Marks: The Wilson's Warbler is a rather plain yellow warbler without distinctive marks other than its black cap, which is often hard to see, and the yellow sides of its head.

Food: The Wilson's Warbler feeds primarily on insects.

A Canada Warbler (*Wilsonia canadensis*). Photograph by B. D. Cottrille for the Cornell Laboratory of Ornithology.

Canada Warbler
Wilsonia canadensis (Linnaeus)

Status: The Canada Warbler is an uncommon migrant in eastern Kansas and casual in the western part of the state, perhaps more common in the fall than in spring.

Period of Occurrence: This streaked-breast warbler is a late spring migrant, arriving around 10 May and departing northward by 20 May. The date of extreme spring arrival is 6 April and extreme de-

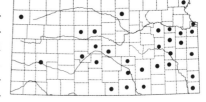

parture 28 May. The fall passage begins around 3 September and ends by 20 September. The extreme dates of autumnal migration are 17 August and 1 October.

Habits and Habitat: The name Canada Warbler is a misnomer, since the species nests south into northern Georgia. The Canada Warbler is an inhabitant of dense understory or edges along riparian forest in migration through Kansas.

Field Marks: The gray upperparts without white markings in the wing or tail, yellow eye ring, and black necklace on a yellow breast help to identify this warbler. The female is slightly duller than the male.

Food: This warbler feeds primarily on insects.

A Yellow-breasted Chat (*Icteria virens*). Photograph by John S. Dunning for the Cornell Laboratory of Ornithology.

Yellow-breasted Chat
Icteria virens (Linnaeus)

Status: The Yellow-breasted Chat is an uncommon migrant throughout the state. It was previously a common nesting species in the state, but present distribution needs to be reassessed.

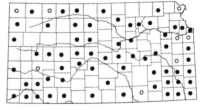

Period of Occurrence: The spring arrival of the Yellow-breasted Chat begins about 20 April and fall departure around 1 October. The extreme date of spring arrival is 15 April, with an extreme fall departure of 24 October. There is one unverified winter record on 1 January from Ford County.

Breeding: The present distribution of breeding in the state by the Yellow-breasted Chat is uncertain. It formerly bred throughout the state, but indications are that it is now restricted. The Yellow-breasted Chat

was a common breeding bird along the Arkansas River in 1960 in
Cowley and Sumner counties but now appears to no longer be breeding in the area.

The Yellow-breasted Chat nests low in thickets of dogwood, willow,
rose, or other types of low-growing shrubbery or trees. The four eggs
are laid the first week of June and hatch in 12 days. The young leave
the nest in about nine days.

Habits and Habitat: This chat is an aberrant wood warbler and may well
be placed in some other family in the future. It inhabits riparian woodlands, usually dense thickets of roughleaf dogwood, coralberry, rose,
or other types of thick shrubbery. Although large as wood warblers go,
it is an inconspicuous bird despite the bright yellow breast. The song
is the easiest way to find the Yellow-breasted Chat. The calls are quite
varied, and it may sound like almost anything but a warbler.

Field Marks: This is the largest of all the wood warblers. Its olive green
upperparts, the white stripe over the eye, and the bright yellow throat
and breast contrasting with the white abdomen help to identify it.

Food: The food of the Yellow-breasted Chat is varied. It is an insect eater
but in the fall may rely upon berries such as chokecherry for a major
part of its diet.

Tanagers (Family Emberizidae, Subfamily Thraupinae)
Summer Tanager
Piranga rubra (Linnaeus)

Status: The Summer Tanager is an uncommon transient and summer resident in the eastern third of the state and a rare to casual transient westward.

Period of Occurrence: This melon red tanager arrives in the state around 25 April and departs by 28 September. The earliest date of arrival is 21 April, and the latest departure date is 27 October.

Breeding: The Summer Tanager reaches the northwest edge of its breeding range in the state. It nests west to Sumner County in the south and probably Saline County in the north. Although there are many counties with sightings in the breeding period, very few nests have been discovered. The nest is usually placed about 20 feet high in deciduous forest. The four eggs are laid around 5 June. The young birds hatch in 12 days and depart the nest on the eighth day. The adults continue to feed the young for up to three weeks.

Habits and Habitat: The Summer Tanager occurs primarily in hardwood forest in the eastern part of the state and in almost any type in the west. In Morton County, when present, it utilizes cottonwood or locust. The male typically sings from the tops of trees. The dense foliage can sometimes make the bird very difficult to see, despite the intense color. The red color is sometimes mottled with yellow in young males.

Field Marks: The adult male Summer Tanager is melon red from head to tail.

Food: The primary food of the Summer Tanager is insects. It has a particular appetite for bees and wasps, especially the larva (Bent 1958). This species will also consume fruit when available.

Scarlet Tanager
Piranga olivacea (Gmelin)

Status: The Scarlet Tanager is an uncommon transient and rare nesting species in the eastern third of Kansas. It is rare to casual westward.

Period of Occurrence: This tanager arrives around 28 April and departs by 18 May on its northward passage. Some migrants may linger until 7 June. Those birds that remain to nest in the state depart for the south by 20 September. The 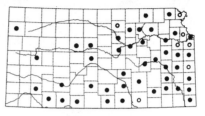 dates of extreme occurrence are 20 April and 13 October.

Breeding: There are few actual nesting records of this species for Kansas. However, if summer records are taken into account, the Scarlet Tanager nests as far west as Saline County in the north and Sumner County in the south. Thompson banded a pair in Cowley County that were utilizing oak trees for a nest site. The nest was never discovered. The birds returned the second year to nest again. The third year someone cut the oaks for firewood, and the pair could not be found. The nest is placed 10 to 50 feet high in hardwood forest. The four eggs are laid around 1 June, but it may be as late as July. The incubation period is 13 days. The young fledge in 15 days.

Habits and Habitat: The Scarlet Tanager is one of the most spectacularly colored birds that occurs in Kansas. It is also one of the most difficult to observe. Its habit of remaining in the tops of trees to sing complicates the birders' observations. Like many brightly colored birds these tanagers seem to blend into their environment. The Scarlet Tanager is most readily observed in the northeastern part of the state.

Field Marks: The adult male is brilliant scarlet and has contrasting black wings.

Food: The Scarlet Tanager also seems to have a fondness for bees, although it also consumes other types of insects. Like other tanagers it does utilize berries in its diet.

A Western Tanager (*Piranga ludoviciana*). Photograph by Roger Boyd.

Western Tanager
Piranga ludoviciana (Wilson)

Status: The Western Tanager is a casual transient in the extreme west and a vagrant eastward. It is more common in the west in fall.

Period of Occurrence: There are very few records of this tanager in Kansas. Our present records indicate this tanager arrives around 1 May and completes its spring passage by 20 May. The dates of extreme spring occurrence are 10

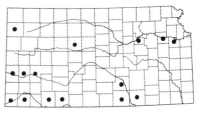

April to 27 May. There is one summer record on 8 July. The fall arrival begins around 8 September with an early fall arrival of 19 August. The fall departure is usually complete by 21 September. There is a late date of 18 December.

Habits and Habitat: This is another beautiful tanager found in the state, with most records coming from Morton County. The birds were observed mainly along the Cimarron River north of Elkhart. The birds have been observed in cottonwood along the river and in tamarisk on the sandbars.

Field Marks: The adult male has an orange head and throat and yellow underparts contrasted with the black back and wings.

Food: The food habits are similar to the other species of tanagers in Kansas.

A Northern Cardinal (*Cardinalis cardinalis*). Photograph by Gerald J. Wiens.

CARDINALS AND GROSBEAKS
(FAMILY EMBERIZIDAE, SUBFAMILY CARDINALINAE)
Northern Cardinal
Cardinalis cardinalis (Linnaeus)

Status: The Northern Cardinal is a common resident in eastern Kansas, becoming uncommon to rare in the west.

Period of Occurrence: This cardinal is resident and occurs all months of the year.

Breeding: The Northern Cardinal breeds in most areas in which it occurs, except the extreme western part of the state. We have good data on its nesting habits because of its close affiliation with human habitations. Probably no other 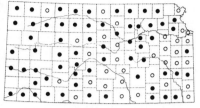 species in the state nests over such a long span of time. There are nesting records for 1 April and 20 September. Johnston (1964b) had 117 records and found that three eggs are laid around 1 May. Nesting after 1 May shows no definite pattern. Most nests are placed low in trees or shrubs, usually not over six feet high. However, in towns, cardinals may choose such places as flowerpots, hanging baskets, or shrubs on patios. Incubation takes 12 days, and the young leave the nest about nine days later. In three weeks the young are totally independent, and the parents go about raising another brood. Some cardinals may rear as many as four broods in one season (Johnsgard 1979).

Habits and Habitat: The Northern Cardinal is a ubiquitous bird. It is commonly found in yards in town, in the country, and just about anywhere there is enough cover for shelter. The male is treasured by those who feed birds in the winter and puts on a brilliant show against a white background of snow. He seems tolerant of other male cardinals at the feeder until about March, when they again set up breeding territories.

Field Marks: The adult male cardinal is familiar to most observers in Kansas. It is the only all red bird with a crest.

Food: The Northern Cardinal feeds primarily on seeds. It particularly favors the small, black sunflower seeds at feeders.

A Pyrrhuloxia (*Cardinalis sinuatus*). Photograph by Dan Gish.

Pyrrhuloxia
Cardinalis sinuatus Bonaparte

Status: The Pyrrhuloxia is a vagrant in the state. There is but one record. A female was observed in Morton County at the U.S. Forest Service service area north of Elkhart, 6 November 1989, by Sebastian Patti and Max C. Thompson. Subsequently, several bird watchers observed the bird in the same area. Patti and Thompson returned there on 30 December and 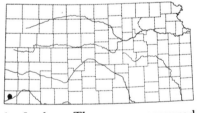 searched the area but found only the feathers. These were recovered and compared to specimens in the Southwestern College collection. They were clearly feathers of a female Pyrrhuloxia and have been cataloged into the Southwestern College collection. There are at least two winter records for Cimarron County, Oklahoma. However, the normal range of this species is along the Mexican border from Texas to California.

A Rose-breasted Grosbeak (*Pheucticus ludovicianus*). Photograph by Bob Gress.

Rose-breasted Grosbeak
Pheucticus ludovicianus (Linnaeus)

Status: The Rose-breasted Grosbeak is a common transient and an uncommon summer resident in the eastern half of the state. It is an uncommon transient in the west.

Period of Occurrence: This rose-splashed grosbeak returns from the wintering grounds around 25 April, and most depart for more northerly breeding areas by 15 May. The extreme date for spring

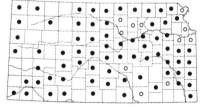

arrival is 13 April. The fall departure begins about 1 September and finishes around 10 October. The fall departure extreme is 4 November.

Breeding: The Rose-breasted Grosbeak breeds at least west to Republic County in the north and Cowley County in the southern part of Kansas but is most common breeding in the northeast. On the western fringes of the breeding range it meets the western Black-headed Grosbeak and frequently interbreeds with it. Johnston (1964b) listed the egg-laying date as 5 June, with some birds nesting as late as 11 July. It can be assumed with some certainty that June records are probably breeding birds. The nest is placed in trees from six to 30 feet high. The clutch size is around four eggs. The incubation period is 13 days, and the young leave the nest in about 10 days.

Habits and Habitat: The Rose-breasted Grosbeak is found primarily in hardwood forest in the east and riparian woodlands in the west. It is also frequently found in towns with a lot of trees. In Elkhart it is frequently seen in the cemetery in Siberian elms. Grosbeaks get their name from their enormous bills, which they use to crack seeds. As any bird-bander will testify, the bill has the power to give a strong pinch.

Field Marks: The adult male is unmistakable with its massive bill, black back, and white underparts with pink on the breast.

Food: This grosbeak divides its food between animal and vegetable. It is particularly fond of insects, seeds, and the tender buds on the spring growth of trees.

A Black-headed Grosbeak (*Pheucticus melanocephalus*). Photograph by Roger Boyd.

Black-headed Grosbeak
Pheucticus melanocephalus (Swainson)

Status: The Black-headed Grosbeak is an uncommon transient and summer resident in the western half of Kansas and a rare migrant in the east.

Period of Occurrence: This grosbeak arrives about 25 April and departs around 15 September. There are migrants passing through to more northerly breeding grounds, but their passage dates are hard to determine because of the resident breeding population. However, we can assume that most birds that are still in Kansas by 5 June are probably breeding. The dates of extreme occurrence are 17 April and 11 October.

Breeding: The Black-headed Grosbeak nests mainly in the western part of the state but has been recorded breeding east to Pottawatomie and Cloud counties. In the eastern part of its range, it interbreeds with the Rose-breasted Grosbeak.

The nest is placed in the fork of a tree approximately 10 feet high. It is a bulky nest made of twigs, stems and roots and lined with rootlets and small twigs. The eggs are gray to light blue with blotches at the larger end. Usually about four eggs are laid in late May to early June, and incubation takes 12 days. The young remain in the nest for about 11 days.

Habits and Habitat: The Black-headed Grosbeak occurs in woodland areas of the west. In migration it utilizes shelterbelts, city parks, and wooded streams. It frequently feeds upon the ground on plant buds. Sometimes it is tame and confiding. A bird at Elkhart was observed feeding on flower buds on the ground by numerous birdwatchers. It seemed unconcerned to be watched by 10 pairs of binoculars, 15 feet away. Its bill, like that of its close kin the Rose-breasted Grosbeak, is a powerful seed cracker.

Field Marks: The adult male has a rusty breast, black head with a massive bill, and black and white wings.

Food: The food of this grosbeak is about 50 percent insects and 50 percent seeds and fruits.

A Blue Grosbeak (*Guiraca caerulea*). Photograph by Roger Boyd.

Blue Grosbeak
Guiraca caerulea (Linnaeus)

Status: The Blue Grosbeak is an uncommon transient and summer resident in the eastern half of the state to common in the west.

Period of Occurrence: The normal arrival date of this breeding grosbeak is about 25 April and departure about 10 September. The dates of extreme occurrence are 12 April and 14 October.

Breeding: The Blue Grosbeak appears to be a more common breeding bird in the western half of Kansas. It breeds in riparian woodland, shelterbelts, cities, and scrub woodland. The nest is placed three to 12 feet high, usually in edge situations, in trees, vines, thickets, or even in hedgerows. The nest is composed of grasses interlaced with bark and stems and lined with fine grass. Occasionally, a piece of snakeskin will be used.

The four eggs are white to pale blue and are laid in late May or early June. Incubation takes 12 days, and the young birds fledge in another 12 days. In Kansas the species rears two families per year.

Habits and Habitat: The Blue Grosbeak inhabits woodland, scrub woodland, towns, and shelterbelts. It is frequently seen around edge habitat, where it nests in the denser vegetation. In southwest Kansas, it can
be found in ravines with dense scrub vegetation.

Field Marks: The male is one of the more brightly colored birds in Kansas.
Even so, the male may look black unless you see it in the sunlight. The
male can be confused only with the male Indigo Bunting, from which
it differs in being larger and having a larger bill and rusty wing patches.

Food: The Blue Grosbeak feeds on insects and seeds, with the former
about 70 percent of its diet.

A Lazuli Bunting (*Passerina amoena*). Photograph by Dale and Marian Zimmerman.

Lazuli Bunting
Passerina amoena (Say)

Status: The Lazuli Bunting is an uncommon transient and a rare summer resident in the west. It is rare in the central part and casual in the east.

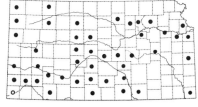

Period of Occurrence: This western bunting arrives in Kansas around 5 May and is finished with its spring passage by 20 May. The dates of extreme spring occurrence are 23 April and 27 May. The fall passage begins around 20 August and is finished by 15 September. The earliest arrival date in fall is 10 August, and the latest departure is 16 September. More information is needed on the period of occurrence in the state.

Breeding: Although the Lazuli Bunting undoubtedly breeds with some regularity in Kansas, the only actual breeding record comes from Morton County. A pair bred just east of the Cimarron River bridge north of Elkhart, Morton County, in 1958 (Thompson 1958). Johnsgard (1979) listed it as a common breeder in Morton and Hamilton counties, but this is certainly not the case.

The nest is usually placed about four feet high in scrub trees or other vegetation. The four pale bluish white eggs are placed in a nest composed of grass, twigs, and bark. The nest is lined with soft grasses and other materials. The eggs hatch in about 12 days, and the young fledge in another 12 days. The parents usually rear two broods in one season.

Habits and Habitat: The Lazuli Bunting occurs in riparian forest in the east and in riparian woodland and scrub in the west. These buntings seem to be somewhat regular in occurrence in Cowley County, where they are regularly netted and banded along the Arkansas River. In Ellis County they are netted and banded regularly during migration along Big Creek in Hays.

Field Marks: The adult male Lazuli Bunting is easily recognizable with the azure blue head, upperparts, and throat; cinnamon band across his breast; white belly; and white wing bars. The female is more difficult but is brown and has a hint of wing bars. She is smaller in size than the female Blue Grosbeak, which she resembles in color.

Food: The Lazuli Bunting's diet consists of insects and seeds, with the insects furnishing about 70 percent of the diet.

An Indigo Bunting (*Passerina cyanea*). Photograph by Roger Boyd.

Indigo Bunting
Passerina cyanea (Linnaeus)

Status: The Indigo Bunting is a common migrant and summer resident throughout the state and is perhaps somewhat less common as a breeding bird in the west.

Period of Occurrence: The Indigo Bunting arrives in spring around 1 May and departs in the fall about 25 September. The dates of extreme occurrence are 21 April and 16 October.

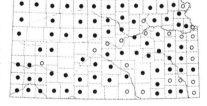

Breeding: This blue bunting breeds throughout the state but at a higher density in the east than the west. The nest is placed about three feet high in low trees, thickets, brambles, vines, weeds, and grasses. The nest is composed of dried grasses, dead leaves, and stems. The inside is lined with fine, soft material. Occasionally, snake skin is found incorporated into the nest. The three pale bluish white eggs are laid around 15 June. The eggs hatch in about 12 days, and the rapidly growing young fledge in nine days.

The Indigo Bunting is thought to rear two broods of young a year.

Habits and Habitat: This deep blue bunting is found mainly along wooded streams, where the male stakes out his territory for the breeding season. The male is a strong defender of his territory. During the breeding season he sings relentlessly from the highest perches in his territory. If telephone or power lines transit his territory, he will frequently utilize them for perches.

Field Marks: This species frequently hybridizes with the Lazuli Bunting in the west. However, most male Indigo Buntings are pure enough that they can be told by their bright blue feathers over all of the body. They are about one-half the size of the Blue Grosbeak, with which they might be confused. The brown females closely resemble the Lazuli Bunting female, but the latter has white wing bars.

Food: The Indigo Bunting feeds on both seeds and insects in approximately a 50-50 ratio.

A Painted Bunting (*Passerina ciris*). Photograph by Roger Boyd.

Painted Bunting
Passerina ciris (Linnaeus)

Status: The Painted Bunting is an uncommon summer resident in the southeast, becoming less common as you move westward to Sumner County and north to Douglas County. It is a rare summer resident west to at least Meade County and north to Douglas County.

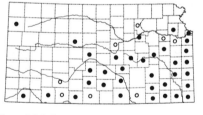

Period of Occurrence: This bright bunting arrives around 5 May and departs by 1 September. The dates of extreme occurrence are 25 April and 21 September. There are two feeder reports for winter from Reno and Douglas counties. Arrival and departure dates for this species are meager, and more information is needed.

Breeding: The Painted Bunting breeds in the southern tier of counties at least as far west as Clark County. West of Sumner County the density of breeding pairs is quite low. The density from Sumner eastward increases, and the species is common in Cowley County in riverine scrub. Breeding elsewhere in the state is sporadic. In Cowley County it nests on hillsides covered with scrub oak and sumac with much undergrowth or along river bottoms with extensive plum thickets. The nest—made of grasses, leaves, and twigs and lined with soft grasses—is placed about three feet high in shrubs or short trees in edge habitat.

Three pale bluish white eggs with reddish brown spotting are laid. Incubation lasts for 12 days, and the young leave the nest in approximately 10 days. Although information is scarce, the species may be double brooded.

Habits and Habitat: This is undoubtedly the most beautiful of all the Kansas songbirds. As the name implies, the male looks as if someone couldn't decide what color the bird should be: red, blue, yellow, or green. This array of colors should make it highly conspicuous, but it is one of the harder birds to see unless you know the song. The male marks its territory from the tops of trees, making it difficult to observe. The search is certainly worth it when you finally spot the male. Although the male is brilliantly colored, the female is also beautiful in her subtle shades of green.

Field Marks: The red, blue, and green combinations of the male should make its misidentification unlikely. The female is the only small finch-like bird with a light green coloration.

Food: The Painted Bunting feeds primarily on seeds and seems to be especially fond of foxtail (Bent 1968). It does occasionally feed upon insects.

A Dickcissel (*Spiza americana*). Photograph by Frank S. Shipley.

Dickcissel
Spiza americana (Gmelin)

Status: The Dickcissel is a common transient and summer resident in the east and central part of the state. In the west it is a local transient and summer resident. It is a winter vagrant, although its wintering range seems to be moving northward.

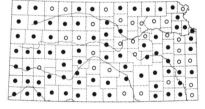

Period of Occurrence: This sparrow arrives around 25 April and remains until 25 September. Because of the large number of summering birds, it is impossible to tell when the last transients pass through the state. The dates of extreme occurrence are 8 March and 26 November. Birds have been observed on 8 December and 4 February; they were probably injured or disoriented.

Breeding: The Dickcissel probably breeds throughout the state but is most common in the central and eastern parts. There can be little doubt that this is one of the more common breeding birds in the state. The species prefers grasslands or cropland areas planted in alfalfa, clover, and wheat. Birds are commonly found along highways sitting upon the fences or on transmission lines.

The Dickcissel is polygynous. Zimmerman (1966) found that 18 percent of the males had more than one mate, 40 percent were monogamous, and 42 percent were unmated. The male usually obtains a second mate while the first lays or incubates the eggs. Unlike most male birds, the Dickcissel male makes no attempt to assist in marital duties. Gross (Bent 1968, pt. 1) states: "One morning as I watched a female returning to her nest with a beak full of food for her 5-day-old young, a sharp-shinned hawk appeared out of nowhere and carried her off. Her mate seemingly paid no attention to the tragedy enacted in front of him, but continued singing from his regular post nearby. He continued to sing the rest of that day, and the next 2 days, while the young slowly starved to death."

The nest is usually placed upon the ground but may be in shrubs or trees. The nest, built in a depression, is of grass, leaves, and weeds and lined with soft grass, rootlets, and hair. The four pale blue, unmarked eggs are incubated for about 12 days. The young remain in the nest for eight to 10 days.

Habits and Habitat: The Dickcissel prefers grasslands and croplands for its breeding areas. It is a common sight in Kansas to see the males neatly spaced on fences along alfalfa fields singing their "dick, dick-cissel, cissel" song. The Dickcissel is one of the species most heavily parasitized by the Brown-headed Cowbird. This could eventually cause a loss in numbers.

Field Marks: The Dickcissel's black V marking on the yellow breast and its rust wings help to identify it, as does the distinctive song.

Food: The food of the Dickcissel varies with the season but averages about 50 percent animal and 50 percent vegetable.

A Green-tailed Towhee (*Pipilo chlorurus*). Photograph by David A. Rintoul.

TOWHEES, SPARROWS, AND LONGSPURS
(FAMILY EMBERIZIDAE, SUBFAMILY EMBERIZINAE)
Green-tailed Towhee
Pipilo chlorurus (Audubon)

Status: The Green-tailed Towhee is a rare migrant in southwest Kansas and a vagrant elsewhere in the state.

Period of Occurrence: This towhee has been observed mainly in spring passage, with most records falling from 27 April to 23 May. The Johnson, Wyandotte, and Shawnee county records are all birds discovered in winter, two of which remained in the area until April.

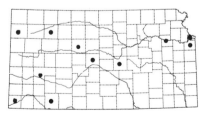

Habits and Habitat: Little is known of the habitat of this bird in Kansas.

The one sighting by Thompson, in Morton County, was in sagebrush. Grinnell and Miller (1944) state: "Forest is avoided; only scattered trees within the brushland are tolerated, but they may be used as song post." Other authors mention sagebrush as a principal habitat. Perhaps the Green-tailed Towhee is overlooked in Morton County because most birdwatchers tend to make their observations in areas with trees.

Food: The primary food of the Green-tailed Towhee is seeds and fruits.

A Rufous-sided Towhee (*Pipilo erythrophthalmus*). Photograph by Bob Gress.

Rufous-sided Towhee
Pipilo erythrophthalmus (Linnaeus)

Status: The Rufous-sided Towhee is a common migrant throughout the state and a rare summer resident in the northeastern counties. It is an uncommon winter resident in the east and rare in the west.

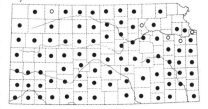

Period of Occurrence: The Rufous-sided Towhee's actual dates are hard to determine because of wintering populations. However, there is a marked increase in numbers around 10 April, with most passing through by 15 May. In the fall it returns to the state about 25 September and remains until 15 October. It has been noted every month of the year.

Breeding: The breeding status of the Rufous-sided Towhee is not well known, but it appears to be a rare breeding species in the northeastern part of the state. The only nest from the west is from Decatur County. Johnston (1964b) listed 19 records of breeding but gave no actual localities. His data indicated that the clutch size is four eggs and that the most common egg-laying date is 5 May but spanning a time from 21 April to 10 August.

The white eggs with reddish brown dots are laid in a nest placed on the ground in dense brush. The birds occasionally build in shrubs, vines, and low in trees. The nest is bulky and is composed of grasses, leaves, and stems and lined with fine grasses and other soft materials. The incubation period is 13 days, and the young leave the nest in nine to 11 days.

Habits and Habitat: This is one of the larger sparrows occurring in Kansas. It is usually found in areas of dense brush where it gives its distinctive call note, sometimes the only indication that it is present. However, its inquisitive nature makes it easy to call in by squeaking on the back of your hand.

Field Marks: The Rufous-sided Towhee is, as the name implies, rufous sided. Two forms occur in Kansas, one with a white-spotted back and the other with a black back. The white-spotted form is the more common one in Kansas. The black-backed form is the eastern race and occurs primarily in the extreme eastern part, but it has been observed in the west at least to Ellis County. The vocalizations of the two forms are easily separated.

Food: This towhee feeds primarily on seeds and fruits.

A Canyon Towhee (*Pipilo fuscus*). Photograph by Dale and Marian Zimmerman.

Canyon Towhee
Pipilo fuscus Swainson

Status: The Canyon Towhee is a casual winter visitor to Morton County, although it may remain well into May and June. A pair was seen from 9 to 11 June, 1972 (Patti 1972). One of the birds was observed to be carrying dried grass, and the pair could have been nesting. This is the only summer record. Canyon Towhees were seen again in Morton County in 1975 and in 1989–90.

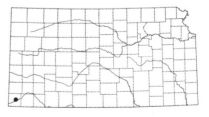

The Canyon Towhee was formerly known as the Brown Towhee, but the latter was split into two species in the 1989 supplement to the American Ornithologists' Union Checklist.

Habits and Habitat: The Canyon Towhee has been observed in only two areas in Morton County. The most likely area to observe them is at Point of Rocks overlooking the Cimarron River north of Elkhart. The other site is the U.S. Forest Service Research Station about three miles north of Elkhart.

Food: The Canyon Towhee feeds upon seeds and fruits.

A Bachman's Sparrow (*Aimophila aestivalis*). Photograph by Charles Platt for the Cornell Laboratory of Ornithology.

Bachman's Sparrow
Aimophila aestivalis (Lichtenstein)

Status: The Bachman's Sparrow was formerly a casual visitor in extreme northeastern Kansas. There are no recent records.

Period of Occurrence: There are only two records: a specimen from Lake Quivira, Wyandotte County, 24 April 1949, and a sighting from Johnson County, 26 April 1948, both by Harold C. Hedges.

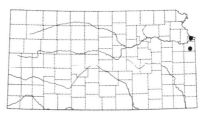

Habits and Habitat: The Bachman's Sparrow nests in the southeastern United States and as far northwest as southeastern Missouri and Illinois, building on the ground under a bush or vine. It prefers open pine woods (hence it is sometimes called the "Pine-woods Sparrow") and brushy fields on hillsides. It spends most of its time on the ground and is difficult to observe or flush. The song, a clear whistled note followed by a trill, is usually delivered from a tall bush or a tree branch. It also has a flight song. This is another of the species that benefited by the arrival of Europeans. In this case the clearing of dense virgin pine forest, which resulted in more open second growth, prompted a great increase in both number and distribution.

Field Marks: This is a reddish, long-tailed sparrow with unstreaked underparts, a reddish eye line, and dark upper mandible.

Food: The food of the Bachman's Sparrow is insects, including beetles, true bugs, and grasshoppers; spiders; snails; and seeds of pines and grasses. At feeding stations it eats such items as raisins, kernels of black walnuts, and cracked corn.

Cassin's Sparrow
Aimophila cassinii (Woodhouse)

Status: The Cassin's Sparrow is a common transient and summer resident in sagebrush in western Kansas, chiefly south of the Arkansas River but also north to Wallace County and east to Edwards county. During irruption years, as in 1974, populations increase greatly in size, and birds occur much farther north and east. Nesting has occurred east to Rice County.

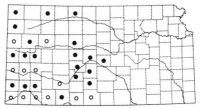

Period of Occurrence: There are sight records from 2 and 14 April to 7 September, with stragglers to 25 September and once to 10 November (Sebastian Patti). There are few fall records, and the status of this species then is uncertain.

Breeding: Nests are placed either on the ground or in a small bush (usually sage) a few inches above the ground and are extremely well hidden. The nest is constructed of grasses, weeds, and plant fibers and lined with small grasses. The clutch is three to five, usually four, pure white eggs. Birds are said to desert their nests at the slightest disturbance.

Habits and Habitats: Within most of its range this is a characteristic species of the short-grass prairie dotted with scattered shrubs. In Kansas the Cassin's Sparrow nests regularly in sagebrush grasslands, chiefly in the southwest. Allen (1872) found it "rather common along the streams" in Ellis County during the summer of 1871. During some years Cassin's Sparrows move north and east of the usual range, and singing males may be conspicuous in grasslands and wheat fields. Except for singing males, birds are usually on the ground. During the breeding season pairs nest in loose colonies. Each male spends most of each morning, from before sunrise until the day becomes hot, repeating its conspicuous flight song—a form of "skylarking." He flies up from one tall shrub, sets his wings, and with head up and tail spread glides to a second shrub 20 to 36 feet distant. The song consists of two low notes followed by a trill and then two short notes. The first two notes are inaudible at a distance, so the song is best described as "sweeeeeeeeet, sweet, sweet." Common calls include a "tsip" and a more rapid "tzee, tzee, tzee." It is a difficult species to observe later in the nesting season, and there are few records from the postnesting period.

Field Marks: The Cassin's Sparrow is a long-tailed, pale grayish sparrow with a streaked back; immatures are similar, with streaking on the underparts.

Food: During summer this species feeds primarily on insects such as beetles and caterpillars and in winter shifts to the seeds of a variety of grasses and forbs. Outside Kansas it has been observed to eat the flowers of blackthorn and to visit feeders for milo and ground corn.

A Rufous-crowned Sparrow (*Aimophila ruficeps*). Photograph by Dale and Marian Zimmerman.

Rufous-crowned Sparrow
Aimophila ruficeps (Cassin)

Status: The Rufous-crowned Sparrow is casual in the extreme southwest and vagrant elsewhere in Kansas.

Period of Occurrence: There are single specimens from Comanche (7 June 1936) and Morton (12 November 1985) counties and a few additional sight records from Morton County on 21 May 1950 and between 27 September and 2 Jan-

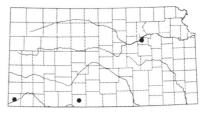

uary (six different years). One was reported from Junction City, Geary County, on 26 December 1982. The species is probably more regular than these records indicate and should be looked for along rocky ravines in southwestern Kansas in late fall.

Habits and Habitat: The Rufus-crowned Sparrow breeds in arid and semi-arid regions of the southwestern United States and Mexico, nesting on the ground. Most of its time is spent on the ground, usually near boulders on dry brushy hillsides or in ravines. It prefers to run rather than fly from one patch of cover to another. The individuals seen in Kansas have usually been shy and difficult to approach a second time. In its usual range many individuals will respond to "pishing." This species is typically nongregarious and rarely occurs in flocks of larger than family size. The song is a feeble jumble of notes or chittering that reminds some observers of a softened House Wren song and others of the song of a Lazuli Bunting. In some areas, at least, nesting activities are closely related to the timing of summer rains.

Field Marks: This is a dark gray sparrow, unmarked below, with streaked back and conspicuous head pattern—reddish crown, white line above eye, and black whisker bordered above and below by white. Immatures are more buff colored, with less distinct markings.

Food: During spring and summer the Rufus-crowned Sparrow feeds primarily on insects, including beetles, crickets, grasshoppers, flies, and caterpillars. During fall and winter it adds seeds of various grasses, forbs, and plant shoots. In some areas, where common, it may visit feeders for baby chick scratch.

An American Tree Sparrow (*Spizella arborea*). Photograph by Bob Gress.

American Tree Sparrow
Spizella arborea (Wilson)

Status: The American Tree Sparrow is a common transient and winter visitor statewide.

Period of Occurrence: This species is most common from late October through late March, with usual arrival and departure dates of about 15 October and about 5 April. Extreme dates are 23 September and 2 October and 29

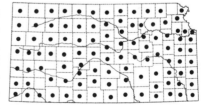

April. Numerous summer records, between 2 May and 21 June and 16 to 18 August, are almost certainly in error.

Habits and Habitat: The American Tree Sparrow nests among stunted trees and shrubs just below the tundra line in central Canada and Alaska, building on the ground or in low shrubs, usually within inches of the ground. In Kansas the species occurs in a wide variety of weedy habitats from old fields to woodland edge and riparian situations. It usually occurs in flocks of from six to eight individuals to as many as several hundred in good feeding areas. The constitution of such flocks changes constantly as some individuals leave and wander to join other flocks. The birds feed by scratching on the ground, by jumping up at overhanging seed heads, and by alighting on the seed heads directly. In western Kansas greatest concentrations are in weedy draws within grassland or cultivated areas, with patches of native sunflowers and ragweed being favored. During particularly inclement weather some individuals move into towns and visit feeders.

Birds frequently sing during the warm days of late winter. The song is a series of clear, sweet notes followed by a warble. Individuals are very sociable within the flock and givie a variety of calls, including a characteristic "twiddley, twiddley" described by Thoreau (1910) as a "tinkle of icicles." The usual call is a soft "zeep." Most migration is at night. During winter, nocturnal flights can frequently be heard just prior to heavy snows. Males winter farther north than do females; in Kansas males slightly outnumber females (Baumgartner *in* Bent 1968).

Field Marks: The most often mentioned field mark is the dark spot on an otherwise unmarked breast, but some individuals lack this spot and it is sometimes difficult to see. A better characteristic is the bicolored bill—dark upper mandible, yellow lower mandible. Our other reddish-crowned winter sparrows have pinkish (immature White-crowned and Field) or dark (Swamp) bills.

Food: During winter the American Tree Sparrow feeds almost entirely on seeds of grasses and weeds, especially ragweed, lambsquarters, and smartweeds. It is noted for the high percentage (about 50 percent) of grass seeds in its diet, chiefly panicgrass and pigeongrass. Baumgartner (*in* Bent 1968) reported 982 seeds in the crop and 200 more in the stomach of a single bird. During summer, other plant foods, including berries, buds, and flowers, are eaten as are such insects as beetles, wasps, ants, caterpillars, and flies and spiders. At feeding stations the birds typically feed on the ground, eating milo, chick scratch, and sunflower hearts.

A Chipping Sparrow (*Spizella passerina*). Photograph by David A. Rintoul.

Chipping Sparrow
Spizella passerina (Bechstein)

Status: The Chipping Sparrow is a common transient statewide. It is a local summer resident in the east and is casual westward. There is one verified winter record from Garden City, Finney County, from December 1991.

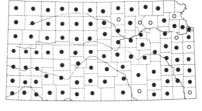

Period of Occurrence: The Chipping Sparrow is most common from late April through early October. Extreme dates (some dubious) in breeding areas are 13 March and 21 November. Extreme dates for transients are 30 March to 2 June and 28 July to 21 November.

Breeding: The nest is constructed of grasses, plant stems, and rootlets and lined with fine grasses and hair. It is placed in a crotch or fork of a branch of a shrub or small tree, usually within 10 feet of the ground. The clutch is two to five, usually four, greenish blue eggs with brown

to blackish spots and with streaks and blotches near the larger end.
The incubation period is 11 to 14 days. The nestling period is 8 to 12
days. The species is double brooded. The nest is built by the female,
who does most of the incubation and sits so closely that she can sometimes be touched by an observer. The male often feeds the female while
she is at or on the nest. Females help defend nesting territories.

Habits and Habitat: This bird was originally a species of open woods and
forest clearings, especially along lakes and rivers and in open pine woods.
With the arrival of Europeans it soon moved into clearings, farmsteads,
and towns, and early workers considered it to be the most domesticated
of our native sparrows. During migration it occurs in large flocks,
often with other *Spizellas,* in all brushy and semiwooded habitats. The
Chipping Sparrow is most conspicuous while feeding on lawns and in
grassy areas near streams or woods. When flushed, birds commonly fly
up into trees until the disturbance is passed, then return to the ground
to feed. The song is a series of chip notes of one pitch that form an
unmusical trill reminding one of a sewing machine.

　　Most winter records are dubious, and those describing a rusty crown
are definitely wrong, because winter birds have streaked crowns! Any
authentic winter record will likely be of a single immature at a feeder,
which should be captured or photographed in detail.

Field Marks: In spring and summer the rufous cap, white line above the
eye, dark line through the eye, and completely dark bill are diagnostic. Adults at other seasons and immatures have the crown streaked;
the gray rump is distinctive. Individuals in juvenile plumage, into early
fall, are browner with streaked underparts and brownish rump.

Food: Insect food of this species includes beetles, leafhoppers, grasshoppers, bugs, wasps, and caterpillars. It also eats spiders and large amounts
of plant food, chiefly seeds of grasses such as crabgrass and pigeongrass and such weed seeds as dandelions, clover, knotweeds, smartweeds,
and pigweeds. On the wintering grounds some birds visit feeders and
take various small grains.

A Clay-colored Sparrow (*Spizella pallida*). Photograph by Calvin L. Cink.

Clay-colored Sparrow
Spizella pallida (Swainson)

Status: The Clay-colored Sparrow is a common transient statewide. It probably nested in Morton County in 1964. There are unconfirmed reports of stragglers into mid-winter (to 5 February) in Crawford, Ford, and Sedgwick counties.

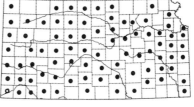

Period of Occurrence: The Clay-colored Sparrow is most numerous from late April through mid-May and late September through mid-October; extreme dates for transients are 24 March to 5 June and 20 August to 15 October with stragglers to 19 November. There are several unverified summer records for western Kansas, and a male with enlarged gonads was taken in Cheyenne County on 12 June.

Breeding: There is one probable nesting record: Two adults were feeding three fledged young in Morton County on the very late date of 4

September 1964 (Trautman 1964). The nest is well hidden in a clump
of dead grass or in a shrub and within three feet of the ground. It is
constructed of grasses, weed stems, and rootlets and lined with fine
grasses and rootlets. The clutch is three to five, usually four, pale
bluish green eggs with black spots and scrawls near the larger end. The
incubation period is 11 to 14 days; the nestling period is seven to nine
days.

Habits and Habitat: This sparrow breeds in second growth and forest
edges in the northeastern United States and central Canada, building
its nest on the ground or in a low shrub. In Kansas it occurs most frequently in brushy fields and such semiopen areas as forest edges,
parks, and roadsides; it often occurs with other sparrows, especially Chipping Sparrows. The Clay-colored Sparrow usually feeds in flocks on the
ground, flying up into low trees or shrubs when disturbed. At other
times individuals glean insects from foliage and twigs and also eat
buds and similar plant parts. The distinctive song consists of two or three
simple notes best described as "buzzz, buzzz," all of one pitch and usually delivered from a tall shrub or low tree branch, sometimes in chorus. Its breeding in the northeastern United States is apparently a
recent phenomenon, and the number of sightings along the East
Coast has increased since the 1940s.

Field Marks: Adults are easily identified by the contrasting head pattern
—white line over eye, brown cheeks outlined by black lines above and
below, a black whisker, and gray nape and sides of neck. Another iden-
tifying mark is a light central median stripe through the darker crown.
Nonbreeding birds are duller and buffier; immatures are still duller
and the rump is brownish. The bill is flesh colored, not bright pink as
in the Field Sparrow.

Food: In summer the Clay-colored Sparrow is largely insectivorous, eating grasshoppers, ants, wasps, true bugs, and caterpillars. It also eats
large quantities of seeds of various grasses and weeds, catkins, buds,
and other plant parts. At feeding stations it eats finely cracked corn,
millet, sunflower hearts, and bread crumbs.

A Brewer's Sparrow (*Spizella breweri*). Photograph by Dale and Marian Zimmerman.

Brewer's Sparrow
Spizella breweri Cassin

Status: The Brewer's Sparrow is a rare transient in western Kansas and a very local summer resident in the extreme southwest. Sight records, especially in fall, should be verified because many fall immature Clay-colored Sparrows closely resemble this species. A sighting from Shawnee County, 30 April 1961, was by many observers.

Period of Occurrence: Sight records of nonsinging birds are questionable. Present sight records (most unverified) are between 8 April and 14 September, with most sightings during May. Most nesting is from mid-May to mid-June, 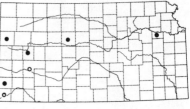 after which birds are difficult to observe.

Breeding: Small colonies were discovered in sand-sage grassland in Morton County in 1978 and in Finney County in 1980. Up to 23 singing males were reported by Mark Ports in 1979. Other colonies probably exist, but the species is difficult to find and to identify. The nest, extremely well hidden, is concealed in sagebrush, usually within three feet of the ground. It is constructed of grass and plant fiber, lined with fine grass and sometimes hair. The clutch is three to five, usually four, bluish eggs with dots, spots, and blotches of dark brown near the larger end. The incubation period is 12 or 13 days. The incubating female sits very closely, then often leaves, silently and unseen.

Habits and Habitat: The Brewer's Sparrow spends most of its time on the ground and is usually shy and difficult to observe. Singing males, however, perch on the top of a shrub. Where abundant on the breeding grounds, males may sing in chorus at dawn. The song is an elaborate series of long, sweet, musical trills varying in speed and pitch and *very* different from that of the Clay-colored Sparrow. Occasional individuals are reported in large flocks of other *Spizellas,* and several have been captured or heard singing at Hays, Ellis County.

Field Marks: This is a nondescript grayish brown sparrow lacking any conspicuous head pattern. It shares the slim, long-tailed build and unstreaked breast of other *Spizellas.* Adults have a finely streaked crown, pale brown cheeks bounded by darker lines, a faint white line over the eye, and a faint eye ring. This species lacks the contrasting gray nape of the Clay-colored Sparrow. Immatures are paler and buffier, with less contrasting head pattern. Both sexes have a pale pinkish bill.

Food: In spring and summer the Brewer's Sparrow eats many insects, including beetles, aphids, and caterpillars, and spiders. In fall and winter it eats large amounts of weed seeds. In California some individuals visit feeding stations and eat "chick scratch." It is said to be one of the few species capable of fulfilling all of its water requirements from dry seeds.

A Field Sparrow (*Spizella pusilla*). Photograph by Mike Hopiak for the Cornell Laboratory of Ornithology.

Field Sparrow
Spizella pusilla (Wilson)

Status: The Field Sparrow is a common transient and summer resident in the east and an uncommon transient and local summer resident in the west. It is rare in winter, seen chiefly in eastern Kansas.

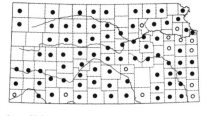

Period of Occurrence: Transients are most common from mid-April to mid-May and during October. The usual extreme dates are 10 March and 5 November, but a few individuals overwinter locally at many localities.

Breeding: Individuals are strongly territorial. The nest, usually well concealed, is placed on the ground or in a shrub within three feet of the ground. It is a cup of grass, weed stems, and leaves lined with fine grasses. Only the female builds, but the male may accompany her as she works. First nests require four to five days for completion, later nests only two to three days. The clutch is three to five bluish eggs dotted and spotted with reddish brown and lavender, especially at the larger end. The incubation period is about 11 days. The nestling period is seven or eight days, and the young can fly by about 12 days of age. The species is double brooded.

Habits and Habitat: There is some evidence that the Field Sparrow increased its original range following the clearing of virgin forests by Europeans and that it recently has been declining as many small abandoned farms have been lost to succession or urban development. In Kansas this species nests in old fields and prairies with shrubs or thickets and is local in distribution. In the central and western part of Kansas, habitat that looks good is not utilized. During migration it occurs in any brushy or "edge" habitat from dooryards to edges or open woodland. Small numbers overwinter, often in company with Tree Sparrows and juncos, in brushy or riparian habitat.

Even during migration this sparrow rarely occurs in flocks of more than a few individuals. Males sing from elevated perches, usually the tops of bushes or low trees. The song is a series of three or four whistled notes followed by a trill and can be expressed as "sweeet, sweeet, sweeet, sweeet, wee-wee-wee-wee-wee." The call is a sharp "chip." Walkinshaw (*in* Bent 1968) reported a male that with its mate raised two broods at six years of age. A second six-year-old male, however, was unable to retain its territory. The species is subject to considerable predation, and one female in Michigan built seven nests in one summer, none of which was successful. Hoyt (*in* Bent 1968) reported nests of a Field Sparrow and a Rufous-sided Towhee 18 inches apart in a tree with parents of both species feeding the young in both nests!

Field Marks: The adult can be distinguished by its rusty crown, white eye ring, rusty eyebrow and ear patch, and conspicuous pink bill. The immature is duller with faintly streaked underparts. Wintering birds are sometimes confused with the immature of the much larger White-crowned Sparrow, but the latter has a distinct buffy line through the eye and a light stripe through the middle of the crown.

Food: While nesting the Field Sparrow feeds chiefly on invertebrates, including beetles, grasshoppers, caterpillars, leafhoppers, ants, and spiders. During the rest of the year seeds predominate, especially those of crabgrass, pigeongrass, various weeds, and rarely waste grain. The young, as in most songbirds, are fed invertebrates exclusively.

A Vesper Sparrow (*Pooecetes gramineus*). Photograph by David A. Rintoul.

Vesper Sparrow
Pooecetes gramineus (Gmelin)

Status: The Vesper Sparrow is a common transient statewide and is casual in summer in the west. It is casual in winter, chiefly in the south and east.

Period of Occurrence: This species is most common during April and the last half of October. Spring transients have been reported between 10 March and 18 May, with stragglers to 13 June (singing male, Jefferson County). Fall dates are from 7 and 23 August to 22 November, with scattered winter records statewide between 2 December and 17 February. There are also summer records of 28 June (Russell County) and 17 July (Morton County, specimen).

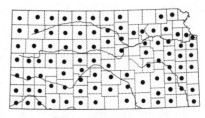

Habits and Habitat: Vesper Sparrows prefer fallow fields, stubble, and overgrazed pastures. In spring flocks are common along roadsides, often with Savannah Sparrows. They feed on the ground in open areas, often alighting on a fence wire or post when alarmed, thereby making observation fairly easy. The Vesper Sparrow is said to be especially fond of dust bathing. Despite the term *vesper,* males sing commonly during early morning, usually from an elevated location such as a fence post, overhead wire, or tree. The song has been described as plaintive and sweet—two long notes, two higher ones, and a descending trill. There are no nesting records for Kansas, but all midsummer reports should be investigated as occasional nesting is possible.

Field Marks: In all plumages the Vesper Sparrow has streaked underparts, white outer tail feathers, and usually a white eye ring. A chestnut patch on the "shoulder" (lesser wing coverts), responsible for the earlier name of "Bay-winged Bunting," is often visible at close range.

Food: During the summer this species feeds on a variety of invertebrates, including beetles, grasshoppers, and caterpillars. At all seasons it eats a wide variety of grass seeds, weed seeds, and waste grains.

A Lark Sparrow (*Chondestes grammacus*). Photograph by David A. Rintoul.

Lark Sparrow
Chondestes grammacus (Say)

Status: The Lark Sparrow is a common transient and summer resident statewide and is casual in winter.

Period of Occurrence: Peak migrations are late April–early May and mid-October. The usual arrival is in mid-April, with usual departure in mid-October. Extreme dates are 11 March and 29 October. Fall departure is poorly documented. There are a few winter records (27 November to 18 February) from southern and eastern Kansas.

Breeding: The nest is placed either in a depression on the ground or in a shrub or tree. Ground nests are usually in disturbed areas (rocky outcrops in prairies are favorites) partially hidden by a grass clump or forb. Nests in trees and shrubs are larger and bulkier. The nest is constructed of weed stems and grasses and lined with rootlets or fine grass. Only the female builds and incubates. During incubation she sits very "tightly" and may sometimes be touched or even captured by hand. The clutch is three to five, usually four, creamy white eggs with brown, black, and purple spots and scrawls at the larger end, sometimes forming a wreath. The incubation period is 11 or 12 days, and young leave the nest in nine or 10 days. The Lark Sparrow is probably single brooded in Kansas, though replacement nesting may stretch the breeding season to three months.

Habits and Habitat: Shortly after the turn of the century the species greatly expanded its range in the eastern United States, but more recently it is regressing westward to the prairie states. Lark Sparrows prefer areas with low or sparse vegetation interspersed with bushes. Large lawns, golf courses, and edges of fields and ravines in grasslands are favored habitats. During migration this sparrow occurs in smaller flocks than most common sparrows, but it is an active, conspicuous species and is one of our better-known sparrows. The song is a long variable series of clear notes, buzzes, and trills delivered from a low perch or the ground or occasionally in flight. During courtship the male is very active, with much chasing of rivals and singing. Courtship includes a strutting display in which the male droops his wings and spreads his tail. Although combative during courtship, Lark Sparrows are generally tolerant of other species. Baepler (*in* Bent 1968) reported active nests of a Lark Sparrow, an Orchard Oriole, and a Scissor-tailed Flycatcher in the same tree. Wooster (*in* Ely 1971) found a nest with eggs within the base of a Swainson's Hawk nest in Ellis County. The Lark Sparrow feeds chiefly on the ground by gleaning insects and seeds as it moves about through vegetation.

Field Marks: No other species has its conspicuous face pattern — a "quail face" that includes a chestnut ear patch and a black malar stripe separated by a broad white stripe. The white breast has a conspicuous black patch, and the tail is bordered with white on its outer margins. Immatures are duller, with lightly streaked underparts.

Food: About 75 percent of the food of this species is seeds of grasses and weeds; most of the remainder consists of grasshoppers, with smaller proportions of beetles, caterpillars, and other small invertebrates.

A Black-throated Sparrow (*Amphispiza bilineata*). Photograph by David A. Rintoul.

Black-throated Sparrow
Amphispiza bilineata (Cassin)

Status: The Black-throated Sparrow is a vagrant, chiefly in the west.

Period of Occurrence: The single specimen was taken in a garage north-east of Garden City, Finney County, on 25 November 1952 by Marvin D. Schwilling. There are unverified sight records from Cowley (13 April 1971), Morton (1 July 1969), and Sedgwick (27 October 1979) counties.

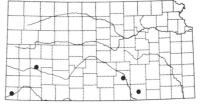

Habits and Habitat: This is a species of arid regions of the Great Basin south into Mexico. Nesting is in a low shrub such as creosotebush or juniper. The species occurs in the Black Mesa area of Oklahoma and

Colorado and has strayed north and east to Massachusetts. It probably occurs occasionally in Kansas during late fall. It usually occurs near the ground, often flying up into low bushes when approached. It is an active, vocal species uttering soft, metallic bell-like notes. The song is a series of clear notes followed by a trill, sometimes described as "canarylike." In the Big Bend country of Texas the Black-throated Sparrow is limited to areas of *Opuntia* cactus. It occurs in small flocks in winter.

Field Marks: The adult is unmistakable with its gray upperparts, bold face pattern (including white line over eye and white mustache) and black throat. The immature has brownish upperparts; white throat; a browner, less distinct head pattern; and lightly streaked underparts.

Food: The Black-throated Sparrow feeds on the ground and in low shrubs, eating insects such as grasshoppers and aphids, seeds, and various plant parts.

Sage Sparrow
Amphispiza belli (Cassin)

Status: The status of the Sage Sparrow is uncertain. It is either a vagrant or a rare winter visitor to the southwest.

Period of Occurrence: Two specimens were taken in Morton County on 1 November 1956 and one in Seward County on 11 January 1957. Sight records in summer from Comanche (13 and 14 May and 5 July) and Morton (1 July) counties 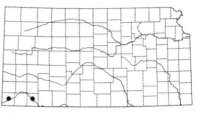 are unlikely. One such sighting (April) proved to be of Lark Buntings in molting winter plumage. There are recent sight records from Morton County between 31 December and 8 January.

Habits and Habitat: The Sage Sparrow is a shy species that spends most of its time on the ground under sagebrush and similar vegetation. It often occurs in small flocks. It usually feeds on the ground, gleaning food from the surface rather than by scratching. It may fly to the top of a bush when alarmed, in response to "pishing," or while singing. The song, unlikely to be heard in Kansas, has been described as a series of high-pitched tinkling notes. The call, a musical "tink," can be heard from a considerable distance.

Field Marks: The adult is gray, lightly streaked with black above, with browner wings and white wing bars. The tail is darker, contrasting sharply with the back and with white in the outer feathers and at the tip. The tail may be cocked upward while the bird is running and is flicked frequently while the bird is perched. The Sage Sparrow also has a gray cheek, white line over the eye, white malar, and black whisker and breast spot. Immatures are duller and more heavily streaked below.

Food: During the summer this species feeds largely on small invertebrates, chiefly grasshoppers, true bugs, caterpillars, and ants. At other seasons it feeds on a variety of weed seeds.

A Lark Bunting (*Calamospiza melanocorys*). Photograph by Roger Boyd.

Lark Bunting
Calamospiza melanocorys Stejneger

Status: The Lark Bunting is a common transient and summer resident east to Ellis County and is casual in summer (occasionally nesting) eastward to Franklin County. It is ca-sual to regular in winter, chiefly in the southwest. Nesting has been documented east (sporadically) to Barton County and at least once each to Riley, Shawnee, and Franklin counties.

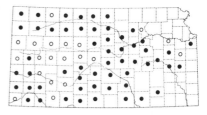

Period of Occurrence: In the southwest most migration is from mid-April to mid-May and during early September. In central Kansas arrival is two weeks later, and most birds depart soon after completing nesting. A few flocks remain into late December. This species has been locally common in Morton County in recent winters, with stragglers to Sher-man and Jewell counties. Extreme dates for transients are 26 March and 7 November. Vagrants have been reported eastward at all seasons.

Breeding: The following comments are from a study by Jerry Wilson

(1976) undertaken in Ellis County near the normal eastern border of the Lark Bunting's nesting range. The birds nested singly or in loose colonies, with nests sometimes within 35 feet of one another. Males arrived about two weeks before females, courted females for two weeks, and displayed until late July. Preferred habitat was fallow fields, but as annual vegetation became taller and more dense, later nests were built in native grassland, usually on a hillside with sparse vegetation. Each nest was built on the ground under a plant but with good visibility in at least two directions. The nest was a very loose structure, built flush with the ground, constructed of grass blades and fine rootlets, and lined with finer vegetation. Nest building probably required two or three days. The clutch was two to six, usually five, unmarked pale blue eggs. The incubation period was 12 days, and the females did most of the incubating. Farming activities, especially discing of stubble fields, and predation caused most nest failures.

Habits and Habitat: The Lark Bunting is one of the most conspicuous grassland birds in western Kansas. It frequents stubble fields, fields of wheat and other small grains, alfalfa fields, mid-grass prairie, and sand-sage grasslands. Except when actually nesting, Lark Buntings usually occur in small to large flocks of both sexes. Males deliver their flight song from spring arrival into mid-July, being especially vocal in early morning. The bird delivers the first half of its song as it ascends in a steep curve and the last half as it slowly "floats" earthward to its next perch. Occasionally one sings from a low perch. Where numerous, a great deal of chasing occurs. Populations fluctuate considerably from year to year; for example, a fivefold increase occurred in Ellis County in 1969. On occasion birds have appeared outside the usual range and have taken advantage of local conditions. Orville Rice (1965) described a colony that nested unexpectedly in the open disturbed areas of an alfalfa field in Shawnee County in 1964.

Field Marks: The male in breeding plumage is unmistakable—jet black with large white wing patches. Females are brownish above with dark streaking, a brown cheek patch bordered above and below by white, and a faint wing patch. Immatures are duller, with heavier streaking below. Winter males resemble the female but have a larger wing patch, darker wing, and often some black mottling below.

Food: Summer food of the Lark Bunting is primarily small invertebrates, including grasshoppers, caterpillars, bugs, ants, and bees. Some weed seeds are also eaten. In winter weed seeds, especially smartweeds and goosefoot, predominate, and some waste grain is eaten.

A Savannah Sparrow (*Passerculus sandwichensis*). Photograph by David A. Rintoul.

Savannah Sparrow
Passerculus sandwichensis (Gmelin)

Status: The Savannah Sparrow is a common transient statewide and is casual in winter.

Period of Occurrence: Most migration is during April and October. Extreme dates of presumed transients are 14 March and 26 May and 6 September and 16 November. There are a number of summer sightings, including one from

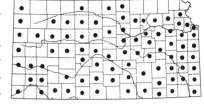

Stafford County on 17 July. A few apparently winter (28 November to 9 February) in southern Kansas during mild winters.

Habits and Habitat: The Savannah Sparrow nests throughout Alaska, Canada, and most of the United States except for the southern Great Plains and the southeast. It winters from the central United States southward. In this huge area it occurs in habitats as diverse as tundra, salt marshes, and short-grass prairies. While migrating through Kansas it occurs in a variety of grasslands, from overgrazed prairies to wet meadows and marshes. During spring this species is common in stubble fields and along roadsides, often in small flocks; in fall it prefers more dense vegetation. It spends most of its time on the ground under or near dense vegetation and when approached usually runs along the ground. The Savannah Sparrow feeds while hopping through vegetation, where it gleans food from surfaces and also scratches like a towhee. It also roosts on the ground. When flushed it usually flies a short distance just above the vegetation and then dives into thick cover. Individuals often respond to "pishing," and one may get a brief glimpse as a bird perches briefly on a weed stem, on a fence, or in an open area of the ground. The song, described as "tip, tip, ti, seee, saaay" (Terres 1980), is usually delivered from a bush or other low perch.

Field Marks: Darkness of color and size vary considerably depending on which race is involved. This is a short-tailed sparrow with streaked underparts and often with yellow or white above and before the eye.

Food: The Savannah Sparrow is one of our more insectivorous sparrows. In summer its food is a wide variety of invertebrates, with beetles, grasshoppers, true bugs, ants, spiders, and snails predominating. At other seasons a wide variety of grass seeds and weed seeds is eaten.

Baird's Sparrow
Ammodramus bairdii (Audubon)

Status: The Baird's Sparrow is probably a rare transient. There are scattered reports statewide.

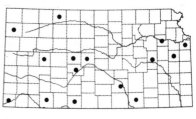

Period of Occurrence: At present all specimens (over half from TV tower kills!) were taken during the periods 25 to 28 April and 25 August to 7 October. Sight records are from the periods 6 April to 9 May and 11 September to 27 October and possibly November. All sight records need verification. Summer sightings are undoubtedly in error.

Habits and Habitat: The Sparrow is a relatively common breeder in grasslands of the northern Great Plains and is not particularly difficult to find there. However, as a transient through Kansas, it is elusive and rarely seen. Birds usually migrate as individuals or in small flocks and, being quiet and secretive, are difficult to find. Since most of the well-documented records are of birds killed at TV towers, it is also possible that most individuals overfly the state at night. The Baird's Sparrow is one of the truly grassland sparrows, spending most of its time on the ground and preferring to evade pursuers by running through vegetation rather than by flying. On the breeding grounds the beautiful song is diagnostic—a series of high pitched "zip" notes followed by a low pitched trill often expressed as "zip-zip-zip-zrr-r-r-r-r-r" (Farrand 1983).

Field Marks: In spring the Baird's Sparrow's dull ocher crown and nape, dark posterior spot on its ear coverts, and black whisker are diagnostic. Fall birds are buffier, with less distinct markings and more ventral streaking. Some juveniles migrate before molting, and these especially resemble Grasshopper Sparrows. However, they generally have lighter edges to the feathers on the back, which gives them a "scaly" appearance.

Food: During summer this species eats a wide variety of invertebrates, including grasshoppers, true bugs, caterpillars, and spiders. Large amounts of grass seeds and weed seeds are eaten at all seasons. The latter include many annual weeds such as ragweeds, plantains, and pigweeds.

A Grasshopper Sparrow (*Ammodramus savannarum*). Photograph by Bob Gress.

Grasshopper Sparrow
Ammodramus savannarum (Gmelin)

Status: The Grasshopper Sparrow is a common transient and summer resident statewide, with nesting documented from all except the extreme southwest. It is a vagrant in winter.

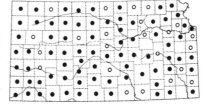

Period of Occurrence: Spring arrival is usually mid-April, and fall departure is about early October. Stragglers occur to mid-November and rarely into mid-winter. Extreme dates are 23 March and 31 January (Kearny County).

Breeding: This sparrow sometimes nests in loose colonies, but within these colonies territories are defended by singing. The nest is on the ground in a depression, typically very well concealed under a clump of grass or forb and often domed, making it even more difficult to find. In addition the female typically alights (or flushes) some distance from the nest and approaches (or leaves) it on foot. At times an injury-feigning display is used also. Nests are most easily found by following adults carrying food to the young. The nest is constructed of dried grass and lined with finer grass. The clutch is three to six, usually four or five, creamy white eggs with sparse reddish brown spots and blotches and gray undermarkings. The amount of spotting is variable but usually concentrated at the larger end. Incubation is by the female alone. The incubation period is 12 or 13 days; the nestling period is nine or 10 days. The species is probably two brooded in Kansas.

Habits and Habitat: The Grasshopper Sparrow occurs in all grassland habitats and has increased its range within historical times following deforestation. During the breeding season it prefers natural grasslands and fields of wheat or other small grains. During migration it occurs in a wider variety of areas, including brushy fields. On 7 October 1988 Scott Seltman observed a flock of over 100 birds that were in such extensive molt as to be nearly flightless. The Grasshopper Sparrow is most easily observed along roadsides, where it commonly perches on fence wires, posts, or other log perches while singing. The song is a characteristic short, thin, high-pitched insectlike trill. The bird also has a more sustained, more musical song of up to five-seconds duration that it gives during the courtship period (Smith *in* Bent 1968). Its typical flight is weak with rapid, buzzy wingbeats and is usually erratic and of short duration; it reminds one of the flight of a wren.

Field Marks: The Grasshopper Sparrow is a small, flat-headed, short-tailed sparrow with buffy face and buffy, unmarked underparts. At close range the yellow lores and yellow on the bend of the wing may be visible. Fall birds may be much brighter, with heavy streaking, and are sometimes confused with other species. Juveniles show little contrast above and are lightly streaked below.

Food: In summer food is primarily insects, especially grasshoppers, and other small invertebrates such as spiders, snails, and small earthworms. Seeds of various grasses and annual weeds are eaten at all seasons, and some waste grain is taken in fall and winter.

A Henslow's Sparrow (*Ammodramus henslowii*). Photograph by B. D. Cottrille for the Cornell Laboratory of Ornithology.

Henslow's Sparrow
Ammodramus henslowii (Audubon)

Status: The Henslow's Sparrow is an uncommon transient and very local summer resident in eastern Kansas.

Period of Occurrence: Specimens have been taken from 14 April through 15 October. Many more migration data are needed. The relatively few sight records of transients are from 10 April to 4 May and 3 August to 26 October. Nesting has been documented from Anderson, Geary, Morris, Riley, and Shawnee counties, and singing males have been observed during the breeding season at other localities in eastern Kansas.

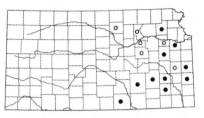

Breeding: The largest and most stable population in Kansas is at the Konza Prairie. The nest is well hidden on the ground under a grass clump that overhangs and covers the nest. It is composed of grass and lined with finer grasses. The female builds the nest alone in four or five days. The clutch is three to five creamy white eggs thickly dotted and spotted with reddish brown, chiefly at the larger end. The incubation period is about 11 days; the nestling period is nine or 10 days. Incubation is by the female alone. In some areas the species is at least semicolonial.

Habits and Habitat: Henslow's Sparrow is primarily a breeder in the northeastern United States and winters in the Gulf States. It is a very local summer resident in Kansas, but it is probably more widespread as a transient and is probably often overlooked. It is usually very secretive but has a distinctive song, a sharp "tis'-lik'" delivered from the top of a grass stem or stalk and audible only at close range. It frequently sings at night. A courting male sings to the female while holding dead grass in his bill and rapidly fluttering his wings. This species spends most of its time on the ground in dense vegetation and is a difficult species to flush and observe. In much of its range it prefers moist areas, but in others, as at Konza Prairie, it occurs in dry upland prairie.

Field Marks: The Henslow's Sparrow is a flat-headed, short-tailed sparrow resembling a dark Grasshopper Sparrow but with a more olive (often greenish) head, streaked flanks, and rusty wings. Juveniles are very similar but less distinctly marked.

Food: This species feeds on grasshoppers, crickets, beetles, caterpillars, ants, and other invertebrates and, during the nonnesting season, on seeds of a variety of grasses, sedges, and weeds.

Le Conte's Sparrow
Ammodramus leconteii (Audubon)

Status: The Le Conte's Sparrow is an uncommon transient and winter resident in eastern Kansas and is casual westward.

Period of Occurrence: Specimens have been taken between 30 September and 10 May. Most migration is during April and October. Extreme dates of transients are 20 March and 16 May and 18 September and 16 November. The

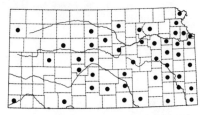

Le Conte's Sparrow winters locally in the east and extreme south.

Habits and Habitat: This species breeds in marshes and moist grasslands from central Canada south through the Great Lakes and winters from southern Missouri to the Gulf Coast. It is primarily a transient across Kansas, but small populations appear to winter regularly in the east. It is secretive and difficult to observe, so it is probably often overlooked. In Kansas the Le Conte's Sparrow occurs in a variety of grassland habitats but appears to favor "old fields" and weedy areas. It spends most of its time on or near the ground and when alarmed prefers to run along the ground under dense cover. When flushed it flies a short distance before diving back into heavy cover. The song is a short insectlike buzz delivered from under cover, from the top of a grass stem, or occasionally in flight.

Field Marks: The Le Conte's Sparrow resembles a Grasshopper Sparrow with a more contrasting face pattern—buffy or pale orange face, throat, and breast; gray ear coverts; and white median crown strip. There are also distinct dark streaks on the flanks and less distinct pinkish streaks on the nape. Juveniles are less distinctly patterned.

Food: In summer this species feeds on a variety of insects, spiders, and other small invertebrates. At other seasons food is largely seeds of grasses and weeds.

A Sharp-tailed Sparrow (*Ammodramus caudacutus*). Photograph by T. Perry for the Cornell Laboratory of Ornithology.

Sharp-tailed Sparrow
Ammodramus caudacutus (Gmelin)

Status: The status of the Sharp-tailed Sparrow in Kansas is uncertain. It is probably a rare, irregular transient through the eastern and central regions.

Period of Occurrence: Specimens have been taken between 6 and 26 October. Sight records (most unverified) are between 20 April and 8 May and between 3 September and 28 October and possibly 24 November. All sight records need

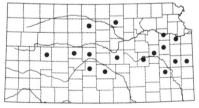

careful verification. The report by Goss (1891) of nesting in Kansas is almost certainly in error.

Habits and Habitat: The inland race breeds in freshwater marshes and meadows from central Canada to North Dakota, and some migrants cross Kansas enroute to the Gulf Coast. This race is the freshwater representative of a species that otherwise occurs in coastal salt marshes. It is very secretive, spending much of its time walking or running on the ground under vegetation and flying up only a short distance before diving again into thick vegetation. It will respond to "pishing," however. The Sharp-tailed Sparrow is rarely seen in Kansas; when seen, it is usually in or near marshes. Although not territorial on its breeding grounds, it is most easily located by its song, a high, thin trill, that is also heard during spring migration.

Field Marks: The Sharp-tailed Sparrow resembles a Le Conte's Sparrow but has a solid, dark crown, contrasting gray collar, and white dorsal streaks; it is also longer tailed.

Food: This species eats a variety of small invertebrates, including grasshoppers, beetles, caterpillars, spiders, small snails, and amphipods; it also eats seeds of grasses, sedges, and weeds.

A Fox Sparrow (*Passerella iliaca*). Photograph by Gerald J. Wiens.

Fox Sparrow
Passerella iliaca (Merrem)

Status: The Fox Sparrow is a common transient and uncommon winter resident in eastern Kansas and a rare transient and casual winter resident in the west.

Period of Occurrence: Most migrants are seen from mid-March to early May and from mid-October through mid-November. Extreme dates for transients are 3 March and 24 May and 11 October and

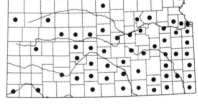

20 November. There are also reports for 28 August and 22 September. Most wintering birds are in eastern and southern Kansas.

Habits and Habitat: The Fox Sparrow breeds in central and western Canada and our intermountain west and winters along the Pacific Coast and throughout the eastern and southern United States. In Kansas it spends most of its time on the ground, usually under dense vegetation. It characteristically feeds by scratching through leaves and litter using both feet simultaneously, like a towhee. It is considered one of the finest singers among sparrows, delivering a series of clear, melodious, flutelike notes from within undergrowth.

Field Marks: Although very variable as a species, all Kansas birds are likely to be the eastern race, which is characterized by a rusty face contrasting with a gray crown and collar, rusty wings and back, and a reddishbrown tail. Fox Sparrows are sometimes confused with various thrushes, especially the Hermit Thrush. However, Fox Sparrows have short, thick bills; streaked, not spotted, underparts; and very different behavior.

Food: The Fox Sparrow feeds on beetles, flies, spiders, millipedes, and other small invertebrates as well as grass and weed seeds and small fruits such as elderberries and wild grapes.

A Song Sparrow (*Melospiza melodia*). Photograph by David A. Rintoul.

Song Sparrow
Melospiza melodia (Wilson)

Status: The Song Sparrow is a common transient statewide. It is common in winter in the east but is uncommon in the west. It is a local summer resident in the extreme northeast and is casual elsewhere during summer.

Period of Occurrence: The Song Sparrow is most common from early October through early April. Extreme dates for nonbreeding birds are

28 August and 24 May. Mid-summer sightings (21 June to mid-
July) have been reported from
Jefferson, Linn, and Phillips counties. Nesting is documented from
Wyandotte County, and according to O. Smock, it probably
"nested about 1929" near Arkansas City, Cowley County.

Breeding: In 1966 and 1967 Ted Anderson (1982) found four nests in
a willow thicket bordering the Missouri River near Walcott, Wyandotte
County. One clutch was completed on 2 May; in a second nest the first
egg hatched on 13 May. No other recent nestings are known. The nest
is typically placed on the ground under a tuft of grass or small shrub
or in a bush or low tree, usually within six feet of the ground. The nest—
a cup of grasses, weed stems, and leaves lined with fine grasses, rootlets,
and hair—is built by the female. The clutch is three to six, usually three
to five, greenish white eggs heavily dotted and blotched with reddish
brown and purple and underlain with gray. Some eggs may be so heavily marked as to appear light brown. Incubation is by the female. The
incubation period is 12 or 13 days, the fledgling period is about 10 days,
and the young can fly a few days later. The Song Sparrow is probably
two brooded in Kansas.

Habits and Habitat: The species breeds over most of North America except the Great Plains and Southeast and winters north to the central
United States. In Kansas, during migration, it prefers brushy cover near
water, woodlands, roadsides, and residential gardens. In winter it usually occurs near water. The Song Sparrow usually occurs singly or in
small, loose flocks. The song is quite variable, often beginning with three
clear notes—"sweet, sweet, sweet"—followed by a descending trill. It
is usually delivered from a bush, low tree, or similar perch.

Field Marks: This is a long-tailed sparrow streaked both above and
below and with a striped head pattern that includes a mustache mark.
The breast streaks commonly merge to form a blotch or "stickpin." Immature birds are washed with buff, show less contrast, and may lack
the breast spot. Birds from the Rockies are much grayer in color. The
Song Sparrow commonly pumps its tail in flight and has a very distinctive
call note.

Food: This sparrow's summer diet is at least half invertebrates, chiefly
beetles, grasshoppers, and caterpillars. The remainder is seeds of

grasses and weeds and wild fruits such as elderberries, blackberries, and grapes. At other seasons weed seeds predominate. Some individuals visit bird feeders and eat cracked corn and milo.

A Lincoln's Sparrow (*Melospiza lincolnii*). Photograph by Gerald J. Wiens.

Lincoln's Sparrow
Melospiza lincolnii (Audubon)

Status: The Lincoln's Sparrow is a common transient statewide. It is a rare and local winter resident.

Period of Occurrence: Most migration is from early April to early May and from mid-September through October. Extreme dates for transients are 3 March and 16 June in the spring and 5 September and 25 November in the fall.

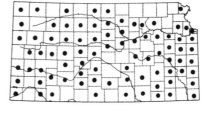

Small numbers regularly winter in eastern and southeastern Kansas and rarely elsewhere.

Habits and Habitat: The Lincoln's Sparrow breeds in Canada and much of the mountainous western United States and passes through Kansas enroute to the Gulf Coast and Central America. In Kansas it occurs most commonly in brushy habitats, especially riparian situations, and in brushy tangles in fields and woodlands. It is usually a shy species but will often respond to a "pish" by hopping into the open for a brief look, then darting back into cover. This species feeds on the ground under vegetation by scratching like a towhee—kicking backward with both feet at once. It is probably more common than many birders realize— 41 were killed at a TV tower near Topeka on 30 September 1954.

Field Marks: This is a nervous, dark sparrow with moderate-length tail and a white throat contrasting with a buffy breast band. Immatures show less contrast in markings.

Food: Food of the Lincoln's Sparrow consists of a variety of insects and seeds of weeds and grasses.

A Swamp Sparrow (*Melospiza georgiana*). Photograph by Mike Hopiak for the Cornell Laboratory of Ornithology.

Swamp Sparrow
Melospiza georgiana (Latham)

Status: The Swamp Sparrow is a common transient and uncommon winter resident in eastern Kansas. It is an uncommon to rare transient and a rare winter resident in the west.

Period of Occurrence: This species is most common from October through April, with extreme dates of 23 September and 21 May.

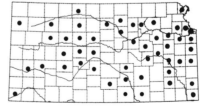

Habits and Habitat: The Swamp Sparrow breeds in marshes and swamps in the northeastern United States and much of Canada and winters throughout the eastern half of the United States. In Kansas it is most often observed in dense cover in marshy areas or in riparian habitat. In winter it is most often associated with marshy areas near open water. This sparrow does much of its feeding in shallow water, where it picks up floating insects (Terres 1980). The song, similar to that of a Chipping Sparrow but louder and more musical, is delivered from a low perch such as a cattail stalk, bush, or small tree.

Field Marks: The Swamp Sparrow resembles the Lincoln's Sparrow in behavior and a short-tailed Chipping Sparrow in general pattern. It differs from the latter in lack of wingbars, contrasting white throat, pale median crown stripe, and rusty wings. Immatures show less contrast and have the throat and upper breast unstreaked.

Food: This species feeds on a variety of invertebrates, including beetles, ants, and grasshoppers, and on seeds of grasses, weeds, and sedges.

A White-throated Sparrow (*Zonotrichia albicollis*). Photograph by Gerald J. Wiens.

White-throated Sparrow
Zonotrichia albicollis (Gmelin)

Status: The White-throated Sparrow is a common transient and uncommon winter resident in eastern Kansas and an uncommon transient and rare winter resident in the west.

Period of Occurrence: Most migration is from mid-April through early May and during October. Extreme dates for transients are 15 March and 31 May (a straggler on 6 June) and 9 September and 22 November. The White-throated Sparrow is regular in winter in eastern Kansas and occurs less regularly in the west.

Habits and Habitat: This Sparrow breeds throughout much of Canada and the northeastern United States and winters in the southeastern and south-central United States. It migrates and winters in small flocks in various shrubby situations such as woodlands, roadsides, hedgerows, shrubs in parks, and residential areas.The White-throated Sparrow sings occasionally in winter and commonly during spring migration. The song is a series of clear whistled notes almost universally described as "Old Sam Peabody, Peabody, Peabody." It feeds on the ground, where it scratches through leaf litter.

Field Marks: The White-throated Sparrow is a large, long-tailed sparrow with striking black and white or tan and white stripes on the crown, yellow lores, and a white throat that contrasts with gray upper breast. The duller immatures have dark bills.

Food: This species eats a variety of invertebrates such as beetles, flies, and ants; a wide variety of weed seeds and small fruits of dogwood, elderberries, and similar shrubs; and tree buds.

A Golden-crowned Sparrow (*Zonotrichia atricapilla*). Photograph by David A. Rintoul.

Golden-crowned Sparrow
Zonotrichia atricapilla (Gmelin)

Status: The Golden-crowned Sparrow is apparently a winter vagrant in Kansas, but we still lack verification in the form of a photograph or specimen.

Period of Occurrence: There are presently seven sight records between 1 January and 13 May for Cowley, Harvey, Morton, Pottawatomie, Russell, and Scott (two) counties.

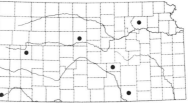

Habits and Habitat: The Golden-crowned Sparrow breeds from western Alaska south in the mountains to Washington and winters in extreme western Canada and along the Pacific slope. A few individuals straggle eastward. It forages chiefly on the ground. It is most likely to be seen in late fall at a feeder with other sparrows. Others have been reported with flocks of White-crowned Sparrows in brushy habitat in western Kansas.

Field Marks: The Golden-crowned is a large, dark, long-tailed sparrow with a dark bill and a dull yellow crown broadly bordered with black. Immatures vaguely resemble long-tailed female House Sparrows but have the crown streaked with brown and with dull yellow on the forehead.

Food: In its normal range this sparrow's food consists of a variety of insects, weed seeds, small fruits, buds, and other plant parts.

A White-crowned Sparrow (*Zonotrichia leucophrys*). Photograph by David A. Rintoul.

White-crowned Sparrow
Zonotrichia leucophrys (Forster)

Status: The White-crowned Sparrow is a common transient and winter resident, especially in the west. It is local in winter in much of the central region.

Period of Occurrence: Birds usually arrive in late September and depart by mid-May. Peak movements are late October to late November and late April to early May. Extreme dates are 16 September and 26 May.

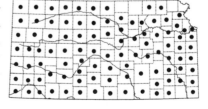

Habits and Habitat: The White-crowned Sparrow breeds in Canada, south through the mountains of the western United States; it winters throughout the central and southern United States. It is one of our most conspicuous migrants since it frequents yards and parks as well as brushy fields, woodland-edged roadsides, and riparian situations. It is locally common in winter in western Kansas in riparian habitats and hedgerows. Conversely, in most years this sparrow is absent, or winters in low numbers over large parts of the state. Its song is a series of whistles similar to that of the White-throated Sparrow, but less melodious. It feeds on the ground, vigorously scratching through leaf litter. The White-crowned Sparrow can often be induced to hop into view by imitating its song or by pishing.

Field Marks: This species has a pale pink bill and conspicuous black and white or tan and brown head stripes. The throat is gray, concolor with breast and face. Fall birds are often confused with the much smaller *Spizellas*, especially the Field Sparrow.

Food: During summer the White-crowned Sparrow eats a variety of invertebrates, including beetles, flies, caterpillars, and spiders. Seeds or various weeds and grasses are eaten throughout the year and make up the bulk of the winter diet. The birds also eat willow catkins and tree buds in spring. In winter some individuals visit feeders for "chick feed," cracked corn, and ground milo.

A Harris' Sparrow (*Zonotrichia querula*). Photograph by Bob Gress.

Harris' Sparrow
Zonotrichia querula (Nuttall)

Status: The Harris' Sparrow is a common transient and winter resident statewide but especially in the south-central region. It is least common in the far west. It is casual in summer.

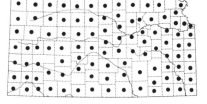

Period of Occurrence: This species usually arrives about 20 October and departs by 10 May. Extreme dates are 26 September and 9 June. There are valid summer records (17 June to 28 August) from Barton, Douglas, Riley, Russell, Sedgwick, and Sumner counties.

Habits and Habitat: The Harris' Sparrow breeds in north-central Canada, west of Hudson Bay, and winters in the Great Plains, especially in southern and eastern Kansas. Individuals regularly straggle to both coasts. Its preferred habitats are thickets along streams, woodland edges, brushy

fields, and windbreaks. Smaller numbers occur in thickets in subur-
ban areas. It is often a regular visitor to feeding stations, chiefly after
snow covers its feeding areas. Much of this sparrow's feeding is on the
ground, often in patches of annual weeds such as sunflowers. At such
times birds converse with each other. In spring they commonly sing a
melodious series of simple, clear whistles. Individuals respond to imi-
tations of the song by hopping into the tops of shrubs or low trees, where
they can be easily observed.

This is one of the most common wintering sparrows in south-central Kansas. On several occasions the Udall-Winfield Christmas Count
has had the highest total in the nation. Individuals typically return to
the same wintering area in successive years.

Field Marks: The adult is a large, long-tailed sparrow with bright pink
bill and black face and throat. The face is brown during fall and winter and gray during spring. Immatures lack the black face and throat
but share the pink bill and heavy black streaking on the flanks.

Food: While in Kansas the food of the Harris' Sparrow is chiefly seeds
of weeds, grasses, and waste grain. In summer it takes a variety of insects. Individuals visit feeding stations regularly for small grains, millet, bread crumbs, and suet.

A Dark-eyed Junco (*Junco hyemalis*). Photograph by Bob Gress.

Dark-eyed Junco
Junco hyemalis (Linnaeus)

Status: The Dark-eyed Junco is a common transient and winter resident statewide.

Period of Occurrence: Fall arrival is usually in late September with spring departure by mid-April. Extreme dates are 13 September and 3 May, with stragglers to 13 May. A report for 27 August is very unusual.

Slate-colored Junco

Habits and Habitat: As a species, the Dark-eyed Junco breeds in boreal

and mountainous coniferous
forests throughout North America. It winters throughout southern Canada and the United States.
The various races of Dark-eyed
Junco are similar in habits and
frequently occur in mixed flocks
during winter and possibly during migration. "Oregon" juncos
predominate westward; "slate-colored" juncos eastward, together
with great numbers of individuals that cannot be identified in
the field. Easier to identify are the
"white-winged" and "pink-sided"
races, which winter primarily in
the west, and the rarer "gray-
headed" race that has been reported nearly statewide.

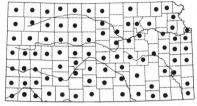

Oregon Junco

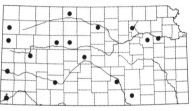

White-winged Junco

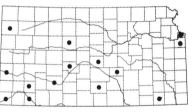

Gray-headed Junco

Juncos occur in small flocks in
various brushy habitats from riparian growth and woodland edge
to parks and gardens. Individuals
frequently visit feeding stations,
and the junco or "snowbird" is one of our most frequently recognized
winter birds. Juncos tend to arrive at a feeder very early in the morning and late in the evening and usually feed on the ground, picking
up small food items discarded by other birds. Like many sparrows they
visit feeders most frequently during periods of snow cover. While feeding, a junco frequently flicks its tail, flashing the white outer tail feathers, probably in a type of aggressive display. In late spring males sing
from a tree or other perch. The song is a long trill similar to that of a
Chipping Sparrow but often more musical. It is interesting that a number of hybrids between the "slate-colored" junco and the White-throated
Sparrow are known.

Field Marks: Members of this highly variable species can be recognized
by their white or pink bills, unstreaked backs, white bellies, and conspicuous white outer tail feathers. Males and well-marked females of
the five races occurring in Kansas can be identified in the field: "slate-
colored"—slate to black hood and flanks; "Oregon"—black hood and
brown back and flanks; "pink-sided"—gray hood, black lores, and pink
sides; "white-winged"—very pale gray overall, including sides, and

white wing bars; "gray-headed"—gray hood and sides and reddish back.

Food: The Dark-eyed Junco eats a variety of insects, such as caterpillars, beetles, and bugs, and other invertebrates during the nesting season. At other seasons it feeds primarily on seeds of grasses; annual weeds including pigweed, ragweed, and lambsquarters; and waste grain. Individuals commonly visit feeders for cracked corn, crushed milo, and small seeds.

A McCown's Longspur (*Calcarius mccownii*). Photograph by Roger Boyd.

McCown's Longspur
Calcarius mccownii (Lawrence)

Status: The McCown's Longspur is probably an uncommon to rare transient and sporadic (sometimes abundant) winter resident in the west. It is casual in the east.

Period of Occurrence: Specimen records are from 7 to 22 October and 5 December to 3 April. Most recent sight records are during mid- to late October and between late December and early March. Extreme dates are 7 September and 31 May.

Habits and Habitat: The McCown's Longspur breeds on the northern

Great Plains south to Colorado and winters from Arizona and Oklahoma into northern Mexico. Its breeding range (and perhaps total numbers) have decreased considerably since settlement of the plains. It prefers short-grass 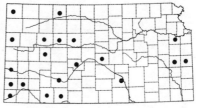 prairies and overgrazed rangeland. During migration it usually occurs in pure flocks, but in winter this species may occur with Lapland Longspurs and less often with Chestnut-collared Longspurs. When feeding, birds are often scattered, and individuals may crouch motionless until approached very closely. On the breeding grounds males fly 20 to 30 feet into the air and deliver a beautiful flight song while parachuting back to earth. Courting birds often lift their wings, thus flashing the contrasting white linings.

Field Marks: This is our palest longspur. The male in breeding plumage is unmistakable with its gray head and black crown and chest. Winter males and females can be identified by the rufous on the shoulders (not wing coverts) and extensive white in the tail. The flight calls are a "kittip," a "dick," and a rattle similar to that of the Lapland Longspur.

Food: Food of this species, at all seasons, is primarily seeds of weeds and grasses but includes insects such as grasshoppers, beetles, and caterpillars in summer.

A Lapland Longspur (*Calcarius lapponicus*). Photograph by David A. Rintoul.

Lapland Longspur
Calcarius lapponicus (Linnaeus)

Status: The Lapland Longspur is a common to abundant transient and winter resident in western and central Kansas. It is uncommon to common and often an erratic transient and winter visitant in the east.

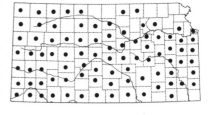

Period of Occurrence: The Lapland Longspur is usually reported from late October or early November to mid-March. Extreme dates are 2 October and 17 April.

Habits and Habitat: In North America this species breeds on the tundra of far northern Alaska and Canada and winters primarily on the Great Plains. This is the most abundant and widespread longspur in

Kansas. In central and western Kansas flocks of tens of thousands are common during most years in irrigated cropland and stubble fields. Prairies and wheat fields are also utilized. In some years the species is so abundant that flocks may literally cover many acres, and hundreds of thousands can be seen in an hour. In open country distant flocks resemble the heat waves of summer, and Ely is certain that he has observed more than a million birds in one day.

During winter large overhead movements can often be heard during nighttime snow storms. During periods of heavy snowfall large flocks may concentrate along recently cleared roads, and many are killed by passing traffic. This is often the best look one gets at a longspur. In earlier times flocks were reported to enter towns during blizzards. On one such occasion Imler (1937) picked up 40 dead and injured birds from the streets of Stockton, Rooks County. Local concentrations depend on local conditions and the extent of snow farther north. The erratic movements of this species were described by Orville Rice ("Woods" 1976) during an invasion of the Kaw River valley near Topeka during the winter of 1970–71. Two hundred were noted on 26 December, and there were thousands, perhaps even millions, present by 23 January; yet two days later not a single bird could be found.

In Kansas the Lapland Longspur usually occurs in huge flocks that walk about under vegetation seeking seeds. When flushed, the birds depart in tight flocks that often form great sweeping circles. When present in small numbers, it is often seen in flocks of other longspurs or Horned Larks.

Large numbers are sometimes destroyed by the natural disasters of the Great Plains. Terres (1948) described the widespread mortality over a three-state area on the night of 13–14 March 1904. Migrating flocks met inclement weather (sticky snow) and were forced down, often crashing into the ground. As many as five million may have perished on that one night. In Minnesota an estimated 750,000 birds were present on the exposed surface of two frozen lakes only two square miles in area, with comparable densities over surrounding areas, including rooftops and streets. Large numbers of injured birds were reported for the next two weeks. This and similar catastrophes seem to have no long-term effect on the total population.

Field Marks: In flight longspurs differ from Horned Larks in their chunkier build, bouncy flight, and call notes. The male of this species is unmistakable in breeding plumage, with its black face and throat and chestnut nape. The female and winter male have a buffy face with darker ear patch, chestnut on nape, and rufous wing coverts. Novice birders often confuse these with Chestnut-collared Longspurs because of the prominent chestnut collar. However, male Laplands usually show some black on the upper chest or face, and both sexes show very little white in the tail. The usual flight call is a three-note rattle "trididit" or a descending "teeer."

Food: In summer the Lapland Longspur eats a variety of small invertebrates, including beetles, flies, caterpillars, and spiders. Large amounts of grass seeds and weed seeds are eaten at all seasons, and seeds of pigweed, ragweed, and grasses such as the foxtails and waste grain are major items during winter.

A Smith's Longspur *(Calcarius pictus)*. Photograph by Mary Tremaine for the Cornell Laboratory of Ornithology.

Smith's Longspur
Calcarius pictus (Swainson)

Status: The Smith's Longspur is an uncommon transient and rare local winter resident, principally in the Flint Hills. Many sight records, especially in the west, need verification.

Period of Occurrence: The actual status of the Smith's Longspur in much of Kansas is uncertain. Specimens have been taken between 5 November and 23 April. Most sightings are during November and from early March through 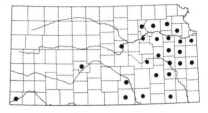 mid-April, with extreme dates of 9 October and 23 April. There is also a sighting for 26 September (Geary County).

Habits and Habitat: Although the Smith's Longspur was considered "common" to "fairly common" by authors as recent as Tordoff (1956), the number of sightings does not support this. For example, there were only five sightings in 25 years in Shawnee County ("Woods" 1976). The species breeds near tree line from central Alaska to north-central Canada and winters chiefly in the southern Great Plains. It is said to prefer short grass, and in some states it seems partial to grassy fields at airports. In Kansas it is most often recorded from pastures in the Flint Hills. This is the least known of our four longspurs and may be overlooked. Except on Christmas Bird Counts it is reported most regularly from Lyon, Coffey, Chase, Cowley, and Douglas counties.

The Smith's Longspur usually occurs in small flocks during migration and has been reported in flocks of mixed longspurs in winter. Birds are most easily found by their call notes, uttered both on the ground and while in flight. Birds scatter widely while feeding and are often difficult to flush. Wetmore (*in* Bent 1968), in describing the activity of a flock in close-cropped pasture near Independence, noted that birds sat so closely and were so well camouflaged that he could pass within a dozen feet without seeing them. Unless disturbed repeatedly, individuals usually fly only a short distance with a zigzag flight and then drop back into the vegetation.

Field Marks: The male in breeding plumage is unmistakable, with his black and white face pattern and clear buffy underparts. Females and winter males are buffy below with faint streaks and often have white on the shoulders. They are easily confused with comparably plumaged Chestnut-collared Longspurs, which are paler above with much more white in the tail. Smith's also has a blackish crown and back (the feathers edged with paler color) and a vague ear patch, and the abdomen is concolor with the breast. The flight call is a dry rattle or series of clicking notes.

Food: The food of this species is not well known but includes seeds of grasses, sedges, and weeds at all seasons and presumably beetles, caterpillars, spiders, and other small invertebrates during summer.

A Chestnut-collared Longspur (*Calcarius ornatus*). Photograph by M. and B. Schwarzschild for the Cornell Laboratory of Ornithology.

Chestnut-collared Longspur
Calcarius ornatus (Townsend)

Status: The Chestnut-collared Longspur is an uncommon transient and winter resident in central and western Kansas and is rare and sporadic in the east. Sight records need confirmation as it is often confused with the Lapland Longspur. The Chestnut-collared Longspur formerly nested in Ellis County and probably elsewhere on the western plains.

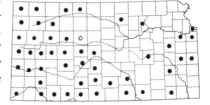

Period of Occurrence: This species is most common during migration, usually mid-October to early November and March through mid-April. Some flocks remain into mid-winter, and some may actually winter. Extreme dates are 27 September and 27 April.

Habits and Habitat: The Chestnut-collared Longspur breeds in the northern Great Plains south to northeastern Colorado and Nebraska and winters on the southern Great Plains west to Arizona. Its breeding range has been greatly reduced by the plowing and overgrazing of native prairie. It is said to prefer taller vegetation than other longspurs and in central Kansas definitely prefers native grassland during migration. During winter this species has been reported from flocks of mixed longspurs in a variety of habitats, including stubble fields, young wheat fields, and fallow fields. It may possibly roost in grassland and visit other areas for feeding. It is likely that many winter reports are of Lapland Longspurs. In migration the Chestnut-collared Longspur usually occurs in small flocks, but Scott Seltman reported a flock of 500 on 17 March. The Grabers reported "large flocks" in southwestern Kansas in spring between 28 February and 23 April.

The species was locally common and nesting near Fort Hays, Ellis County, in 1871. Allen (1872) reported they "were only met with on the high ridges and dry plateaus, where they seemed to live somewhat in colonies. At a few localities they were always numerous, but elsewhere were often not met with in a whole day's drive." He collected a series of adults and at least three clutches of eggs. On the breeding grounds the male has a delightful flight song uttered while flying upward and then descending with rapidly beating wings.

Field Marks: The male in breeding plumage is unmistakable, with its rusty collar, buffy throat, and extensive black underparts. Females and winter males are buffy below, usually with a rusty nape. During spring migration males usually show some black on the underparts. The flight call is very distinctive—"til'-lip" or "cheedlup"—and both sexes show much white in the tail.

Food: Food of the Chestnut-collared Longspur is insects and a variety of weed seeds and waste grain.

Snow Buntings (*Plectrophenax nivalis*). Photograph by L. Page Brown for the Cornell Laboratory of Ornithology.

Snow Bunting
Plectrophenax nivalis (Linnaeus)

Status: The Snow Bunting is a rare and irregular winter visitor, especially in central and eastern Kansas.

Period of Occurrence: The Snow Bunting was considered very rare and sporadic in occurrence prior to about 1965. Since then the number and frequency of sightings have increased dramatically, usually near our larger reservoirs.

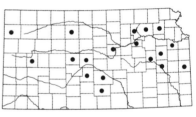

The increase probably reflects both an increased effort by observers and increase in habitat. Sight records have been from 2 November through 19 February.

Habits and Habitat: Formerly considered one of our rarest winter visitors (several sightings and *no* specimens between 1879 and 1965), a few Snow Buntings may now be expected during most winters. In Kansas most birds have been seen in bare areas near large reservoirs, even on parking lots. It is a bird of open country and even roosts on the ground, sometimes in soft snow. Occasionally one or more is found in a flock of longspurs or Horned Larks.

In the northern states the species often arrives with winter storms and occurs in large flocks in open areas. Flocks swirl from field to field, and the early vernacular name, "snowflake," is very descriptive. It is attracted to recently manured fields, where it feeds on weedseeds and waste grain. In the northeastern United States flocks also frequent ocean beaches, lake margins, and salt marshes. This is the most northerly breeding song bird in North America.

Field Marks: Winter birds are largely white but with buff edges to the feathers of head, sides, and upperparts. In flight this species also shows large white wing patches and white in the tail and appears completely white from below. The call is a short descending whistle.

Food: Summer food of the Snow Bunting includes beetles, caterpillars, true bugs, flies, and spiders. At all seasons it feeds on seeds of grasses, sedges, and such weeds as smartweed, ragweed, and pigweed.

A Bobolink (*Dolichonyx oryzivorus*). Photograph by O. S. Pettingill for the Cornell Laboratory of Ornithology.

BLACKBIRDS AND ORIOLES
(FAMILY EMBERIZIDAE, SUBFAMILY ICTERINAE)
Bobolink
Dolichonyx oryzivorus (Linnaeus)

Status: The Bobolink is an irregular transient and summer resident in eastern and central Kansas. It is casual westward, where it may possibly breed very locally. Nesting has been confirmed from Barton, Cloud, and Stafford counties.

Period of Occurrence: Most spring migration dates fall within the period 2 to 20 May. The fall migration is poorly documented, with

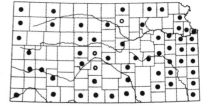

dates from 15 August to 13 October. Extreme dates are 2 April and 13 October.

Breeding: The Bobolink nests in southern Canada and the northern United States, south to eastern Oregon, Kansas, and West Virginia. It winters in southern South America. In Kansas nesting is restricted to dense, moist grassland. Males are not strongly territorial, but nests are usually spread out over the nesting area. The nest, in a shallow depression on the ground and extremely well hidden, is a loose cup of weed stems and grass and is lined with fine grasses. The adult typically alights some distance from the nest and approaches it on the ground, masking the location of the nest even more. The clutch is four to seven, usually five or six, eggs with a pale gray or buff ground color almost completely obscured by brown splotches and spots. Only the female incubates, but the male assists in feeding the young. The incubation period is 13 days, and young leave the nest in seven to 14 days, often before they can fly. There is a single brood.

Habits and Habitat: Bobolinks prefer tall grasslands such as wet meadows, hayfields, and moist tall-grass prairie. Migrants frequently visit alfalfa fields. Early in the nesting season males are very conspicuous as they utter their flight songs or sing from tall perches. The song, a bubbling, tinkling warble with notes tumbling over the previous ones, defies description. By July males cease singing, soon molt, and become inconspicuous. During the late nineteenth and early twentieth centuries huge flocks of southbound migrants ravaged southern rice fields, earning them the name "ricebird." Birds became very fat, and thousands were killed as game birds under the name "reedbird." Before departing, our birds congregate in marshy and reedy areas and are usually overlooked. Most migration is to the east of Kansas.

Field Marks: The male is uniquely patterned. The female, immatures, and fall males are buffy with streaked upperparts, striped heads, and strongly pointed tail feathers. The call note in fall is a metallic "pink" that can often be heard at night as migrants pass overhead.

Food: In summer this species feeds primarily on beetles, grasshoppers, caterpillars, and other small invertebrates and on seeds of various grasses and weeds. At other seasons it feeds primarily on domestic and wild grains and on weed and grass seeds.

A Red-winged Blackbird (*Agelaius phoeniceus*). Photograph by Bob Gress.

Red-winged Blackbird
Agelaius phoeniceus (Linnaeus)

Status: The Red-winged Blackbird is a common transient and summer resident statewide. It is a locally abundant winter resident.

Period of Occurrence: This bird is regularly reported in all months. Non-wintering birds are reported most regularly between late February and early November. In Ellis County males are on territory in mid-March, and females join them by mid-April. Immatures are already forming roosting flocks by late June or early July.

Breeding: Nests are placed in a variety of situations—often in loose colonies—in marshes, roadside ditches, brushy fields, and wheat fields and along streams in any type of habitat. Nests are usually built within three feet of the ground but may be as high as 12 to 17 feet in trees. In wheat fields nests are usually placed in a weed such as dock or mustard. The nest is usually bound to the surrounding vegetation and consists of sedges, rushes, grasses or cattail leaves, rootlets, and plant fibers woven together and lined with fine grasses. The female builds and incubates. The male is usually polygamous with two or three females. The clutch is three to five, usually four, pale greenish blue eggs that are spotted, blotched, and scrawled with brown, purple, and black, chiefly at the larger end. The incubation period is 10 or 11 days. Some individuals are double brooded. Young leave the nest in about 10 days and clamber about in nearby vegetation for several days until able to fly.

Habits and Habitat: The Red-wing breeds throughout most of North America, including the Mexican highlands. Northern birds winter in the southern part of the range. The male, with his yellow-bordered red "epaulets," is one of our best-known birds, but casual observers frequently confuse females and immatures with "sparrows." The arrival of individual males in wet areas where they erect and display their red shoulders and give their "konk-la-reee" song is a sign that spring is fast approaching. Nonbreeding males and females are still in large flocks at this time. A common sight in late spring is of a hawk or crow flying over a colony hotly pursued by a succession of Red-wings.

This is one of the most abundant songbirds in North America, and in winter huge numbers congregate (often with other species of blackbirds) at certain roosting sites. One roost in the Dismal Swamp, Virginia, held an estimated 15 million individuals (Terres 1980). The winter flock at Cheyenne Bottoms has been conservatively estimated at 3.5 million birds during some winters. As dusk approaches, long more or less continuous streams of birds converge on the roost site. They typically assemble in nearby trees and then drop into the cattails before dusk. When approached the birds leave with a roar of wings, and one can feel the warmth of their collective bodies. One also notes the mass of feces and feathers on the ground. Natural predators are as attracted to such assemblages as are birders. Less spectacular, but more of a nuisance, are the postbreeding assemblages of blackbirds in general that form in towns in late summer. Large flocks of Red-wings and other blackbirds feed in grain fields, feedlots, pastures, and freshly planted fields.

Field Marks: The red epaulets of the male are conspicuous during display but at other times may be largely hidden. The female and immatures are brown and heavily streaked and have pointed beaks. There is usually a trace of pink on the throat (females) or a hint of red on the shoulders (young males). The call note, a sharp "chack," is usually distinctive.

Food: During the nesting season the birds consume much invertebrate food, including the nymphs and adults of aquatic insects (mayflies, dragon flies), caterpillars, grasshoppers, beetle larvae, spiders, and snails. At other seasons plant food dominates, including weed seeds, waste grain, small fruits, and berries. A few visit feeding stations.

An Eastern Meadowlark (*Sturnella magna*). Photograph by David A. Rintoul.

Eastern Meadowlark
Sturnella magna (Linnaeus)

Status: The Eastern Meadowlark is a common transient and widespread summer resident in and east of the Flint Hills. West of the Flint Hills it follows humid grasslands along major rivers to at least Jewell, Lincoln, and Gray counties. It occurs casually westward and may breed occasionally west of this line.

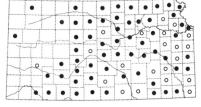

Period of Occurrence: The Eastern Meadowlark occurs all year at most localities, but there seems to be a turnover of individuals. Information on migration periods is currently unavailable for most of Kansas. In Shawnee County the spring migration begins in February, and summer flocks are forming by early August ("Woods" 1976). Sight records of nonsinging birds are unreliable.

Breeding: The nest is in a depression in the ground, usually near a grass clump or forb and often arched over to form a dome. Dead grass is often interwoven with the covering vegetation, concealing the nest even more. It is built of grass lined with finer grasses and typically has an opening on one side. The clutch is two to six, usually four or five, white eggs with brown and lavender spots and blotches, concentrated at the larger end. Nest building and incubation are by the female alone. The incubation period is 13 to 15 days, but some females begin incubating before the clutch is complete. The nestling period is 11 or 12 days. The species is two brooded in Kansas.

Habits and Habitat: The Eastern Meadowlark is primarily a species of tall-grass prairie, moist meadows, and fields of small grains. In central Kansas it is possible to hear both easterns and westerns singing in the same field, but farther west easterns are typically restricted to moist situations such as below impoundments, along rivers, and in subirrigated grasslands. At Cheyenne Bottoms, for example, easterns occur in the bottoms proper but are replaced by westerns on the rim. The Eastern Meadowlark has expanded its range westward since about 1950 and is probably still expanding (Rohwer 1972).

Meadowlarks are truly grassland species at all seasons. The Eastern Meadowlark typically feeds on the ground, walking about while probing with its beak, scratching with its feet, and picking seeds and insects from standing vegetation. The brilliant yellow breast is prominently displayed during courtship, but often when alarmed the bird turns its back on the observer and only the flashing of the white outer tail feathers and the sharp alarm chatter are noted. The song, though less complex than that of the western, is quite variable. Saunders (*in* Bent 1958) once recorded 53 different songs (variations) in less than an hour. Singing may be heard on warm, sunny days in mid-winter.

Field Marks: The two meadowlarks are very similar in appearance. In fact there is more seasonal difference in plumage within either species than between the two species. The Eastern Meadowlark is best recognized by song, a whistled "spring-of-the-yeear." The cheek is completely gray, and the horizontal black bars on the tail feathers meet along the midrib.

Food: About three-fourths of the food of this species is caterpillars (especially cutworms), beetles (including larvae), grasshoppers, spiders, and other invertebrates. In New York State one was reported feeding on a freshly road-killed, smashed carcass of a meadowlark (Terres 1956). The plant food includes barnyard grass, smartweed, ragweed, waste grain, and occasionally fruits and berries.

A Western Meadowlark (*Sturnella neglecta*). Photograph by Bob Gress.

Western Meadowlark
Sturnella neglecta Audubon

Status: The Western Meadowlark is a common transient and summer resident in western Kansas east to the western edge of the Flint Hills. It breeds eastward regularly to at least Clay, Geary, and Reno counties, and individuals are present in summer farther east, chiefly in drier uplands. It is common to uncommon in winter in the west, and its exact status in eastern

Kansas is uncertain. The two species (identified by song types) occur in the same fields at the western edge of the Flint Hills, but farther west separation is usually ecological. A current review of meadowlark distribution in Kansas is needed.

Period of Occurrence: The Western Meadowlark breeds chiefly in the central and western United States but has been expanding its range to the north and east since the beginning of the century. In Kansas it is reported during all months, but sightings of nonsinging birds are unreliable. Wintering birds move southward and probably also east of the breeding range. The extent and periods of migration in Kansas are unclear.

Breeding: The nesting habits, nest, and eggs of this species are identical to those of the Eastern Meadowlark. See that account.

Habits and Habitat: The Western Meadowlark was elected the state bird of Kansas by school children in 1925 by a 40 percent vote. Second and third places went to the Bobwhite and Northern Cardinal respectively (Bergman *in* Goodrich 1946).

The Western Meadowlark occurs in all grassland habitats in the western four-fifths of Kansas but is most numerous in native grassland. Where it overlaps with the Eastern Meadowlark, the western species usually occurs in drier areas, and very little inbreeding between the two species has been documented. During heavy snows many birds move to farmyards, where they feed among cattle and roost in buildings or among hay bales. During particularly severe storms many are killed at such locations. Males sing from perches and also have a very different flight song that is given less frequently. The song, one of the most characteristic sounds of the western prairie, was described by Bent (1968) as having "the flute-like quality of the Wood Thrush with the rich melody of the Baltimore [Northern] Oriole."

The habits of the Western Meadowlark are very similar to those of the Eastern Meadowlark. Ely once watched one that was carrying a choice morsel (unfortunately unidentified) repeatedly drop it while capturing and eating other food, then reclaim the item while it continued foraging. After several minutes the bird flew out of view with the item. Unusual behavior was exhibited by a very spectacular albino that he flushed in Morton County. It dropped to the grass, ran 20 to 30 yards in a circuitous route, and when closely approached, flushed suddenly from an unexpected direction. After a short flight it again dropped to the ground and disappeared. This was repeated several times until Ely lost the bird completely. It was a glistening white bird in vegetation less than knee high! Creighton and Porter (1974) noted three incidents of nest molestation by Western Meadowlarks, including the eating of eggs in a Horned Lark nest. This appeared to be a response to an unexpected food supply but may occur more frequently than we realize.

Field Marks: This species is best recognized by song—a series of bubbling, flutelike notes, speeding up at the end. Westerns are usually paler; the yellow of the throat extends up onto the cheek, and the black horizontal bars on the tail are separated by brown.

Food: The insect food of this species includes grasshoppers, caterpillars (especially cutworms), and beetles.

A Yellow-headed Blackbird (*Xanthocephalus xanthocephalus*). Photograph by Frank S. Shipley.

Yellow-headed Blackbird
Xanthocephalus xanthocephalus (Bonaparte)

Status: The Yellow-headed Blackbird is a common transient and local summer resident in western and central Kansas. It is casual eastward and may nest sporadically wherever it occurs. There are large nesting colonies east to Barton and Republic counties. A few winter, often in flocks of other blackbirds, in central and southern Kansas.

Period of Occurrence: Transients are most frequent from mid-April to mid-May and during September. Extreme dates are 2 March and 6 November.

Breeding: The Yellow-headed Blackbird breeds in the central and western United States, Canada, and Mexico from Oregon and southern Ontario to Baja California, northern Texas, and northwestern Ohio; it breeds casually eastward. It winters chiefly in the Southwest and western Mexico. This species typically nests in large colonies in cattail marshes, but small colonies and even single nestings have been reported in Kansas. All nests have been in cattails, usually over water, and within three feet of the water. It is a bulky structure of water-soaked leaves of cattails, grass, or 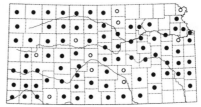 strips of narrow vegetation, typically anchored to the surrounding vegetation. It is lined with narrow and finer strips of similar vegetation. Females often start several nests before completing one. The clutch is three to six, usually four, pale grayish white or greenish white eggs profusely dotted and blotched with brown and gray. Incubation is by the female alone and lasts 12 or 13 days; the nestling period is nine to 12 days, but birds are unable to fly for an additional eight to 12 days. The species is single brooded. Males are often polygynous, having two or three females, but participate in brood care more than do male Red-wings.

Habits and Habitat: At Cheyenne Bottoms, where the Yellow-headed Blackbird occurs with Red-wings, it typically nests over deeper water than do Red-wings. The Yellow-headed Blackbird feeds among aquatic plants near water level and along shorelines as well as in drier environments such as pastures. It also follows machinery preparing fields, accompanies grazing cattle, and visits feedlots and barnyards with cowbirds and other blackbirds. Whether walking on the ground or in flight, this species tends to move slowly in a deliberate manner. It can, however, be very noisy and sometimes pugnacious in defense of its nest or recently fledged young. Like the Red-winged Blackbird, males defend their territories from cattail stalks and low trees. The song is an unmusical series of notes followed by a squawk, described as "klee, klee, klee, ko-kow-w-w" by Terres (1980). During the nonbreeding season, males occur in flocks seperate from those of females and immatures. In spring flocks of males typically precede those of females and young males.

Field Marks: The breeding male is unmistakable; immature males show some yellow on the head and usually white on the wing. The much smaller female is brown with yellow or buff on the face and white stripes on the belly.

Food: Food of this species is about one-third animal material such as beetles, caterpillars (including cutworms), dragonflies, aquatic insects, spiders, and snails. Its plant food includes seeds of numerous grasses and weeds (especially smartweeds) and grain.

A Rusty Blackbird (*Euphagus carolinus*). Photograph by Bob Gress.

Rusty Blackbird
Euphagus carolinus (Muller)

Status: The Rusty Blackbird is an uncommon transient and local winter resident, especially in the east.

Period of Occurrence: Specimen records are from 31 October to 28 December and 4 February to 17 April. Extreme dates, including sight records, are 13 September and 5 May. Sight records need verification because of confusion 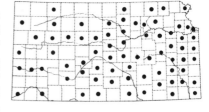 with the Brewer's Blackbird and even the Common Grackle (during period of tail molt).

Habits and Habitat: The Rusty Blackbird breeds in wooded areas of Alaska, Canada, and the extreme northeastern United States. Most birds winter east of the Rockies to the Gulf Coast and Atlantic seaboard. Most migration occurs east of Kansas. Transients and wintering birds prefer wooded thickets along streams and often occur in pure flocks. These flocks are often very noisy, expressing a variety of chuckles, squeals, and whistles together with the usual call, a low "chuck." In western Kansas wintering flocks frequently return to the same favorable sites (often near water) in subsequent winters. Such flocks are quieter and less active than are flocks of most blackbirds. This species feeds on the ground as do other blackbirds. One very striking individual observed in western Kansas had symmetrical white wing patches and a white back.

Field Marks: Fall birds have broad rusty tips to most feathers, and both sexes have yellow eyes. By spring the rusty tips have worn off, and males are black with a greenish gloss to the head; females resemble the Brewer's but are grayer (slate-colored) with yellow eyes.

Food: In summer this blackbird eats beetles, caterpillars, grasshoppers, crustaceans, snails, and other invertebrates and sometimes salamanders and small fish. Weed seeds, grain, berries, and fruit are eaten at all seasons.

A Brewer's Blackbird (*Euphagus cyanocephalus*). Photograph by Bob Gress.

Brewer's Blackbird
Euphagus cyanocephalus (Wagler)

Status: The Brewer's Blackbird is an uncommon transient and local winter resident.

Period of Occurrence: Specimens have been taken from 5 October to 28 November, on 3 January and 2 February, and from 25 March to 9 May. Extreme dates, including sight records, are 8 September and 28 May. Most transients pass

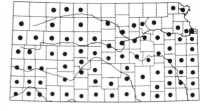

through from mid-March to early April and from mid- to late October, but flocks have been seen during June in Mitchell (200 birds, E. and E. Lewis) and Stafford counties. Sight records need verification because of confusion with the Rusty Blackbird and even the Common Grackle.

Habits and Habitat: The Brewer's Blackbird breeds across southern

Canada and the western United States east to Texas, Nebraska, and Michigan. Most winter in the western United States and from Kansas and the Gulf states into Mexico. This is one of the species expanding its range northward and eastward with the increase in cultivated land, pasture, and irrigated land. There are scattered populations in the Great Plains, including reported breeding in the Oklahoma Panhandle and eastern Colorado, and the species may someday start nesting in western Kansas. It nests in loose colonies, preferring grasslands with scattered trees (often near water), residential areas, and marshes. During migration it often occurs in large flocks in open country, and during winter many frequent farmyards with other blackbirds. The call note is a hoarse "check!" This blackbird feeds on the ground, often in large flocks in cultivated fields and pastures, and is often observed following farm machinery preparing fields.

Field Marks: The male is black, often with a purplish gloss on the head and a greenish gloss to the body, and has yellow eyes. The female is medium gray with dark eyes.

Food: The Brewer's Blackbird's animal food includes beetles, grasshoppers, true bugs, caterpillars, and other invertebrates. It also eats weed seeds, waste grain (especially oats), and fruit, including cherries.

A Great-tailed Grackle (*Quiscalus mexicanus*). Photograph by David A. Rintoul.

Great-tailed Grackle
Quiscalus mexicanus (Gmelin)

Status: The Great-tailed Grackle is a recent immigrant from the south. It was first seen in Kansas in 1963, and the first reported nesting was in 1969. It is now widespread (but often local) through the central part of state and is casual elsewhere. It breeds chiefly in central and southern Kansas. It winters regularly at Cheyenne Bottoms and in the Wichita area and casually elsewhere.

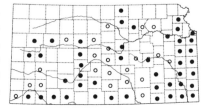

Period of Occurrence: The Great-tailed Grackle has been reported all months but most frequently from 23 April to early August.

Breeding: Most Kansas nests have been in small groves of trees in wind-breaks, around buildings, or along highways, often some distance from water. Most were 10 to 20 feet above ground. The nest has a loose but bulky foundation of twigs and weed stems surrounding a cup of grasses or rushes and mud that is lined with finer vegetation. The clutch is two to five, usually three, light blue or bluish gray eggs strongly spotted or scrawled with brown, gray, purple, and black. Incubation is by the female and may begin before the clutch is complete. Males may be polygynous. The species is single brooded in Kansas.

Habits and Habitat: Colonization of this species of Kansas has been rapid. The first report was on 6 August 1963 in Harvey County (Dwight Platt); the second in early April 1964 near Sedan, Chautauqua County (John C. Humphrey). Successful nesting was reported in 1969 in Barton and Sedgwick counties. By 1971 (Schwilling 1971) colonies were established near Cheyenne Bottoms, at Wichita, and at Haven (Reno County), and birds were present at two future nest sites, near Dodge City and near Russell. The species now nests north to at least Finney, Trego (since 1982), Mitchell, Pottawatomie, and Douglas counties. It has bred in south-central Nebraska since 1977. In Kansas, most nesting colonies are in parklike areas such as pumping stations, industrial sites, and roadside rest stops. Flocks of 200 to 400 birds have wintered at Wichita and Cheyenne Bottoms in recent years.

The Great-tailed Grackle is a very noisy species, especially at roosts and in the nesting colonies. The male calls from the top of a tree or other perch, giving a variety of whistles, squawks, and guttural sounds. It feeds by walking on the ground, with tail held high, while it probes the earth, flips leaves, and gleans insects from the ground surface and low vegetation. It prefers marshes, mudflats, and shallow pools but feeds as well on lawns and in newly worked fields.

Field Marks: The Great-tailed Grackle is noticeably large for a blackbird, with strong sexual dimorphism. The male is black with an extremely large tail that is most noticeable when the bird is walking on the ground or in flight. The female is much smaller and is dark brown with a lighter line over the eye and a lighter-colored throat.

Food: The Great-tailed Grackle is omnivorous. It eats a great deal of animal food—from grasshoppers, caterpillars, beetle larvae, and other insects to crawfish, small fish, tadpoles, birds' eggs, young birds, small snakes, and even mice. Plant food, taken primarily in winter, includes grain, small fruits, and berries.

A Common Grackle (*Quiscalus quiscula*). Photograph by Bob Gress.

Common Grackle
Quiscalus quiscula (Linnaeus)

Status: The Common Grackle is a common transient and summer resident and local winter resident statewide. It is most common in eastern Kansas.

Period of Occurrence: There are sight records from all months, but this grackle is most regular between 12 March and 14 November. In Ellis

County males usually arrive by mid-March, pairing occurs by early April, and roosting flocks form by early July. Large flocks pass through from early October to mid-November.

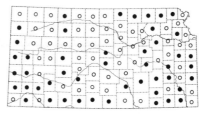

Breeding: The Common Grackle breeds in North America east of the Rockies from central Canada southward and winters chiefly from the Great Lakes to the Gulf. It often nests in small, loose colonies. In Kansas, windbreaks, ornamental plantings (especially conifers), and roadside parks are favorite sites. Nests are usually placed in a tree crotch or fork from seven to 35 feet above ground. In some areas the species nests in tree cavities. Unusual nest sites include the exterior of Osprey nests and a beaver lodge. The nest is a,bulky mass of weed stems and grass with a mud cup and lined with finer grasses. The clutch is three to six, usually five, pale greenish to buffy eggs blotched, scrawled, and spotted with brown, black, and purple. Most nest building and incubation is by the female. The incubation period is 11 or 12 days; the nestling period is 11 to 13 days. It is probably single brooded in Kansas.

Habits and Habitat: The Common Grackle is a sociable bird and occurs in flocks during much of the year. Early in the nesting season many nonincubating birds still return to communal roosts. After the breeding season flocks frequently gather in shade trees in towns and become a nuisance. In the control process that frequently follows not only grackles but also their companions (often martins, robins, and other blackbirds) suffer. The Common Grackle feeds chiefly on the ground, where it walks about probing beneath vegetation and chasing insects. It is very fond of bathing in lawn sprinklers. It visits feeders and has been reported to soften hard bread in water before eating it. Flocks feed in a characteristic "rolling" motion as the birds at the rear of the flock constantly fly forward and alight just ahead of their companions. Its call, likened to the sound of a rusty gate, is usually given as the bird bows and spreads its wings and tail.

Field Marks: Both sexes are black with yellow eyes and have long, wedge-shaped tails that are frequently keeled in flight. Immatures are dark brown with brown eyes. Molting immatures present a very mottled appearance. Flight of the Common Grackle is steady and direct.

Food: This species eats a variety of arthropods, including earthworms, spiders, caterpillars, cicadas, and other insects, and small vertebrates, including tadpoles, frogs, small snakes, birds' eggs, and nestling birds.

It has been reported as killing sparrows, mice, and even bats (Terres 1980). Its vegetable food includes acorns, weed seeds, grain, small fruits, and berries. At feeders this species eats sunflower seeds, bread, corn, and suet.

A Brown-headed Cowbird (*Molothrus ater*). Photograph by Bob Gress.

Brown-headed Cowbird
Molothrus ater (Boddaert)

Status: The Brown-headed Cowbird is a common transient and summer resident and local winter resident statewide.

Period of Occurrence: This species has been reported in all months but is most regular from 20 March to 1 November. Large concentrations occur in late summer, and a few flocks overwinter.

Breeding: The Brown-headed Cowbird breeds throughout North America from tree limit to central Mexico and winters from the Great Lakes to the Gulf. It is our only brood parasite, laying its eggs in the nests of other species and relying on the host to hatch and rear its young. At least 121 species have been successfully parasitized, including about 50 species in Kansas (Lowther 1988). The most important hosts vary with locality and season. In Ellis County, Horned Larks and Pine Siskins are important hosts early in the season, replaced later by Red-winged Blackbirds, orioles, and grassland sparrows.

Each female is believed to lay about six eggs in a clutch, delay several days or more, and then lay another clutch. Peak egg laying is from about 21 April to mid-July. Eggs are usually laid at dawn, probably one egg per nest. The egg is grayish white dotted with brown, especially at the larger end, and often contrasts visibly with the host clutch. The female removes a host egg before or after laying. Some hosts, such as the Yellow Warbler, build a new floor over the egg. Harrison (1975) reported a six-story nest with a cowbird egg buried in each layer. Other species, such as the American Robin, usually eject the cowbird eggs. Most species, however, either desert the nest or accept the cowbird egg. The incubation period is 11 or 12 days; the fledgling period is about 10 to 11 days.

Habits and Habitat: This species is most abundant in edge habitats such as brushy fields and wooded ravines in grassland; it is often, but by no means always, associated with domestic livestock. Cowbirds often travel with livestock and capture insects flushed by them. Occasionally they even ride on an animal's back. During hot days the birds wisely remain in the shade of the moving animals. During spring cowbirds are most often in small flocks of three to six birds, predominately males, which seem as eager to display to each other as to the females. The displaying male ruffles his breast feathers, lifts his wings, stretches on tiptoe, and utters a gurgling call while "bowing" deeply, nearly falling as he does so.

Presumably our native grassland birds have evolved adaptations to survive losses by nest parasitism, whereas species only recently coming into contact with cowbirds (such as the Kirtland's Warbler in Michigan) have not. In a study in Ellis County, Hill (1976) found a 21percent frequency of parasitism in 520 nests of 14 species. Five of six native grassland species were moderately to highly parasitized, and cowbird nesting success was high in two of these—Lark Sparrow and Grasshopper Sparrow. Overall, parasitism decreased nesting success of the host species by one chick per nest. Cowbirds (of three species) are increasing in numbers and range nationwide, and we anticipate corresponding reductions in the numbers of native species, especially vireos, wood warblers, and other nesters in deciduous woods.

Hill (1976) studied a large concentration of cowbirds utilizing a feedlot near Hays during 1973 and 1974 and banded and color-marked over 10,000 individuals. Adults began congregating at the feedlot in late July, and most were gone by early August. Immatures, including a huge transient element, peaked in early August and left by mid-August. One of the marked birds was already in central Mexico by 4 September! The birds utilized two distinct wintering areas—west central Mexico (a livestock-growing and irrigated-crop region) and the southern Great Plains. In subsequent summers marked birds were reported north to Saskatchewan, North Dakota, and Minnesota.

Field Marks: The Brown-headed Cowbird is a small slender blackbird with a heavier, almost sparrowlike bill. The male is black with a coffee-brown head. The female is dark brown or dark gray, and immatures are similar but with ventral streaking. With experience, silhouette and flight pattern allow identification at a distance.

Food: During the summer this species feeds primarily on insects, especially grasshoppers, caterpillars, ants, beetles, and true bugs. It eats smaller amounts of plant material, especially in fall and winter. This includes grass seeds, weed seeds, waste grain, standing grain, small fruits, and berries.

Orchard Oriole
Icterus spurius (Linnaeus)

Status: The Orchard Oriole is a common transient and summer resident statewide.

Period of Occurrence: The usual dates of occurrence are about 25 April through 15 September. Extreme dates are 15 April and 12 October.

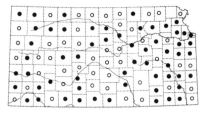

Breeding: The Orchard Oriole breeds east of the Rockies from the Canadian border to the Gulf and winters in Central America and northern South America. The nest is typically hung from the horizontal fork of a branch or from a group of downward projecting branches, usually seven to 25 feet above the ground. The nest is typically much less pendulous than the nest of the Northern Oriole and is well concealed within the vegetation. It is constructed entirely of fresh grasses that turn light yellow as they dry, making the nest easy to identify. It is thinner walled and shallower than a Northern Oriole nest and is lined with fine grasses and plant down. Fuzzy willow infloresences are often incorporated into the walls. The nest is built by the female in three to six days. The clutch is three to seven, usually four or five, pale bluish white eggs that are spotted, blotched, and scrawled with brown, purple, and gray, often concentrated at the larger end. The species is single brooded. The incubation period is 12 to 14 days; the fledgling period is 11 to 14 days.

Habits and Habitat: The Orchard Oriole is most common along roadsides, in brushy fields, and in riparian areas. It is usually secretive (except vocally) and remains hidden by foliage, so it is often overlooked even where common. Most of its foraging is in trees and shrubs, where it gleans insects and fruit. In prairies birds are often seen in isolated groves or perched on roadside fences. Birds visit grasslands and forage among tall grasses and forbs at two seasons, once during nest building and later when feeding nestlings. The very energetic song is usually delivered from the canopy, but the species also has a conspicuous flight song. Bent (1958) described the song as "robin-like in quality, usually with a down slurred note" at the end.

Field Marks: The male Orchard Oriole is unmistakable, chestnut and black. The female is smaller and more uniformly yellow than our other orioles. The first-year male resembles her but with a black face and throat.

Food: Food of this species is about 90 percent invertebrates, chiefly grasshoppers, caterpillars, beetles, ants, spiders, and flies. It eats a small amount of fruit, chiefly pokeweed, blackberries, mulberries, and when available, nectar of flowers.

Hooded Oriole
Icterus cucullatus (Swainson)

Most authors have included the Hooded Oriole on the Kansas list on the basis of a banded bird from Los Angeles, California, that was found dead near Garden City, Finney County (Lincoln 1940). However, Allan R. Phillips has questioned this account and we concur. The bird was banded on 22 January 1939 and found dead about 5 August of that year. The leg with the band was saved but has since been lost. The bander identified the bird as a Hooded Oriole but noted that it was the heaviest he had banded (40.4 grams) and the first he had banded earlier than March. This bird may well have been another species of oriole that wintered in California, then visited Kansas. The movement of any passerine between California and southwest Kansas is so unusual as to be worthy of note.

A Northern Oriole (*Icterus galbula*). Photograph by Bob Gress.

Northern Oriole
Icterus galbula (Linnaeus)

Status: The Northern Oriole is a common transient and summer resident statewide. It is casual in winter, usually at feeders. The area of hybridization between "Baltimore" and "Bullock's" Orioles is along a line from roughly Meade and Seward counties north through Scott and Cheyenne counties.

Period of Occurrence: According to numerous data, spring arrival of "Baltimores" at a given locality varies within a 10-day span in various years. In general, first arrival is around 20 April in southern and eastern Kansas and 25 April in the north and west. Fall departure is during the third week of September, with stragglers into October. Extreme dates are 16 April and 24 October. A few birds have survived, usually at feeders, until at least 15 January. Extreme dates for "Bullock's" Orioles are 21 April and 19 September.

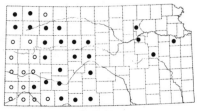

Bullock's

Breeding: The species nests throughout North America, except for the Gulf Coast, and winters from the Gulf States to northern South America. It usually nests in a residential area, along

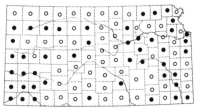

Baltimore

a roadside, in a park, or in a riparian situation and less often in woodland edge. The nest is usually eight to 32 feet above ground and attached to the drooping limbs of a cottonwood, elm, or maple. The nest is a pendant affair attached by its rim to several branches. It is a deep, intricately woven pouch of plant material, usually fibers of milkweed and dogbane and whatever string, yarn, hair, or similar materials are available locally. Ely has seen one woven completely of black horsehair, another built completely of aluminum icicles from a discarded Christmas tree, and one woven completely of monofilament fishing line. The nest is lined with hair, plant down, and similar soft materials. Though open at the top, the nest is usually built in such a way that the weight of the incubating bird partially closes the entrance. The clutch is four to six, usually four, pale grayish white eggs, streaked, scrawled, and blotched with brown and black, often concentrated at the larger end. Incubation is by the female and lasts 12 to 14 days. The nestling period is about 12 to 14 days. The species is single brooded.

Habits and Habitat: This confiding and colorful bird is one of our best-known species. It is attracted to bird baths, feeders that feature fresh fruit, and sometimes hummingbird feeders. While wintering in the tropics it feeds avidly on the nectar of trees and shrubs such as hibiscus. Females visit yards for nesting material and often accept lengths of colored yarn or string. The male has a loud and highly variable song that is easily recognized but difficult to describe. Young birds become very noisy just before and just after leaving the nest and provide a characteristic sound of tree-lined streets in early July. After nesting the adults become more secretive and gather in small flocks, often in riparian situations and in the vicinity of fruiting trees and shrubs. At such times their faces become stained with juices. The "Bullock's" Oriole is the most conspicuous bird in the cottonwood groves bordering the Cimarron River in southwestern Kansas.

Field Marks: Males are conspicuously black and orange. The "Baltimore" has a completely black face, and the "Bullock's" has an orange face with black eye line and more white in the wing. Females have olive backs, yellowish tails, and a variable amount of black on the head and throat. Immatures are duller. First-year males in spring have mottled black and orange but usually retain the dull tail feathers.

Food: Food of the Northern Oriole is largely insects, with caterpillars predominating, and smaller numbers of beetles, flies, true bugs, spiders, and insect galls. It eats a considerable amount of fruit, including pokeberries, cherries, and mulberries. It has been reported to be fond of green peas. Nectar and fruit are important food items on the wintering grounds.

Scott's Oriole
Icterus parisorum Bonaparte

Status: The Scott's Oriole is accidental or vagrant in southwestern Kansas.

Period of Occurrence: The only confirmed record is a female collected in Morton County, 16 April 1977, by Larry W. Anthony.

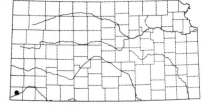

Habits and Habitat: The Kansas specimen was taken in open cottonwoods bordering the Cimarron River north of Elkhart. It is interesting that the resident orioles had not yet arrived at that date. The Scott's Oriole is typically a bird of pinyon-juniper and yucca grasslands of the southwestern United States but has also been reported from Colorado.

Field Marks: The male is a black and yellow oriole with yellow patches in the tail. The female resembles a female Orchard Oriole but has a streaked back and a dusky cheek. The first-year male is similar but has veiled black on the face and throat.

Food: The Scott's Oriole feeds primarily on insects, with some fruit and nectar taken as well.

A Pine Grosbeak (*Pinicola enucleator*). Photograph by J. Surman for the Cornell Laboratory of Ornithology.

FINCHES (FAMILY FRINGILLIDAE)
Pine Grosbeak
Pinicola enucleator (Linnaeus)

Status: The Pine Grosbeak is a casual winter visitor. There seems to be no pattern to where they are going to appear, as a glance at the map will attest. Pine Grosbeaks are well known for periodic irruptions that are apparently due to the lack of food on their normal wintering grounds.

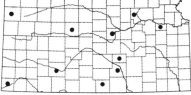

Most observations of Pine Grosbeaks in Kansas seem to be of the rosy pink form from the north (Ely 1961). However, Kingswood's (1979) description of birds seen in Morton County indicates that the Rocky Mountain race might occasionally occur in Kansas.

Habits and Habitat: The summer habitat of this rosy grosbeak is normally pine woodlands. In Kansas, they have been found in areas that have pines and redcedars, such as cemeteries, shelterbelts or city parks. They occasionally come to feeders for sunflower seeds. The periodic irruptions are unpredictable this far south of the normal wintering area.

If they get this far south (or east) it is usually in small numbers, and luck is needed to find them.

Food: The Pine Grosbeak feeds extensively on tree buds, fruits, seeds, and occasionally insects.

A Purple Finch (*Carpodacus purpureus*). Photograph by Frank S. Shipley.

Purple Finch
Carpodacus purpureus (Gmelin)

Status: The Purple Finch is an irregular winter visitor, most common in the east. There are reports most years of at least a few wintering birds. However, some years they may be abundant.

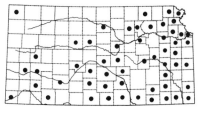

Period of Occurrence: The irregular nature of the Purple Finch's migration patterns make it difficult to state dates of occurrence. However, if an irruption is going to occur, it usually arrives in Kansas by the end of December or in January. Birds may remain well into the spring. The earliest recorded date is 3 October, and the latest spring departure is 3 May.

Habits and Habitat: What a thrill to look out and see this bright rose-colored finch feeding at your bird feeder. In years when it is common, dozens may remain at a feeder for weeks. The birds may be abundant, as they were one winter in Winfield, Cowley County. These birds remained well into April, thousands fed on the budding trees, and you were never away from singing males. It is generally found wherever there are trees and shrubs to feed in.

Field Marks: The three red to rose-colored finches that occur in Kansas might be confused. The Purple Finch is intermediate in size between the Cassin's Finch and the House Finch. The male Purple Finch is rose colored and has a dark rose cap that blends into the back; the under-tail coverts are usually unstreaked. The male Cassin's Finch is larger; its red crown patch contrasts abruptly with the brown neck, and the undertail coverts are heavily streaked. The male House Finch is the smallest of the three and is red on the streaked breast.

Food: The Purple Finch feeds on seeds in the winter and in spring may utilize tree buds. In the summer it eats berries if available.

A Cassin's Finch (*Carpodacus cassinii*). Photograph by Allen Cruickshank for the Cornell Laboratory of Ornithology.

Cassin's Finch
Carpodacus cassinii Baird

Status: The Cassin's Finch is an occasional winter visitor in the west. It was first recorded in 1960 and has only been found in six counties.

Period of Occurrence: The records for this species occur from 16 October to 28 April.

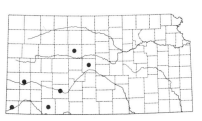

Habits and Habitat: Most of the Cassin's Finch records for Kansas come from towns, especially around bird feeders or in cemeteries.

Field Marks: See Purple Finch account.

A House Finch (*Carpodacus mexicanus*). Photograph by David A. Rintoul.

House Finch
Carpodacus mexicanus (Muller)

Status: The House Finch is a common resident in western Kansas. It is rapidly making its way eastward, with regular breeding as far east as Cowley County in the south and Saline County in the north. Recent breeding in Shawnee and Lyon counties could be from the introduced eastern populations moving westward, but there is much to be learned about the dispersal of this species within the state.

Period of Occurrence: The House Finch occurs throughout the year in the state.

Breeding: The House Finch has probably bred in southwestern Kansas for a number of years. Tordoff (1956) reported it common north to Hamilton County and east to Finney County. He was not sure of its breeding status. He also noted that most records were for the winter months. M. Lohoefener (1977) observed the first known nest in 1976 in Decatur County. By 1979 it was nesting in Ellis County, where it is now a common breeding bird. However, most breeding dates are for

1981 to 1985. The breeding records for Shawnee County were in 1988, in 1987 for Lyon County, and in 1990 for Wyandotte County.

Observations of Kansas birds suggest a very early nesting date. In Decatur County a pair started nest construction by early March. The female was incubating four eggs by 20 March, and the eggs hatched on 5 April. The young fledged on 22 April. The same nest underwent renovation on 15 May, with egg laying on 18 May. The four eggs hatched on 2 June, and the young fledged on 25 June.

The above data suggest that in Kansas the breeding season begins very early in the spring and that the House Finch is double brooded. This evidence is corroborated by observations at Hays, Ellis County.

The nest of the House Finch is placed in trees, in cavities, on ledges, or in and about buildings. Spruce trees seem to be a particular favorite in Kansas. The nest is highly variable but is usually composed of stems and leaves. The four bluish white eggs are spotted or streaked with black or brown. The eggs are incubated for 14 days, and the young fledge in 20 to 25 days or so.

Habits and Habitat: The House Finch is rapidly becoming a common bird in towns in western Kansas and has now even spread all the way to the eastern border. The birds that were introduced into New York had moved almost to or into eastern Kansas by 1990. With the rapid eastward expansion of the native Kansas population, the two populations should be meeting shortly in the eastern third of the state.

Field Marks: See Purple Finch.

Food: The food of the House Finch is almost entirely vegetable matter.

A Red Crossbill (*Loxia curvirostra*). Photograph by JoAnn S. Garrett.

Red Crossbill
Loxia curvirostra Linnaeus

Status: The Red Crossbill is an irruptive species that is common some winters and rare or entirely absent in others. There are two breeding records for the state.

Period of Occurrence: This crossbill usually spends only the winter in Kansas,

but it has been found in every
month of the year. The normal
occurrence is from 15 November
to 25 March.

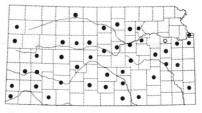

Breeding: The first breeding record
was in 1917 in Topeka, Shawnee
County. The second record was
from the same county in 1943. The nesting cycle elsewhere is highly
irregular, and breeding has been recorded nearly every month of the
year. Breeding apparently is timed to coincide with an abundance of
spruce seeds.

The nest is a bulky structure composed of twigs, stems, and needles
and is lined with grass. It is usually placed in a conifer away from the
trunk. The four eggs are pale bluish to greenish white with dark spots.
The incubation period is 15 days, and the young fledge in 20 or more
days. The period of time in the nest may be dictated by food supply.

Habits and Habitat: The thrill of finding Red Crossbills is unique. No
matter how many times you have seen them, you are still energized by
another observation. The bizarre crossed bill that the bird utilizes to
pry open spruce or pine cones is a wonder of nature. The birds are
usually tame and easy to approach. Frequently, the first sign that they
may be in your area is the popping sound as they open the cones and
drop the pieces to the ground. They usually give a flight call when the
flock is moving. Look for them in cemeteries, shelterbelts, or other areas
with extensive groves of conifers. Southwestern College campus, in Winfield, is a favorite site because of the extensive grove of arborvitae, the
seeds of which the birds relish. Fort Hays State University campus, Hays,
is another regular haunt of this species.

Field Marks: The red coloration of the male and the crossed bill are excellent field marks. The female is greenish yellow and also has the crossed
bill. The only other bird with which it can be confused is the White-
winged Crossbill, which has two wing bars. The male White-wing is pinkish rather than brick red. The females resemble each other except for
two white wing bars in the White-winged Crossbill.

Food: The Red Crossbill feeds almost entirely on cones of conifers. It
can be attracted to bird feeders with sunflower seed.

A White-winged Crossbill (*Loxia leucoptera*). Photograph by Bob Gress.

White-winged Crossbill
Loxia leucoptera Gmelin

Status: The White-winged Crossbill is a rare, irruptive winter visitant. There have been some irruptions where it was common, such as the early 1950s.

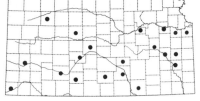

Period of Occurrence: Sporadic dates are available, but unlike the Red Crossbill, the records are scanty. This species has been recorded from 15 September through 14 May. The last big invasion was in 1961–1962, although it has been sporadic since then.

Habits and Habitat: Like its close cousin the Red Crossbill, this cross-bill prefers conifers as its habitat. It will sometimes flock with Red Crossbills, and those flocks should be scanned carefully. They also will sometimes feed at feeders on sunflower seeds.

Field Marks: See Red Crossbill.

Food: The White-winged Crossbill feeds almost entirely upon seeds from conifers.

A Common Redpoll (*Carduelis flammea*). Photograph by Gerald J. Wiens.

Common Redpoll
Carduelis flammea (Linnaeus)

Status: The Common Redpoll is generally a rare, irregular winter visitor throughout the state. However, it was common to abundant in Cheyenne County on 26 January 1969, when 20 specimens were collected.

Period of Occurrence: Most sightings of the Common Redpoll are in winter from 18 November through 10 March. There is a late date of 13 April.

Habits and Habitat: The Common Redpoll is another one of the wintering northern finches that are so irregular this far south. They are usually found in patches of sunflowers, often in the company of goldfinches or siskins. They also 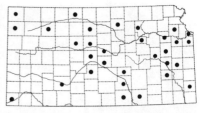 utilize conifers for feeding. However, most reports in Kansas seem to come from feeder stations, where the Common Redpolls are conspicuous among the other feeding birds.

Henry David Thoreau (1910), in remarking about the Common Redpoll, wrote: "Standing there I am reminded of the incredible phenomenon of small birds in winter,—that ere long amid the cold powdery snow, as it were a fruit of the season, will come twittering a flock of delicate crimson-tinged birds, lesser redpolls, to sport and feed on the seeds and buds now just ripe for them on the sunny side of a wood, shaking down the powdery snow there in their cheerful social feeding, as if it were high midsummer to them. These crimson aerial creatures have wings which would bear them quickly to the regions of summer, but here is all the summer they want. What a rich contrast! tropical colors, crimson breasts, on cold white snow! Such etherealness, such delicacy in their forms, such ripeness in their colors, in this stern and barren season!"

Field Marks: The adult male Common Redpoll has a breast suffused with dark pink, a black chin, and a red cap. It is sometimes confused with male House Finches. The female Common Redpoll is duller but also possesses a red cap.

Food: The Common Redpoll feeds on a wide variety of seeds including sunflower, small grasses, various weeds, birches, and most anything else that is available. The birds will take insects during the summer.

A Pine Siskin (*Carduelis pinus*). Photograph by Gerald J. Wiens.

Pine Siskin
Carduelis pinus (Wilson)

Status: The Pine Siskin is a common but irregular winter visitor and local summer resident throughout the state.

Period of Occurrence: This streak-breasted finch generally arrives in Kansas around 15 October and remains until 15 May. Since the species breeds in Kansas and has been recorded every month of the year, extreme dates cannot be assessed.

Breeding: The Pine Siskin is an irregular breeder in the state. In years that it is a numerous winter resident, a few seem to remain and breed. It has expanded its breeding areas from the northwestern part of Kansas south to Cowley County and eastward as far as Douglas County. The breeding season ends by 15 June, and the adults and young leave the area.

The Pine Siskin selects areas of conifers for its nesting sites. The courtship and nest building start in late March. The nest is constructed of twigs, grasses, and bark strips and is lined with soft grasses or other materials. The normal clutch size is four pale greenish blue eggs with black specks or spots. Incubation lasts for 13 days, and the young fledge in 14 days.

Habits and Habitat: The Pine Siskin seems to prefer areas with conifers for its wintering sites, although it is found feeding in fields of sunflowers and weeds. It frequents bird feeders in yards and sometimes becomes abundant. In prime years, it is not uncommon to see as many as 200 to 300 birds in a flock at the feeders. In a poor season like 1990–91 the Pine Siskin may be nearly absent from the state. Birds become exceedingly tame and may actually sit upon your head or hand when you refill feeders. They frequently fly in flocks with the American Goldfinch.

Field Marks: The Pine Siskin may be rather difficult to distinguish from goldfinches or redpolls at a distance. It frequently flocks with them, but it is a dusky-streaked bird on a grayish brown base with two light wing bars. It usually has considerable yellow on the basal portions of its wings and tail flight feathers.

Food: The Pine Siskin feeds primarily on seeds and is attracted to home feeders by using niger "thistle" seed or small, black sunflower seeds.

A Lesser Goldfinch (*Carduelis psaltria*). Photograph by John S. Dunning for the Cornell Laboratory of Ornithology.

Lesser Goldfinch
Carduelis psaltria (Say)

Status: The Lesser Goldfinch is a casual migrant in the state in the southern tier of counties from Cowley westward. Although there are no specimen records, there is one photograph (not seen by the authors) taken by Hazel Chaplin in Arkansas City, Cowley County. There were several sightings in Morton County in 1989. One of the Morton County birds was seen

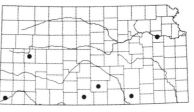

feeding with American Goldfinches on the wild sunflowers along the Cimarron River.

Breeding: There is some reason to believe that it might be a casual nesting species in the state. Hazel Chaplin had a pair in Cowley County, and the female was seen carrying nesting material on 15 August 1961, but both birds disappeared on 21 August.

Habits and Habitat: The Lesser Goldfinch occurs in weedy growths along river courses and forests. It would probably come to feeders along with the American Goldfinches, but there are too few records from Kansas to state much about its habits and habitat.

Field Marks: The Lesser Goldfinch might easily be mistaken for the American Goldfinch by the inexperienced observer. The male in summer plumage has a black back, not yellow as in the American Goldfinch. In winter plumage, the male has a greenish back, not brownish as in the American Goldfinch. The overall size is somewhat smaller than that of the American Goldfinch. The females of the two species resemble one another, but the Lesser Goldfinch female has a greenish—not brownish—back.

Food: This goldfinch primarily eats seeds.

An American Goldfinch (*Carduelis tristis*). Photograph by Gerald J. Wiens.

American Goldfinch
Carduelis tristis (Linnaeus)

Status: The American Goldfinch is a common resident in the eastern half of the state and probably a low-density breeder in the west. It becomes more common in the west in winter. In winter local birds are augmented by more northerly populations.

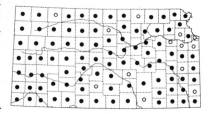

Period of Occurrence: This goldfinch is found throughout the year.

Breeding: Despite the abundance of this species in the winter, there are few substantiated breeding records. It probably breeds in many counties, but there is documentation for only 13! The American Goldfinch is one of the latest of all species to breed in the state, waiting until at least mid-June. Most egg laying probably takes place in July and August. Johnston (1964b) found the average laying date to be 5 August, but this was based on meager data.

The nests of the American Goldfinch are made of woven plant fibers lined with thistle and cattail down. Spiderwebbing is frequently bound around the rim. The four to five pale bluish white unmarked eggs are incubated for 13 days. The young leave the nest in about 12 days. They frequently are double brooded.

Habits and Habitat: This "Prairie Canary" is one of the most colorful birds of the state and one easily recognized by most observers. It frequents bird feeders in the winter and well into early summer. Some years it is more common than others, and it takes a somewhat deep pocket to keep the feeders full of niger seed and black sunflower seeds. Flocks of 200 to 300 birds are not uncommon around feeders in the winter. When you combine these with Pine Siskins in the same year, you will have a yard full of finches. This is of course the time to look for the oddball finch that might come to the feeder and be lost in the crowd. When not feeding at feeders, many goldfinches feed in weed patches, particularly sunflowers.

Field Marks: See Lesser Goldfinch.

Food: The American Goldfinch feeds primarily on weed seeds. It is occasionally seen eating dandelion heads in the spring.

An Evening Grosbeak (*Coccothraustes vespertinus*). Photograph by Bob Gress.

Evening Grosbeak
Coccothraustes vespertinus (Cooper)

Status: The Evening Grosbeak is an irregular winter visitant through-out the state.

Period of Occurrence: There are records of this grosbeak from 19 October to 20 May, but most records fall after 15 November. The spring departure is irregular, but most have moved on by 15 March.

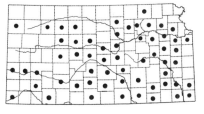

Habits and Habitat: How exciting to look at your feeder and see this bright golden brown species feeding. When Evening Grosbeaks find a feeder that they like, they may stay most of the winter. At least two feeders in Cowley County have had flocks that have remained for three months feeding upon sunflower seeds. This robin-sized bird is another of the northern finches that Kansans should look for each win-ter. They are reported most winters in Kansas but only in very small numbers. In other winters they can be quite common.

Field Mark: The large size, big yellowish bill, and the golden brown color contrasting with the black wings with large white patches make this bird unmistakable. The female is a drab olive but also has the large bill. It is the only large-billed finch liable to be seen in winter.

Food: The Evening Grosbeak feeds primarily on seeds and is especially fond of sunflower seeds at feeders.

A House Sparrow (*Passer domesticus*). Photograph by David A. Rintoul.

OLD WORLD SPARROWS (FAMILY PASSERIDAE)
House Sparrow
Passer domesticus (Linnaeus)

Status: The House Sparrow is a common, sometimes abundant, resident of the state.

Period of Occurrence: This European import is a resident throughout the state.

Breeding: The House Sparrow probably breeds throughout the state. The nests are placed in any cavity, be it barn, house, tree, or

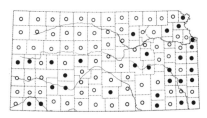

martin house. If the birds can't find a cavity, they will build a bulky nest directly in a tree. They nest most commonly around human habitation. Nests are usually made of grasses, leaves, and whatever else seems to be available. They are lined with a variety of soft materials, including feathers, grasses, toilet paper, string, and other man-made materials. The birds start laying their four white spotted eggs by 20 March and may continue until 20 July. The incubation period lasts 12 days, and the young leave the nest in 14 to 18 days. The House Sparrow is commonly double brooded, but there are records of four broods in a year.

Habits and Habitat: The House Sparrow (not really a sparrow but rather a weaver finch) is found primarily around human habitation. "Woods" (1972) published the introductory history of the House Sparrow in Kansas. The following information is largely from his paper. An article on p. 4 of the 27 June 1904 *Atchison Daily Globe* of Atchison, Kansas, read in part:

"R. J. Groves recalls that Henry Brandner turned four [English Sparrows] loose in Atchison in 1865: three males, and one female. He had imported three pairs, but two of the females died. That fall, Mr. Groves saw eleven English sparrows down by the river, picking up grain. Mr. Groves believes the original Topeka supply was secured in Atchison. In 1865, there was great excitement in the country over the English sparrow. It was claimed that they would rid the fields of insects. English sparrows were talked of everywhere and Mr. Brandner sent for three pairs. There are millions and billions of the birds in this vicinity now."

Another excerpt from Woods shows how rapidly they multiplied:

"In the month of March, 1874, F. W. Giles, C. W. Jewell, Samuel Davidson, and a few others, purchased and had shipped to them from the city of New York twenty-eight sparrows." [These were kept until all but five died, then released in 1874.] "The following autumn there were twelve birds, in the second autumn sixty, and in the third about three hundred."

By 1894, 20 years later, they were considered abundant in Finney County.

Field Marks: Probably little needs to be said about what a House Sparrow looks like, but nonbirders seem to still not understand the plumages. Males in the fall acquire a subdued plumage; as the winter wears on, the feathers wear down until the birds have the black throat and the rusty head and back that is the breeding plumage.

Food: The House Sparrow feeds mainly on seeds, with a supplement of insects in the summer. It certainly is not the insect controller that had been hoped in the 1800s.

LITERATURE CITED

Allen, J. A.
  1872.   Notes of an ornithological reconnaissance in portions of Kansas, Colorado, Wyoming, and Utah. Pt. 2. Bull. Mus. Comp. Zool. 3(6):113–183.
Anderson, Ted R.
  1982.   Song Sparrow nesting in Kansas. Kansas Orni. Soc. Bull. 33(2):23–24.
Anthony, Larry W.
  1969.   The breeding ecology of the Barn Swallow in Ellis County, Kansas. M.S. thesis, Fort Hays Kansas State College. 34 pp.
Bagg, Aaron Clark, and Samuel Atkins Eliot, Jr.
  1937.   Birds of the Connecticut Valley in Massachusetts. The Hampshire Bookshop, Northhampton, Mass. 813 pp.
Bent, Arthur Cleveland
  1942.   Life histories of North American flycatchers, larks, swallows and their allies. U.S. Natl. Mus. Bull. 179. 555 pp.
  1946.   Life histories of North American jays, crows, and titmice. U.S. Natl. Mus. Bull. 191. 495 pp.
  1948.   Life histories of North American nuthatches, wrens, thrashers, and their allies. U.S. Natl. Mus. Bull. 195. 475 pp.
  1949.   Life histories of North American thrushes, kinglets, and their allies. U.S. Natl. Mus. Bull. 196. 454 pp.
  1950.   Life histories of North American wagtails, shrikes, vireos, and their allies. U.S. Natl. Mus. Bull. 197. 411 pp.
  1953.   Life histories of North American wood warblers. U.S. Natl. Mus. Bull. 203. 734 pp.
  1958.   Life histories of North American blackbirds, orioles, tanagers, and their allies. U.S. Natl. Mus. Bull. 211. 549 pp.
  1968.   Life histories of North American cardinals, grosbeaks, buntings, towhees, finches, sparrows, and allies. U.S. Natl. Mus. Bull. 237, Pts. 1–3. 1889 pp.
Boyd, Roger L.
  1985.   First nesting record of the Ash-throated Flycatcher in Kansas and an additional nesting record for the Black-billed Magpie. Kansas Orni. Soc. Bull. 36(4):34.
  1986.   First nesting record of the Cerulean Warbler in Kansas. Kansas Orni. Soc. Bull. 37(3):37–38.
Branan, W. V., and H. C. Burdick
  1981.   Bird species composition in a Missouri park 1916 vs 1973. Kansas Orni. Soc. Bull. 32(4):41–45.
Cink, Calvin L.
  1975.   Mourning Dove incubates robin eggs. Kansas Orni. Soc. Bull. 26(4):19–21.
Cink, Calvin L., and Roger L. Boyd
  1982.   Ovenbird nesting in Douglas County, Kansas. Kansas Orni. Soc. Bull. 33:17–19.
Creighton, Philip D., and David K. Porter
  1974.   Nest predation and interference by Western Meadowlark. Auk 91:177–178.
Ely, C. A.
  1961.   Cassin's Finch and Pine Grosbeak in west-central Kansas. Condor 63:418–419.

1970.   Migration of Least and Traill's Flycatchers in west-central Kansas. Bird-Banding 41:198–204.

Ely, Charles.
1971.   A history and distributional list of Ellis County, Kansas, birds. Fort Hays Studies, New Series, Science Series no. 9. 115 pp.

Farrand, John, Jr.
1983.   The Audubon Society master guide to birding. Pt. 3. Warblers to sparrows. Knopf, New York. 399 pp.

Gaunt, Abbot S.
1959.   Behavior in the Purple Martin. Kansas Orni. Soc. Bull. 10(4):14–16.

Godfrey, W. Earl
1979.   The birds of Canada. Natl. Mus. of Canada, Ottawa. 428 pp.

Goodrich, Arthur L., Jr.
1946.   Birds in Kansas. Rept. Kansas State Bd. Agri. 44(267). 340 pp.

Goss, Nathaniel S.
1891.   History of the birds of Kansas. Crane & Co., Topeka. 692 pp.

Graber, Jean W.
1957.   A bioecological study of the Black-capped Vireo (*Vireo atricapillus*). Ph.D. dissertation, Univ. of Oklahoma. 203 pp.

Graber, Richard S., and Jean Graber
1950.   New birds for the state of Kansas. Wilson Bull. 62(4):206–209.

Gress, Robert J.
1982.   Red-breasted Nuthatch nesting in Sedgwick County. Kansas Orni. Soc. Bull. 33(4):37–39.

Grinnell, Joseph, and Alden Holmes Miller
1944.   The distribution of the birds of California. Pacific Coast Avifauna, No. 27. Cooper Orni. Soc., Berkeley, California. 608 pp.

Hailman, J. P.
1960.   A field study of the mockingbird's wing-flashing behavior and its association with foraging. Wilson Bull. 72(4):346–357.

Harrison, Hal H.
1975.   A field guide to birds' nests. Houghton Mifflin Co., Boston. 257 pp.

Heppner, F. H.
1965.   Sensory mechanisms and environmental clues used by the American Robin in locating earthworms. Condor 67(3):247–256.

Hill, Richard A.
1976.   Host-parasite relationships of the Brown-headed Cowbird in a prairie habitat of west-central Kansas. Wilson Bull. 88:555–565.

Imler, R. H.
1936.   An annotated list of the birds of Rooks County, Kansas, and vicinity. Trans. Kansas Acad. Sci. 39:295–312.

Jenkinson, Marion Anne
1984.   Correction of a purported nesting of the Chestnut-sided Warbler from Kansas. Kansas Orni. Soc. Bull. 35(2):22.

Johnsgard, Paul A.
1979.   Birds of the Great Plains. Univ. of Nebraska Press, Lincoln. 539 pp.

Johnston, Richard F.
1964a.   Traill's Flycatcher breeding in Kansas. Kansas Orni. Soc. Bull. 15:7.
1964b.   The breeding birds of Kansas. Univ. Kansas Publ. Mus. Nat. Hist. 12(14):575–655.

Kalmbach, Edwin Richard
  1927.   The magpie in relation to agriculture. U.S. Dept. of Agri. Tech. Bull. 24.
          29 pp.
Kaufman, Kenn
  1990.   A field guide to advanced birding. Houghton Mifflin Co., Boston. 299
          pp.
Kennard, John H.
  1975.   Longevity records of North American birds. Bird-Banding 46:55–73.
Kingswood, Steven C.
  1979.   A late May record of Pine Grosbeaks in southwest Kansas. Kansas Orni.
          Soc. Bull. 30(3):28–29.
Klaas, Erwin E.
  1962.   Nesting success and cowbird parasitism in the Eastern Phoebe in Kansas.
          Kansas Orni. Soc. Bull. 13:17–19.
Lincoln, Frederick L.
  1940.   Arizona Hooded Oriole in Kansas. Auk 57:420.
Lohoefener, Mary
  1977.   Nesting of the House Finch in northwestern Kansas. Kansas Orni. Soc.
          Bull. 28(1):9–10.
Lohoefener, Renne R.
  1977.   Comparative nesting ecology of solitary and colonially nesting Barn
          Swallows in west-central Kansas. M.S. thesis. Fort Hays State University,
          Kansas. 55 pp.
Lowther, Peter E.
  1977.   Chestnut-sided Warbler nesting record from Kansas. Kansas Orni Soc.
          Bull. 28:32.
  1988.   Kansas cowbird hosts, a catalogue update. Kansas Orni. Soc. Bull. 39:36–37.
Ohlendorf, Harry M.
  1974.   Comparative relationsltips among kingbirds (*Tyrannus*) in Trans-Pecos,
          Texas. Wilson Bull. 86:357–373.
Olmstead, Roger
  1955.   Observations on Purple Martins. Kansas Orni. Soc. Bull. 6:8–10.
Parkes, Kenneth C.
  1951.   The genetics of the Golden-winged X Blue-winged Warbler complex.
          Wilson Bull. 63:5–15.
Patti, Sebastian T.
  1972.   Brown Towhee—a species new to Kansas. Kansas Orni. Soc. Bull. 23(3):14.
Raney, Edward C.
  1939.   Robin and Mourning Dove use same nest. Auk 56:337–338.
Rice, Orville O.
  1965.   Lark Bunting nesting colony, Shawnee County, 1964. Kansas Orni. Soc.
          Bull. 16:1–2.
Rising, James D.
  1974.   The status and faunal affinities of the summer birds of western Kansas.
          Univ. Kansas Sci. Bull. 50(8):347–388.
Rohwer, Sievert A.
  1972.   Distribution of meadowlarks in the central and southern Great Plains and
          the desert grasslands of eastern New Mexico and west Texas. Trans.
          Kansas Acad. Soc. 75:1–19 + errata.
Schuckman, John M.
  1971.   Comparative nesting ecology of the Eastern Phoebe (*Sayornis phoebe*)

and Say's Phoebe (*Sayornis saya*) in west-central Kansas. M.S. Thesis, Fort Hays State College, Kansas. 29pp.

Schwilling, Marvin D.
1956.   Bird notes and nesting records from the Marais des Cygnes Waterfowl Refuge and surrounding area. Kansas Orni. Soc. Bull. 7(4):21–22.

1971.   Rapid increase and dispersal of Boat [Great]-tailed Grackle in Kansas. Kansas Orni. Soc. Bull. 22:15–16.

1982.   Sedge Wrens nesting into September. Kansas Orni. Soc. Bull. 33:22–23.

1990.   Tree Swallows nesting in bluebird boxes in Kansas. Kansas Orni. Soc. Bull. 41:24.

Schwilling, Marvin D. and Stanley Roth
1987.   Violet-green Swallow nesting in Wallace County, Kansas. Kansas Orni. Soc. Bull. 38:35.

Schwilling, Marvin D., Ed Schulenberg, and Jean Schulenberg
1981.   Southeast Kansas nesting notes. Kansas Orni. Soc. Bull. 32:18–19.

Seibel, David
1978.   A directory to the birds of Cowley and Sumner counties and the Chaplin Nature Center. Wichita Aud. Soc. Misc. Publ. 1:1–74.

Shane, Thomas G., and Robert LaShelle
1974.   Red-breasted Nuthatch apparently breeding in Kansas. Kansas Orni. Soc. Bull. 25(3):22–23.

Shirling, A. E.
1920.   Birds of Swope Park in the heart of America, Kansas City, Missouri. McIndoo Publ. Co., Kansas City. 117 pp.

Snow, Francis H.
1903.   A catalogue of the birds of Kansas. Trans. Kansas Acad. Sci. 18:154–176.

Stein, R. C.
1963.   Isolating mechanisms between populations of Traill's Flycatchers. Proc. American Philos. Soc. 107(1):21–50.

Terres, John K.
1948.   Bird of tragedy. Audubon Mag. 50(2):90–95.

1956.   Eastern Meadowlark (*Sturnella magna*) eating a road-killed bird. Auk 73(2):289–290.

1980.   The Audubon Society encyclopedia of North American birds. Knopf, New York. 1109 pp.

Thompson, Max C.
1958.   Additional nesting records for the state of Kansas. Kansas Orni. Soc. Bull. 9(3):18–19.

Thoreau, Henry David
1910.   Notes on New England birds. Houghton Mifflin Co., Boston. Pp. 419–420.

Tordoff, Harrison B.
1956.   Check-list of the birds of Kansas. Univ. Kansas Publ. Mus. Nat. Hist. 8(5):307–359.

Trautman, Milton B.
1964.   Probable breeding of the Clay-colored Sparrow in Morton County, Kansas. Kansas Orni. Soc. Bull. 15:26–27.

Wilson, Jerry K.
1976.   Nesting success of the Lark Bunting near the periphery of its breeding range. Kansas. Orni. Soc. Bull. 27:13–22.

Wolfe, L.
    1961.   The breeding birds of Decatur County, Kansas: 1908–1915. Kansas Orni.
               Soc. Bull. 12:27–30.

"Woods" (the man who walks in the woods = Robert Sutherland)
    1972.   A note on the early history of the House Sparrow in Kansas. Kansas Orni.
               Soc. Bull. 23:11.
    1976.   The birds of Shawnee County, Kansas. Unpublished manuscript (ca.
               1976). 29 pp.

Zimmerman, J. L.
    1966.   Polygyny in the Dickcissel. Auk 83:534–46.
    1978.   Ten year summary of the Kansas Breeding Bird Survey: an overview.
               Kansas Orni. Soc. Bull. 29:30.

INDEX TO COMMON, GENERIC, AND SPECIFIC
SCIENTIFIC NAMES OF BIRDS